This book challenges conventional opinion by arguing that slaves and Helots played an important part in classical Greek warfare. Although rival city-states often used these classes in their own forces or tried to incite their enemies' slaves to rebellion or desertion, such recruitment was ideologically awkward: slaves or helots, despised and oppressed classes, should have had no part in the military service so closely linked with citizenship, with rule, and even with an individual's basic worth. Consequently, their participation has tended to drop out of the historical record. Focusing on Herodotus, Thucydides, and Xenophon, this study attempts to demonstrate the actual role played by slaves and Helots in warfare, the systematic neglect of the subject by these historians, and the ideologies motivating this reticence. Because of the pervasive influence of both war and slavery, these investigations of an ostensibly marginal practice illuminate several central issues in Greek society and culture.

SLAVES, WARFARE, AND IDEOLOGY IN
THE GREEK HISTORIANS

SLAVES, WARFARE, AND IDEOLOGY IN THE GREEK HISTORIANS

PETER HUNT

Visiting Assistant Professor of Classics at Davidson College

CAMBRIDGE
UNIVERSITY PRESS

PUBLISHED BY THE PRESS SYNDICATE OF THE UNIVERSITY OF CAMBRIDGE
The Pitt Building, Trumpington Street, Cambridge, United Kingdom

CAMBRIDGE UNIVERSITY PRESS
The Edinburgh Building, Cambridge CB2 2RU, UK
40 West 20th Street, New York NY 10011–4211, USA
477 Williamstown Road, Port Melbourne, VIC 3207, Australia
Ruiz de Alarcón 13, 28014 Madrid, Spain
Dock House, The Waterfront, Cape Town 8001, South Africa

http://www.cambridge.org

First published 1998
First paperback edition 2002

Typeface Baskerville 11/12 ½ pt.

A catalogue record for this book is available from the British Library

Library of Congress Cataloguing in Publication data
Hunt, Peter, 1961–
Slaves, warfare, and ideology in the Greek historians / Peter Hunt.
p. cm.
Includes bibliographical references and index.
ISBN 0 521 58429 9 (hardback)
1. Greece – History, Military – Social aspects. 2. Thucydides –
Views on slavery. 3. Herodotus – Views on slavery. 4. Xenophon –
Views on slavery. I. Title.
DF89.H86 1998
938–dc21 97-13721 CIP

ISBN 0 521 58429 9 hardback
ISBN 0 521 89390 9 paperback

Contents

Acknowledgments		*page* ix
Abbreviations		xi
Classical sources		xiii

1	Background: warfare, slavery, and ideology	1
	Classical warfare	7
	Helots	13
	Ideology	19

2	Herodotus: the Persian Wars	26
	Marathon and the Helot Revolt	26
	Thermopylae and Plataea	31
	Salamis	40

3	Herodotus: freedom or slavery	42
	Ancient and modern omission	42
	Slavery and warfare	46

4	Thucydides: Helots and Messenians	53
	Helot soldiers	56
	Athenians and Messenians	62
	Thucydides' attitude	68
	The Messenian question	76

5	Thucydides: manning the navies	83
	Non-Athenian navies	84
	Arginusae	87
	Other objections	96

6	Thucydides: encouraging slave desertion	102
	Desertion and revolt	102
	The fate of fugitive slaves	108
	Recruitment and rebellion	115

7   Thucydides: the ideology of citizen unity   121
    Military prerogatives   122
    Slave and citizen   126
    A threatened ideology   132
    Extremists   135
    Thucydides   138

8   Xenophon: ideal rulers, ideal slaves   144
    The military basis of rule   146
    War as test   153
    Binaries   158
    Xenophon, Sambo, and Nat   160

9   Xenophon: warfare and revolution   165
    Xenophon the soldier   165
    The Neodamodeis   170
    Slave soldiers in the Ways and Means   175
    The foundation of Messene   177

10 Xenophon: the decline of hoplite ideology   185
    Military hierarchies   185
    Hoplite purity   190
    Ignoble battles   194
    The status of soldiers   202

11 Conclusion: Volones, Mamluks, and Confederates   206
    Livy and the Volones   206
    Islamic slave soldiers   209
    Slaves for the Confederacy?   214
    Conclusion   218

Bibliography   222
Index   242

Acknowledgments

This book developed out of a Stanford dissertation, so it is there that my debts begin. I could have wished for no better principal advisor than Susan Treggiari, who was invariably diligent, supportive, and helpful with all aspects of this project. Michael Jameson's wide and profound knowledge and his open-minded yet probing approach have helped me on many points as well as providing a source of inspiration. Keith Bradley's careful reading and useful criticisms would no doubt have improved this work even more than they did but for my obstinacy on certain points.

Victor Hanson, although not a member of my final committee, first suggested the basic direction of the dissertation and has generously read and commented on its entirety. My debt to his expertise and assistance is as great as to any of my readers. Anthony Raubitschek's numerous criticisms and suggestions were useful and welcome. Although I am grateful to all the faculty at Stanford, I owe special thanks to Lisa Maurizio, Steven Johnston, Andrea Nightingale, John Gould and Kenneth Dover during their visits, Michael Wigodsky, and Mark Munn. My gratitude is great for the moral support and intellectual companionship of many graduate and undergraduate students in the Classics department. Denise Greaves deserves special mention for her proofreading, suggestions, and support, but I hope all my friends from Stanford know my sincere gratitude.

My debts outside of Stanford are also numerous. The project began with a paper for Josiah Ober's superb Thucydides seminar at Princeton. John Kelsay kindly commented on my treatment of the Mamluks. J. K. Anderson saved me from several mistakes and gave me valuable suggestions for the Xenophon and Plataea sections. Vincent Rosivach generously let me see his forthcoming article on Athenian slavery. The advisors for Cambridge University Press greatly improved the book with their careful readings, constructive criticisms, and intelligent suggestions. The final revision of the manuscript – especially the footnotes and bibliography – benefited from proof-reading and comments from Elissa Faro, Erika Ihara, and Jie Yuan.

My intellectual debts to various scholars will be clear from my footnotes. I would like to make explicit, however, my special appreciation of the work of Yvon Garlan and Karl-Wilhelm Welwei, the authors who have dealt most fully with slaves in Greek warfare. If I dispute the conclusions of Yvon Garlan more often than those of any other scholar, it is in some sense because his work on the cultural and social side of ancient warfare inspired my own interest in these same issues. I am lucky to have had before me Welwei's thorough, meticulous scholarship, and reasoned judgments even in those cases where we disagree. I have nothing but admiration and respect for these two scholars.

On a more personal level, I would like to thank my parents, sister, and grandmother for their support of and interest in this project. Last but not least, I would like to express my deepest thanks to Rong-Rong Zhu for her criticisms, suggestions, encouragement and love through five years of absorption in ancient slavery and warfare.

Abbreviations

Ancient authors

In the footnotes I abbreviate Herodotus as H. and Thucydides as Th. The works of Xenophon are denoted with abbreviations of their titles alone:

Ages.	*Agesilaus*
An.	*Anabasis, The Persian Expedition*
Ap.	*Apology of Socrates*
Cyn.	*Cynegeticus, On Hunting*
Cyr.	*Cyropaedia*
Eq.	*de equitandi ratione, The Art of Horsemanship*
Eq. Mag.	*de equitum magistro, Cavalry Commander*
HG	*Historia Graeca, Hellenica, History of My Times*
Hier.	*Hiero*
Lac.	*Respublica Lacedaemoniorum, Constitution of the Lacedaemonians*
Mem.	*Memorabilia*
Oec.	*Oeconomicus*
Smp.	*Symposium*
Vect.	*Vectigalibus, Poroi, Ways and Means*
[Xen.]	pseudo-Xenophon's *Constitution of Athens.*

The works of other ancient authors are abbreviated as in S. Hornblower and A. Spawforth eds., *Oxford Classical Dictionary.* 3rd edn., Oxford, 1997.

Modern works

(1) For periodicals I have used the abbreviations of *L'Année Philologique.*

(2) The following modern works are abbreviated:

FGrH	Felix Jacoby, *Die Fragmente der griechischen Historiker.* Berlin, 1926–1957.
GSW	W. Kendrick Pritchett, *The Greek State at War.* 5 vols. Berkeley, 1971–1991.
HCT	A. W. Gomme, A. Andrewes, K. J. Dover, *Historical Commentary on Thucydides.* 5 vols. Oxford, 1956–1981.
IG²	*Inscriptiones Graecae.* 2nd edn. Scholars Reference Edition. Chicago 1974–1977.
IG³	*Inscriptiones Graecae.* 3rd edn. Berlin, 1981–1994.
RE	*Paulys Realencyclopaedie der classischen Altertumswissenschaft.* Stuttgart, 1928.
UAK	Karl-Wilhelm Welwei. *Unfreie im Antiken Kriegsdienst.* 3 vols. Wiesbaden, 1974–1988.

Texts

I have used texts from the Thesaurus Linguae Graecae Compact Disk. The specific texts are listed in the *Thesaurus Linguae Graecae Canon of Greek Authors and Works*. 3rd edn. Edited by Luci Berkowitz and Karl A. Squitier. New York, 1990. When a textual problem is potentially relevant to the argument, I have noted this in a footnote. (I used Pandora 2.5.2 to access the TLG. Pandora was produced at the Perseus Project, Harvard University, Department of the Classics, Boylston Hall 319, Cambridge, MA 02138 by Jeremy Bornstein, Brian Liebowitz, Robert Morris, Elli Mylonas, and Kate Withey.

Translations

I have included the Greek in the footnote when the passage is obscure, particularly interesting, or when my argument depends upon a close reading. In the case of Thucydides and Xenophon I have used the following translations. Where I have found it necessary to alter a translation for the sake of precision, accuracy, or to avoid archaisms, I have indicated this with an A. after the reference. Where the translation of these two authors is my own, I have indicated this with an M. The translations of all other authors are my own.

Reprinted by permission of the Jowett Copyright Trustees:

Thucydides. 2nd rev. edn. Translated by Benjamin Jowett. Oxford: Clarendon Press, 1900.

Reprinted by permission of the publishers and the Loeb Classical Library:

Xenophon. *Hellenica.* 2 vols. Translated by Carleton L. Brownson. Cambridge, Mass.: Harvard University Press, 1918.
Scripta Minora. Translated by E. C. Marchant. Cambridge, Mass.: Harvard University Press, 1925.
The Cyropaedia. Translated by Walter Miller. Cambridge, Mass.: Harvard University Press, 1914.
Anabasis. Translated by Carleton Brownson. Cambridge, Mass.: Harvard University Press, 1922.
Memorabilia and Oeconomicus. Translated by E. C. Marchant. Cambridge, Mass.: Harvard University Press, 1923.

Helots - Serfs in archaic Sparta who were permanently bound to the land they worked for their Spartan Master.

Hoplite - Heavily armed infantry soldiers in ancient Greece who entered battle in a phalanx.

CHAPTER I

Background: warfare, slavery, and ideology

It was not I who wrote the decree, the battle of Chaeronea did.
Hyperides on his proposal to free and arm Athenian slaves to fight
Philip after the defeat at Chaeronea.[1]

War in archaic Greece was as traditional as the society that produced it. The hoplite battle was a limited and conventional way of fighting. Their monopoly of the military reinforced the dominance of independent farmers in political life. With the economic growth and the sophisticated and innovative culture of the classical period, warfare also lost its traditional character. The escalation that Herodotus, Thucydides, and Xenophon document threatened to tear cities apart rather than to bolster their social structures. This book considers the encounter of an ideology rooted in aristocratic and then hoplite combat with the total war of the classical period.

Specifically, the increased manpower needs of a harsher system of war favored the recruitment of slaves and Helots. Chattel slavery had contributed to the economic growth that allowed the transgression of the hoplite ethic; the exploitation of Helots allowed the Spartan army to become the first professional one in the Greek world. Accordingly, large unfree populations were present to fight for their cities or – in another breach of previous practice – to desert or rebel at an enemy's instigation.[2] When the instances of slave participation are viewed in isolation or are falsely assigned to the category of emergency measures, they may appear to be of marginal importance. When the important cases of slave and Helot involve-

---

[1] Hyperides fr. 28 Jensen.

[2] To avoid the frequent use of the awkward expression "unfree," I often use "slave" in a loose sense to include Helots as well. Where the distinction between the two is important, the expressions "Helots" and "chattel slaves" will make this clear.

I

ment are put together, it becomes clear that, during the classical period, the unfree played a decisive role on several occasions and participated on even more.

We will treat these events in the appropriate chapters; a general idea of their significance can be gained by a consideration of the two major Greek powers for most of our period, Athens and Sparta. The single useful piece of epigraphic evidence on the subject suggests that the navy upon which Athens' power rested may have contained about as many slaves as Athenian citizens.[3] The Spartan-led navy that eventually defeated Athens probably contained an even larger proportion of slave rowers. During the height of Spartan power there were as many Neodamodeis, ex-Helot hoplites, on active military service as there were Spartan citizens in total. The fall of Sparta and supremacy of Thebes was sealed as much by the establishment of Messene for Sparta's rebellious Helots as by the battle of Leuctra, which crippled Sparta's army.

All of this was anathema to the traditional link between politics and war. How could slaves, generally considered cowardly items of property, take part in one of the defining activities of the citizen? The participation of slaves in war was not simply immoral. It was not simply a matter for condemnation. Rather, within a certain ideology, it ought to have been impossible. Accordingly, the use of slaves in war receives short shrift in the classical historians. Their world views could not easily accommodate a military role for slaves.

Much of this book will be devoted to demonstrating in detail these two propositions: slaves were important to Greek warfare; classical Greek historians tend to play down their role. The reasons for Greek unease with slaves in warfare turn out to tell us a great deal about classical society, economics, and the places of these three historians within their cultures. In crude terms the use of slaves in warfare was regarded as an abomination because of Greek culture's admiration of martial prowess and contempt for slaves.

The prestige of Greek warfare derived from several sources. Some of these seem obvious and natural: societies tend to reward and to admire their protectors. More sinister, the possession of weapons can be a source of political power. Throughout recorded history, classes

---

[3] *IG* 2² 1951 now *IG* 1³ 1032 a-i. See Laing (1966) and Graham (1992).

that wield military power have often dominated their societies.[4] The ideological counterpart of this domination is the high cultural value put upon the warrior and upon war. Most significant for our investigation, Greece had no warrior class separate from the leaders and citizens of its cities.[5] Thus participation in warfare was linked first with aristocratic rule and then with the egalitarian ethos of hoplite farmers. In the fifth century, the *thetes*, the lowest class of Athenian citizens, gained ideological clout since they rowed in the navy upon which Athens' power rested.[6]

Despite the historic and ideological link between political prerogatives and military service, the Athenians were not about to extend rights to their slaves when they too rowed in the navy. Consequently, the position of slaves presented an awkward anomaly for the Athenian mentality. Although metics, resident aliens, also served Athens – both in the navy and as hoplites – without political rights at Athens, there were additional factors that made fighting slaves more threatening.

Slaves' particular unsuitability for war, which we shall document at length, was essentially due to two factors. First and most directly, the Greeks affected to believe that slaves were cowards. This image of slaves, attested in many other slave societies, to a certain extent merely reflects the reality of slaves' relative powerlessness: slaves could rarely stand up to their masters. Paradoxically, such representations may also assuage the insecurity of masters living in dangerous proximity to their slaves. Second and perhaps more important, slavery played an important ideological role in the relations between sections of the free population. Economically, the relatively peaceful coexistence of rich and poor in Athens was based on slave labor. On the ideological level, slaves were a group against which all Athenians could define themselves as a unity. Thus slaves especially ought to have been kept from the warfare so closely connected with civic rights.[7]

---

[4] Andreski (1968) 26; Howard (1991) 167. Harris (1977) 47–97 finds also a strong connection between the male monopoly of warfare and patriarchy.

[5] Mossé (1985) 221–222; Garlan (1989) 143.

[6] [Xen.] 1.2; Millett (1993) 183, 187, 191; cf. Momigliano (1944), Andreski (1968) 27, and Starr (1978).

[7] In fact, the extension of military roles to every level of the Athenian citizen population may have increased the distaste for recruiting slaves. Vagts (1959) 442–443 points out that the extension of military participation and prestige often requires singling out small groups

Evidence from epic, drama, oratory, and philosophy will help fill out our picture of classical ideologies; post-classical biographers and historians as well as writers on military tactics give us additional evidence about actual military practices. Only the classical historians face both ways. Only Herodotus, Thucydides, and Xenophon both exemplify the thinking of the classical Greek world and systematically narrate its warfare.[8] They were directly confronted with describing wars in which slaves participated within systems of thought that could not easily acknowledge this possibility. Although all three historians faced this same problem, their distinct outlooks, periods, and subject matters ensure that each contributes different perspectives to our understanding of the Greek ideology and practice of slavery and war.

The contrast between slavery and freedom is central to the world of Herodotus. Nations that are soft, cowardly, subject to despotic rule, or defeated in war are likened to slaves. In his story of the Scythians' slaves Herodotus makes it clear that not only metaphorical but actual slavery is incompatible with military prowess. His noble story of Greece's fight for freedom has no place for slave warriors by the side of the victorious Greeks.

Although Thucydides is justly renowned for his unflinching gaze, his narrative too was shaped by the categories of his time and world. These sharply distinguished between slaves and citizens and associated only the citizens with military participation. This dichotomy between slaves and citizens smoothed the uneasy coexistence between rich and poor among the citizens. The Peloponnesian War drove Athens into civil war and gave rise to the widespread use of Helots and slave rowers as well as the incitement of slave revolts. Consequently, the categories of slave and of citizen were increasingly blurred at the very time they were most needed to unite the fractured citizenry. In his history Thucydides maintains these threatened boundaries at the cost of playing down the awkward role of slaves in his war.

Xenophon is best understood in terms of his militaristic justi-

---

without honor: the prestige of fighting, common and thus cheap, could be bolstered by the contrast with a despised class. In classical Athens, slaves may have served this role.

[8] I have used fragmentary historians and the *Hellenica Oxyrhynchia* for military practices; it would be over-ambitious to extract a world view even from the latter. The uncertainties of source criticism would make it unwise to attempt an account of Ephorus or other historians whose narratives must be extracted from the surviving history of Diodorus Siculus.

fication both of leadership and of slave-master relationships. His philosophy equates the virtues which justify rule with those which bring success in war: rulers should also be the best soldiers. In contrast, slaves are anti-warriors: they are soft, feminine, non-Greek, and cowardly. Although this political philosophy had elite or hoplite domination of the city as its primary aim, Xenophon explicitly calls for the exclusion of slaves from warfare, a necessary corollary, on several occasions. Since Xenophon wrote in a variety of genres, he also provides our best evidence for the Greek stereotype of slaves as cowards in ancient Greece. Arming slaves threatened this stereotype, so fragile yet so psychologically necessary for slaveholders.

These specific cultural and social factors made the participation of slaves in war awkward for the Greeks. Other attitudes could accommodate slave warriors: oligarchic thinking did not insist on the primacy of the divide between slaves and citizens; the increasingly hierarchical armed forces of the fourth century included levels considered appropriate to slaves as well as to citizens and to nobles; professional or mercenary armies were tools of the state rather than the citizens-in-arms. So not even in the realm of ideology was the exclusion of slaves from warfare natural or obvious. Rather I suspect that a coincidence between the ancient and the modern Western ideal of citizens and soldiers has led to an overly enthusiastic embrace of only one strand of Greek ideology, the prohibition of slaves from warfare.

The fundamental reason for modern underestimation of the importance of slave participation in warfare is the very reticence of the ancient sources that this book aims to document. Two other lines of reasoning, although often unstated, tend to leave modern scholars skeptical about slaves in war. My specific arguments about the extent of slave use will stand or fall on their own merits. Nevertheless, a discussion of these unspoken grounds for objection may disarm them and will also illustrate the significance of this project. The first set of objections is intellectual, the second political.

Structuralism and the study of mentalities have had great influence in the field of Greek history. Both emphasize the ways that people think about their world rather than attempting to unmask the realities that lie beneath these models. Inspired by structural linguistics, structuralism holds that all societies organize their conceptual worlds according to systems of opposed categories. It is this system of differences rather than any specific events – or even conscious thought – that is the subject of their science.[9] The study of mentalities is just as focused on the way that people understand their worlds. It emphasizes, however, the unique mental worlds of different peoples and periods.[10] Neither school is primarily concerned with the accuracy of the models and interpretive categories it elicits. Historians influenced by these schools of thought emphasize the ideological equivalence of soldier and citizen. They pay little attention to actual practice.[11]

In some ways, this concentration on ancient ideology is salutary. Greek thinking often turns out to have been more complex and various than expected: our authors' slant on fighting slaves is certainly not a screen that we need only to get behind. Nevertheless, no matter how subtle the reading of the Funeral Oration's ideology, Pericles' ideal of "falling in love" with your city needs to be confronted with the blunt realism of Aeneas Tacticus' one thousand and one ways to do in your political enemies – religious festivals, for example, were particularly opportune.[12] What people say is usually interesting and revealing; it is not always true. My goal is to pay attention to the model through which the Greeks understood the world without assuming that it perfectly represents – or creates – their world.

Other objections to my argument may derive from political motives of several sorts. One is the notion that the reputation of the West's admired ancestors, the Greeks, may be contaminated if they turn out to have used slaves in their wars. The undoubted bellicosity of the Greeks, especially the Athenians, has often been palliated by

---

[9] Lévi-Strauss (1963) is the classic introduction to structural anthropology. Pierre Vidal-Naquet (1986) and Hartog (1988) are two works important to our subject influenced by structuralism.

[10] See Lloyd (1990) for bibliography and critical appraisal of the study of mentalities, cf. Williams (1993). Geertz's "thick description," which we discuss below is closely aligned with the study of mentalities.

[11] Loraux (1986) 336 for example, is quite explicit in her distaste for the "historian in quest of *realia*." She has "refused to indulge in the interminable rooting out of illusion." Consequently, Loraux, however perceptive in her reading of ideology, is hardly the scholar to consult for actual practice, e.g., Goldhill (1990) 109.

[12] Pericles in Th. 2.43.1(M): "you should every day look at the true power of the city and should fall in love with the city." Aeneas Tacticus 17.1–2: "In a state full of dissension and mutual suspicion, circumspection is needed about the crowds at torch-races, horse-races, or other contests – indeed, at all religious festivals for the whole people . . . A faction can take advantage even of occasions like these to overcome its opponents. For example . . . " Cf. Arist. *Ath. Pol.* 15.4, 18.4.

the argument that they, at least, put their own lives on the line when they voted for war. That this was only part of the story seems to undermine one of the last claims to simple admiration that the classical Greeks retain.

I have more sympathy for a fear which can perhaps be characterized as leftist in its sympathy for the oppressed: if slaves are shown to have fought for their masters, this could be taken to indicate their attachment rather than resentment or resistance to slavery.[13] Of course, some slaves may have loved their masters. Some may have wanted to risk their lives for the very system of slavery. Many varieties of behavior and belief are likely to occur among large numbers of individuals. I suspect that most slaves were quite smart enough to hate their masters – we will see some hints of this in Xenophon – or felt at best ambivalence. The key point will emerge that fighting does not indicate true feelings or require affection. People can – and usually do – fight for others, for pay, or out of compulsion.

On the one hand, reactionary historians maintain the purity of citizen warfare. On the other, "leftist" historians unnecessarily protect an abstract ideal of discontented slaves. Neither motivation makes for good history. In both cases, we are repeating the gesture of the Greeks themselves for whom the categories of slave and citizen/warrior had to be kept separate.[14]

CLASSICAL WARFARE

Although war and battles have always been the stuff of history, in recent decades historians have paid particular attention to the connections between Greek warfare, culture, and society. Yvon Garlan points out that from 490 to 338, Athens was at war two years out of every three and never experienced ten years of peace.[15] In the absence of a standing, professional army most male citizens could – and did on occasion – experience warfare first-hand. From the fifth to the mid-fourth century, throughout our whole period, the basic divisions of the citizen body at Athens were based on military status:

[13] Fogel (1989) 158 notes a similar "work ethic" of resistance in some work on Southern slavery.

[14] See Bernal (1987) for another interpretation of classical historiography in terms of a concern for purity, in this case racial purity.

[15] Garlan (1975) 15.

the top class provided money for public services including warships, the *hippeis* formed the cavalry, the next class, the *zeugitai*, were hoplites, and the *thetes* rowed in the navy.[16]

Warfare was also central to Greek culture. Vidal-Naquet interprets the coming of age in Athens as the transformation of the anti-hoplite *ephebe* into the hoplite citizen.[17] Winkler argues that tragic festivals were the "occasion for elaborate symbolic play on themes of proper and improper civic behavior, in which the principal component of proper male citizenship was military." In particular, he emphasizes the "quasi-military features of tragic choral dancing."[18] Hanson shows that hoplite warfare was part of the yearly cycle of life for early classical farmers.[19] Furthermore, "the peacetime fascination with the use of shield and spear, the hoplite's ritualistic dance, the competitive race in armor – and the interest of the vase painter, sculptor, and poet" are manifestations of constant anxiety about battles to come.[20]

Some hyperbolic formulations, however, distort the relationship of social status and military participation. Vidal-Naquet insists that the nobility of nobles was "utterly inseparable from their characters as warriors." He implies that there was no social status other than that conferred by fighting.[21] Such a way of thinking may typify some of Xenophon's or Livy's more extravagant moments, but does not characterize any real society. Meier has no trouble showing that the status of Greek nobles depended on factors other than warfare. Some such factors were luxury, music, owning land, and taking part in politics.[22] Similarly, the rough equality of hoplites depended as much on their possession of similar farms as upon their interchangeable places in the phalanx.

The importance of warfare in Greek culture may have been a constant until the mid-fourth century; the nature of armed conflict and its social effects changed dramatically in the fifth century. War in the archaic period had been limited with respect to the means employed and to the parts of society that took part. Throughout the fifth century – culminating in the Peloponnesian War – limits on the way that war was waged broke down.

In appearance Greek land warfare was modern: the Greeks used

[16] Hansen (1991) 116.   [17] Vidal-Naquet (1986c) 120.   [18] Winkler (1990a) 21, 56.
[19] Hanson (1983).   [20] Hanson (1989) 221.
[21] Vidal-Naquet (1986d) 85 followed by Lengauer (1979) 12–13.
[22] Meier (1990) 561, 573ff.

the compact formations usually taken to distinguish "true" from "primitive" war.[23] Nevertheless, the brief, but bloody, battles of early hoplite warfare show more characteristics of traditional – if not primitive – war than of prolonged modern struggles. Early Greek hoplites fought in ways that tended both to limit the killing to one time and place and to reduce the economic impact of war.[24] The decisive nature of Greek battle did not depend upon the magnitude of the victories obtained but rather upon certain conventions. Hanson points out that killing was limited by "the postmortem viewing of the dead, the exchange of bodies, the erection of the battlefield trophy, the lack of organized pursuit and further slaughter, and, above all, the mutual understanding to abide by the decision achieved on the battlefield."[25] Pritchett notes other conventional features such as formal challenges and prearranged battles.[26] Tactical maneuvering or trickery played only a small part in early hoplite warfare.[27] With the exception of Sparta's conquest of Messenia, hoplite war had as its goal merely the acquisition – often temporary – of marginal border lands.[28]

Granted, the idea of the fair and limited fight did not completely dominate Greek thinking about war. In Homer there are hints of an earlier, less conventional view of war. For example, Homer does not consider ambushes unheroic. Odysseus even went looking for poison for his arrows, although the Gods disapproved.[29] Even in the classical age, the dominance of hoplite ideology was never quite complete. In Euripides' *Heracles*, Lycus and Amphitryon argue about the relative merits of hoplite fighting and archery. The villainous tyrant Lycus opposes the stout hoplite to Heracles' cowardly bow; the noble Amphitryon favors killing enemies from a distance without fear of retaliation.[30] It would be over-schematic to imagine a

---

[23] Turney-High (1971) 39.   [24] Hanson (1991a) 6; Ober (1994) 7.

[25] Hanson (1989) 223.   [26] *GSW* 2.147, 2.173.

[27] *GSW* 3.331; Detienne (1974) 180 n. 17.

[28] Connor (1988) 16. Sparta seems also to have tried to interfere in other cities' internal affairs, but see Cartledge (1979) 139–140, 148 for a critical appraisal of Sparta's role as deposer of tyrants.

[29] *GSW* 3.330. Hom. *Od.* 1.260–263. In an older version of the return of Odysseus – who did name his son Telemachus, fighter from afar – Odysseus may have killed all of the suitors with his bow: Homer has Odysseus run out of arrows and rearm to finish the fight with a spear to accommodate the hoplite class's contempt for unsporting combat at a distance (Griffin [1987] 71).

[30] Eur. *HF* 151–204.

Homeric time of acceptance, a hoplite period of strict rules, and then a complete breakdown in the fourth century. Nevertheless, Hanson *et al.* are basically right: the Greeks rarely used tricks and fought largely according to convention during the archaic and early classical period.[31]

Traditional hoplite warfare lasted as long as it did for various reasons. The common Greek culture of the different city-states must have played an important part. The antagonists all shared in a common language, similar customs, and the pan-Hellenic festivals. In contrast, the Greeks did not defend themselves against the Persians by offering fair fights on level ground.[32] Common adherence to the hoplite ethic was in some sense "a wonderful conspiracy" in that loss of life and especially economic harm was minimized.[33] The level of military technology may have abetted the conspiracy: since the Greeks were unable to storm walled cities, the scope of victories was necessarily limited. The costs of escalation may have obviously outweighed the possible benefits.[34] The way that the campaigning season dovetails into the yearly cycle of agriculture suggests that there may not have been the extra time or wealth to fight extended wars requiring the long-term supply of an army.[35]

In addition, hoplite warfare aimed at internal stability as much as at external threats.[36] Indeed, Robert Connor compares a battle to a sacrifice. He concludes that its primary function was civic self-representation.[37] Several scholars argue that the hoplite ethic was a way that the class of farmers who made up the hoplites maintained their power. By limiting warfare to a type that required money for armor, but more men than the aristocracy, and which could be fought and finished during a break in the farming season, the

---

[31] *Pace* Wheeler (1988).

[32] Ober (1994) 8. This contrast is a further piece of evidence that wars between Greek cities were fought within conventional limits.

[33] Hanson (1991a) 6.

[34] Meier (1990a) 569. He also points out that during much of the archaic period expansion via colonization or around colonies was possible without the conquest of neighboring cities (572).

[35] Hanson (1989) 35. Turney-High (1971) 30 considers possession of the economic resources to supply an army as perhaps the key factor that brings a people over the "military horizon." In Thucydides, Pericles contrasts the backward Peloponnesians, whose poverty keeps them from fighting long wars, with the modern Athenians who have the wealth to fight a protracted war (Th. 1.141.3). This supports our argument that Greece was only leaving the realm of primitive warfare in the 5th century.

[36] Cartledge (1977) 24; Garlan (1975) 31: Foxhall (1993) 143.   [37] Connor (1988) 17, 23.

hoplites shut out both the rich and the poor from the symbolic capital that defending the city conferred.[38]

The hoplite ethic broke down for reasons that were no doubt complex. A summary in broad strokes will suffice for here. Economic expansion was a necessary precondition for more intense warfare. States in the classical period could afford to arm greater numbers of people for longer periods. In such a situation, the initial advantage of escalation may have proved too tempting to clever tacticians.[39] The extended war with Persia may have accustomed Greece to war outside of the limits of the hoplite tradition. Finally, naval warfare, which had not developed the same conventions, became more important.[40] For all these reasons fifth-century warfare differed radically from the previous hoplite battles.[41] Early hoplite warfare was like a contest, an *agon*, in that it was conducted according to set rules. The decline of the hoplite *agon* led to conditions that encouraged the use of slaves in war.

In the growing Athenian economy, numerous slaves – perhaps 100,000 – were available to fight.[42] The wealth of Athens enabled it to support numbers of sailors in excess of its citizen population for extended periods. Competition among cities transformed the ability to man large numbers of ships into the necessity for doing so; Athens was not the only wealthy, slave-owning state in Greece. The manpower demands of Greek navies were voracious compared with those of hoplite armies. Athens needed 34,000 men to man the navy that fought against the Persians at Artemisium. At this time, Athens could still only field 8,000 hoplites.[43] From early in the fifth century Athens could no longer man its ships with citizens alone.[44] The casualties suffered in naval warfare were also far higher than those

---

[38] Garlan (1975) 127; Cartledge (1977) 24; Connor (1988) 18; Hanson (1991a) 6; Ober (1994) 4–8. See also Hunt (1994) 268 n. 1035 *contra* Holladay (1982).

[39] Ober (1991) 188.

[40] See Th. 1.13–14 with *HCT* I.120–126 on the growth of Greek navies.

[41] Connor (1988) 29; Meier (1990a) 579.

[42] Garlan (1988) 59. Some other estimates are as follows: Sargent (1924) 126: 67,000–103,000; Gomme (1933) 26: 115,000; Vogt (1975) 4: 115,000; Finley (1982a) 102: 60,000–80,000; Hansen (1991) 93: 150,000; Sallares (1991) 60: 30,000–50,000 (4th century); Cartledge (1993a) 135: 60,000–80,000.

[43] Vidal-Naquet (1986d) 92. Before the Persian Wars Athens manned navies of 70 ships which would require fewer than 14,000 men (H. 6.89). In the Peloponnesian War, Athens manned up to 250 triremes (Th. 3.17.1–2 with Kallet-Marx [1993] 130–134, 150–151 for bibliography and a recent discussion).

[44] Meier (1990a) 584.

in hoplite battles. If 50 ships sank in a battle, up to 10,000 men could die. More than twice that number of ships went down in the largest battles. On the other hand, hoplite casualties in the entire century from 470 to 370 may have totaled only 24,000.[45]

The duration of campaigns also increased. Athenian sieges of recalcitrant allies – not to mention the Egyptian and Sicilian expeditions – could last for years. In contrast, a traditional hoplite battle took up part of one day in a campaign measured in weeks.

Wars became more important to cities.[46] No longer matters of borderlands, wars often determined the political independence, if not the physical survival of a city. Athens itself was usually in the position of dictating terms. At the end of the Peloponnesian War, however, Athens' enemies considered enslaving its whole population.[47]

The combination of wealth and risky wars fought by huge navies led to a situation in which all possible sources of manpower including slaves were used. Slave involvement in the intensification of warfare could work also to the detriment of their masters. As war grew more economic both in its ends and its means, slaves became a particularly vulnerable type of property. In times of war slaves had far greater opportunities to run away – an option they seem to have pursued often enough even in peace. A common tactic was to offer freedom to the fugitive slaves of an enemy city. This could induce mass desertion and cripple an opponent's economy. For instance, Thucydides reports that more than 20,000 slaves, most of them skilled, fled to Decelea. This many slaves could have contributed – as a rough guess – 200 talents per year to the Athenian economy.[48] Such a sum was more than a third of the total tribute paid by the empire.[49] The effort Sparta went to for every defection among Athens' allies points out how relatively effective the tactic of inciting slave desertion was. The Helots of Sparta, especially those in Messenia, were rebellious on their own account. Their discontent

---

[45] Hanson (1995) 308.   [46] Meier (1990a) 583.   [47] *HG* 2.2.19–20; Plut. *Lys.* 15.

[48] Based on an obol of profit per slave per day as in *Vect.* 4.14: the lowest daily pay for a laborer in the Erechtheum work records was 5 obols per day, of which no more than 3 would be needed for subsistence (Randall [1953] 208; cf. Pritchett [1956] 277). As the population of Athens was living largely on the income of the empire during the Peloponnesian War, the comparison of public and private finances is not inappropriate.

[49] Th. 2.13.3 gives 600 talents as the total tribute. Scholars question whether this number may be too large (cf. Kallet-Marx [1993] 99); this would only make our argument stronger.

compounded the effectiveness of an appeal to them by the Athenians. When war rose in ferocity to the level of inciting slaves to revolt, it was far from serving the integrative and stabilizing purposes of the hoplite *agon*.

Historians generally acknowledge that the expansion of warfare led to a breakdown of the citizen-soldier link. Their tendency, however, is to locate this break in the late-fifth or fourth century, to point mainly to the use of mercenary soldiers, and to consider this change a sign of decline.[50] As we shall see, trends in fourth-century land warfare do suggest this pattern. The Athenian navy, however, one of the dominant forces in the Greek world through the fifth century, was manned only in part by citizens. Scholars' elision of the fifth century may derive from a preconception that the citizen-soldier is an ideal not only in some moral sense, but in terms of power. According to this logic it is only in the decadence of the fourth century that the breakdown of the citizen-soldier can be located.

One can make the opposite argument: the most powerful states are those in which the citizens no longer have to do all of their fighting and which have the ability to recruit others for this dangerous work. For example, when Athens mounted its most ambitious campaigns – or showed the depth of its resiliency – its navy probably included the greatest proportion of non-citizens. Similarly, it was during the zenith of Spartan power in the 390s that Sparta sent out armies of Neodamodeis. Citizen armies may dominate the 20th century world, but this has not always been the case. It ceased to be the case in Greece by the mid-fifth century at the latest.

HELOTS

Throughout this book our attention will alternate between the chattel slaves of cities such as Athens, Chios, and Syracuse and the Helots of Sparta. Since the Helots were considered slaves by many Greeks and played a conspicuous part in warfare, both as soldiers and as rebels, their inclusion is unavoidable. They require separate treatment, because their actual status was not that of slaves. Additionally, the justice of their subjugation was contested to a far greater extent than that of chattel slaves. This issue will figure

---

[50] Garlan (1975) 91–93; Mossé (1985) 223, 229: Loraux (1986) 98.

prominently when we consider attempts to instigate revolution among the Helots. Here we need to show that in Spartan and pro-Spartan ideology, the Helots figured as arch-slaves. Their recruitment was favored by practical advantages rather than a lack of ideological difficulties.

Scholars have described the Helots as state slaves, collective slaves, undeveloped or even private slaves, serfs, villeins, or peasant serfs of the state.[51] Helots were different from chattel slaves in several respects. Although some served the Spartans personally either as shield-bearers on campaign or in their houses in Sparta, most Helots lived separately from their masters whose political and military duties kept them in Sparta.[52] Helots were not cut off from their families and homes; they were not, as in Orlando Patterson's well-known definition of slavery, "natally alienated."[53]

The gap between Helots and Spartiates was not as great either socially or legally as that between Athenians and slaves: the children of Helot mothers and Spartiate fathers were given a partial citizenship and were allowed to go through the Spartan education.[54] There does not even seem to have been much prejudice against such offspring: both Gylippus and Lysander were perhaps such half-caste children; yet they rose as high as any non-royal Spartan.[55]

More significant, the amount of produce that the Helots' Spartiate masters could appropriate was limited.[56] Detleff Lotze correctly deduces from this that the Helots had property rights to the remnant

---

[51] M. I. Finley (1982b) emphasizes that Spartan society consisted of a spectrum of statuses whose interpretation in terms of the slave/free dichotomy hinders our understanding. Detleff Lotze (1959) argues that Helots were not serfs since their personal service for the Spartans was identical to slavery; he calls them collective slaves. Older and especially continental scholarship is concisely reviewed in Oliva (1971) 38–43, who eventually opts for "undeveloped slavery." Since then G. E. M. de Ste. Croix ([1981] 149–150, [1988]) has argued for state-serfs. Cartledge ([1985] 40–41, [1979], 161ff.) agrees with Ste. Croix that legally the Helots were state-serfs, but emphasizes that they were slaves in terms of being exploited involuntary producers and were so called by the Greeks. Garlan (1988) 87 sees the difference between Helots and slaves in the fact that the Helots were subjugated as a community rather than as individuals and prefers the expression communal servitude. Ducat (1990) 29, 46–48, 50, 140, 151 tends to emphasize similarities between Helots and slaves, but admits that it was the relative independence of Helots that required the extremely oppressive measures that made some Greeks consider Helotage an extreme form of slavery (182).

[52] Lotze (1959) 35 collects the references.   [53] Patterson (1982) 5ff.

[54] Hooker (1980) 119 on Ath. 6.271 e-f.   [55] Kagan (1987) 298.

[56] Cartledge (1979) 164; Figueira (1984) 108 n. 63.

of their harvest: they could accumulate wealth and leave it to their heirs.[57] Although most Helots were poor, there is even evidence of affluent Helots.[58] At the very least many Helots were in the position of those favored slaves at Athens, "those living separately," who had primarily an economic relationship with their masters.

Since Helots lived with their families in their home country rather than as outsiders in a foreign land, their slavery was collective rather than individual.[59] Some scholars, however, have overemphasized the collective nature of the Helots' subjugation.[60] The evidence concerning the question of whether the Helots were private property is ambiguous. Jean Ducat points out that the references to the punishment of Helots in Myron and pseudo-Xenophon imply that, although the state or the Spartiates in general had broad rights vis-à-vis the Helots, Helots had specific masters.[61] In need Spartans could use each other's slaves, but no more than each other's horses and dogs, certainly private possessions.[62] Helots were freed by state decree, but even at Athens it was the state that freed the slaves who rowed at Arginusae.[63] The link between the possession of Helots and of land is strong. Nevertheless, since the nature of Spartan land tenure is obscure, even this connection provides no firm ground from which to elucidate the ownership of Helots.[64]

Sparta was a society which idealized equality and communality, but permitted individual differences. Accordingly the position of the Helots was a compromise. The view that the Helots were "really" privately owned, but in a state that in general showed little respect for individual rights, and the contrary perspective according to which they were "essentially" state slaves, but lent rather freely to individual Spartans, both describe the same situation. Either description is different from that of chattel slaves. One illustrative difference was that Helots could not be sold individually. For all these reasons no social historian would classify the Helots simply as slaves.

---

[57] Lotze (1959) 32.   [58] Th. 4.26.6; Plut. *Cleom.* 23.

[59] The question of whether the Helots kept their pre-conquest villages is discussed in Cartledge (1979) 163–164.

[60] Garlan (1988) 87.

[61] Ducat (1990) 27–29 on Myron, *FGrH* 106 F 2 and [Xen.] 1.11.

[62] Lotze (1959) 42.   [63] Th. 4.26.5, 5.34.1.

[64] See Hodkinson (1986) and Cartledge (1979) 165ff. for a skeptical view of the tradition that the Spartan *kleroi* were inalienable.

Despite these evident differences, many Greek literary sources including Xenophon, Plato, and Isocrates refer to the Helots as *douloi,* "slaves."[65] Official treaties between Sparta and Athens also use this term.[66] This may well reflect Spartan usage: a scholiast to Thucydides claims that the Spartans called the Helots *douloi* to dishonor and humiliate them.[67] Thucydides himself equates the Helots with the *oiketai* in Chios, who were certainly chattel slaves.[68] Critias goes so far as to assert that in Sparta the free are most free and the slaves most slavish.[69] Insofar as Greeks thought of the Helots as *douloi,* their participation in war would conjure up the same difficulties as that of chattel slaves.

The Greeks commonly derived the word Helot from *helein,* to capture; the Helots were the captured ones.[70] The Helots may have seemed particularly pure slaves since they had lost their freedom because of defeat in war. As we shall see, military inferiority was often considered the ultimate basis of slavery. The Spartan warriors were conversely the ideal master class. So in terms of the distinction between the fighters of wars, the citizens, and the losers in them, the slaves, the Helots appeared perfect slaves and consequently unsuited for fighting.[71]

The use of Helots in war was also contrary to the related idea, found in many slave societies, of slaves as the enemy within.[72] Slaves were incorporated into a society, but always remained outsiders. Thus they were barred from arms. That the Helots fit into this category is explicit in the Ephors' annual declaration of war against

---

[65] *H.G.7.1.13; Ages.* 2.24, *Lac.* 12.4; Isoc. *Archidamus* 28; Pl. *Leg.* 6,776d considers Helots as a subset of *douloi.* In [Pl.] *Alc.* 1.122d, Helots are even assimilated to *andrapodon,* a word which emphasizes that slaves were property like livestock.

[66] Th. 4.118.7, 5.23.3. This official usage guarantees that the use of slave words for Helots was not metaphorical, but that Helots were considered a subset of slaves.

[67] Scholia to Th. 1.101.2 in Hude (1927).   [68] Th. 8.40.2.

[69] Critias, fr. 37 Diels. Cartledge (1979) 162 generalizes that Spartans and most others called the Helots slaves. A little noted exception is [Xenophon] 3.10–11 who implies that the Messenians are ὁμοῖοι to the Athenian demos. This is an example of the oligarchic tendency to lump everyone below the elite together.

[70] Toynbee (1969) 197. Other ancient authors derived the name from the city Helos in Laconia which the Spartans conquered. Ducat (1990) 8ff. contains a full discussion of the naming of the Helots.

[71] The Messenians owed their position to defeat in war. The Laconian Helots may have been the victims of early conquests or of social differentiation.

[72] Patterson (1982) 39.

them.[73] The Helots should always have been enemies rather than fellow soldiers.

As occupants of the bottom rung in the Spartan social hierarchy, the Helots were in a position analogous to that of chattel slaves at Athens. For Athenians to equate the two may have been as natural as for Herodotus to equate the god Amun in Egypt with Zeus.[74] This was especially true since the Helots at Sparta were treated with more pronounced and deliberate disrespect than even chattel slaves at Athens.[75] Greeks may well have been more conscious of the dishonor shared by slaves and Helots than of differences in their economic position, legal relationship to their owners, and the collective or individual nature of their subjection. In this book we are largely concerned with the views of non-Spartans. Even at Sparta, Helots were hardly appropriate material for soldiers.

To compensate for their actual status as Greeks living in their own houses and land, whose economic exploitation was limited, the Spartans pursued a deliberate policy of humiliating the Helots.[76] If the Helots were neither natally alienated nor quite socially dead in Patterson's terms, the Spartans made sure that they were generally dishonored. Ducat's article on Spartan contempt for the Helots brings this out well. The Helots were dressed in hides to distinguish them from the free and to assimilate them to the subhuman realm of animals. Forcing the Helots to do vulgar dances and to get drunk taught Spartan youths to despise the Helots.[77] The story that Helots were beaten once each year regardless of whether they had committed a wrong clearly evokes their status as slaves. This ritual – perhaps a caricature of the heroic beatings endured by Spartan boys at the temple of Artemis Orthia – affirmed the Helots' place in Spartan society.[78]

Especially apropos to our investigation is the report that Helots who became too strong were killed. Ducat explains this on the ideological level: Helots were figured as the weak nourishing part of

---

[73] Plut. *Lyc.* 28.   [74] H. 2.42.

[75] Cf. Dem. 9.3. The aspect of dishonor is emphasized by Patterson as one of the three distinguishing marks of slavery (Patterson [1982] 10).

[76] Cf. Cartledge (1979) 162–165; Cartledge (1985) 40; *contra* Figueira (1984) 108–109.

[77] Ducat (1974) 1456–1458 on Myron in *Ath.* 14.657d; David (1989) 9. The *diphthera*, however, may have rustic rather than bestial connotations. See M. Jameson (1992) 139 n. 22 *contra* Ducat (1990) 111–114.

[78] Ducat (1974) 1458. Ducat underrates the mundane effect of producing terror and submission in his enthusiasm for the symbolic aspect of this ritual.

the state in contrast to the Spartan warriors.[79] For a Helot to be too strong threatened the boundaries that demarcated Helots and Spartans. The same explanation goes for the 2,000 Helots whose death is reported by Thucydides.[80] These Helots had proven their loyalty to the Spartans at the risk of their lives, but they presented a threat in showing the traits of loyalty and courage that were associated with the Spartans.[81] Just as the recruitment of slaves threatened the boundary between citizen and slave, so too the use of Helots undermined the Spartiates' position as the warrior elite.

The recruitment of Helots, as of Greek slaves in general, was antithetical to this whole system of thought. Sparta's recruitment of Helots posed fewer practical difficulties than the employment of Athenian slaves. Helots were a much larger pool of manpower relative to the number of Spartans. The economic effects of the loss or enfranchisement of some Helots was relatively minor. Since all Spartiates had an allotment of land with Helots, the burden of providing slaves for the state could be spread more evenly; at Athens, the freeing of slaves for Arginusae was a heavy tax on the rich; the use of more paid slaves in the navy could displace *thetes* who may have needed the pay. Most significantly, the Spartan state was particularly invasive and controlling of individuals. A government that could dictate where grown men could eat or sleep could easily recruit or free Helots in the common interest.[82]

Helots had homes and families under Spartan control. Although this constraint may have remained implicit, relatives, friends, and communities could serve as hostages for the good behavior of Helot soldiers. Thus, Helots were tied to their Spartan masters in a way that many chattel slaves were not. The same solidarity that enabled the Helots to rebel against the Spartans could force their cooperation while away on campaign.[83]

The number of Helots is no better known than that of Athenian

---

[79] Ducat (1974) 1459.   [80] Th. 4.80.3–4.   [81] Ducat (1974) 1460.

[82] If we formulate the ownership of Helots as collective with individual Spartans exercising some sort of usufruct, then the Spartan state was merely reclaiming its own when it decided to employ Helots for military duties.

[83] An ideological consideration, unrelated to the difference between slaves and Helots, did make it easier for the latter to be recruited. The Spartan army was particularly hierarchical. Thus it could incorporate different classes without disrupting the social structure. Helots could fight as light-armed, in the rear ranks, or in separate brigades of Neodamodeis without establishing a claim to equality with the professional Spartiate hoplites. We shall explore this Spartan or aristocratic conception of the army below pp. 185–189.

slaves, but relative to the much smaller population of Spartiates –
numbered in the low thousands – their military potential is undeni-
able. Some of the lowest estimates of Helot numbers maintain that
there were seven Helots for each Spartiate.[84] Grundy even claims
that a ratio of fifteen to one is a minimum ratio.[85] The considerations that prompt such estimates are the following: the Spartiates
were all men of leisure supported by the work of Helots; the size and
fertility of Laconia and Messenia could support a large population,
but Spartiates were few; Herodotus finds a total of 35,000 Helots at
Plataea plausible; Thucydides implies that the Spartans had the
greatest number of slaves of any Greek state.[86] Even partial mobilization of the Helots could – and sometimes did – double Sparta's
army.

The Helots were a disenfranchised and utterly despised class.
They should have had no part in war, the activity around which the
whole of Spartiate life revolved: in fact, it was the Spartans who had
the stated policy of keeping the *douloi* from arms.[87] Helots and slaves
are considered in parallel in this thesis not because of the likeness of
their social positions, but rather because both presented similar
threats to the ideology of the citizen-soldier. Although practical
factors helped the Spartans to use their vast pool of Helots in war,
ideological considerations similar to those that operated at Athens
would seem to have forbade the use of Helots as warriors.

IDEOLOGY

Since so much of this book treats Greek ideology, a brief outline of
my approach is necessary. I hope merely to situate within different
schools of thought a model of ideology that is far from startling and
whose justification will mainly consist of the persuasiveness of my
arguments about classical Greek authors and practices. Nevertheless,
although I have tried to give examples, the following discussion is
necessarily somewhat difficult and theoretical. Some readers may
prefer to skip ahead and then return to this section: these theories of
ideology will be easier to understand after having first seen their
application to specific cases.

An ideology, like a world view, is a system of intellectual beliefs

---

[84] M. Jameson (1992) 136.   [85] Grundy (1908) 81.   [86] H. 9.10, 9.28–29; Th. 8.40.2.
[87] *Lac.* 12.4.

and emotional judgments that make up a model of the world according to which raw experience is interpreted.[88] As a symbolic system, an ideology has its own internal dynamic; as an account of the social world, it depends on the reality that it seeks to interpret as well as on the interests of social classes. Since ideology is a function of, at least, these three factors – internal structure, social reality, social interests – it cannot be determined by any one of them. Since ideology is neither fully determined nor completely independent of structure, reality, and interest, its relation to these concepts can be described as semi-autonomous.[89]

The challenge of a sufficient theory of ideology is to indicate more precisely the nature of this semi-autonomy. A theory of ideology can incorporate its internal dynamic by considering it as a system of categories, judgments, and metaphors. This symbolic system provides a framework according to which the social world is arranged and given meaning. Social class participates in ideology in that class interests may determine adherence to one of a variety of competing symbolic models of the world.

In a classic article Clifford Geertz details the sense in which an ideology is a symbolic system. He argues that ideologies can be best understood in terms of their cognitive function:

The drive to make sense out of experience, to give it form and order, is evidently as real and as pressing as the more familiar biological needs. And, this being so, it seems unnecessary to continue to interpret symbolic activities – religion, art, ideology – as nothing but thinly disguised expressions of something other than what they seem to be: attempts to provide orientation for an organism which cannot live in a world it is unable to understand.[90]

All people need to understand the world within some sort of conceptual and evaluative framework with its own categories and metaphors. This conceptual framework is not only internal to the mind, but makes up the public language that renders communication possible.[91] All cultural activity including ideology can be seen as utterances within the languages of different symbolic systems. We

---

[88] Although a strict distinction between world view and ideology probably cannot be made, the objects of ideology are usually society and politics whereas a world view can encompass subjects such as time, death, or happiness. For the sake of variety I here use world view and ideology interchangeably.

[89] F. Jameson (1981) 38 uses the expression semi-autonomy in a slightly different context.

[90] Geertz (1973a) 140.   [91] Geertz (1973b) 214–216.

shall see below that many Greeks both thought and communicated about a large variety of unequal relations using the metaphor of slavery. For example, they likened the way despots treated their subjects to the way masters treated slaves. In this case, the comparison with slavery provides a model according to which to understand – and to condemn – arbitrary governments.

Geertz's formulation is most useful in that the idea of an ideology as a model through which to understand the world seems to catch the way that ideology works on the level of the individual. Ideology does not consist of false statements that people are either duped into believing or impose on others. Rather people both understand the world and communicate by using value-laden symbolic systems. Adherence to one system is not being duped nor is expression through another one cynical manipulation.

Mary Douglas's *tour de force* in explaining the Jewish dietary prohibitions shows just how seriously we need to take the desire to keep categories straight: no explanation of the dietary laws in terms of either their objects – lobsters, pigs, rock badgers – or in terms of early Jewish society is sufficient without considering the internal necessities of the Jewish classification system.[92] Similarly, we shall see that the desire to keep slaves out of war is largely motivated by the need to keep the categories of slave and citizen pure.

Geertz's model, however, tends to pay little attention to the connection of an ideology both to the world it interprets and to the groups who adhere to it. In both cases he points out problems with deterministic connections, but does not succeed in severing the links between ideology, truth, and class.[93]

The view that ideologies reflect the interests of social classes can supplement Geertz's view of ideology as a symbolic system, since there are usually several competing ways to see the social world.[94]

---

[92] Douglas (1966) 41–58; *contra* Harris (1979) 190–197. Bernal invokes a similar concern for purity in his controversial *Black Athena* I : "a racist distaste for mixed populations explains the underestimation of Egyptian and Semitic influence on Greece in the Bronze age. There was a desire to keep Greece as the "racially pure childhood and quintessence of Europe" (Bernal [1987] 396, 293, *et passim*).

[93] Geertz (1973b) 202.

[94] In "Ideology as a Cultural System" (Geertz [1973b] originally published in 1964) Geertz proposed an essentially cognitive theory of ideology. However, in "After the Revolution: The Fate of Nationalism in the New States" (Geertz [1973c] originally published in 1971) he emphasizes the power implications of choosing one way of seeing the world rather than another.

Class interest can determine the particular model that a person selects for purposes both of understanding and communication.[95] For example, when would-be oligarchs in Athens went against the predominant slave/citizen dichotomy and put slaves and the free poor in the same category, their elitist, anti-democratic agenda was manifest.

Geertz makes the criticism that Marxist sociology is "too muscular." Ideology is not always a weapon against another class.[96] The interest that motivates the choice of a model through which to understand the world may be the social harmony rather than class war. For example, ideologies in classical Athens can be divided into those that favored the peaceful coexistence of mass and elite and those that tended towards class warfare among the citizens.[97]

Ideology works by presenting a view of the world that justifies certain actions, behaviors or social relations. Such a model of the world often unifies opinion within a class and thus greatly enhances its power. A certain view of the world may also have a persuasive power among those whose interests are either unclear or ambivalent. This, too, is significant since ruling classes often offer perquisites to some of their inferiors. An ideology may convince such inferiors whose interests are mixed: the usually rebellious Helots fought loyally for the Spartans at the battle of Plataea. They may have expected rewards, perhaps even freedom; their interests were mixed. They may also have subscribed to a view of the world that distinguished sharply between Greeks and barbarians. Thus they thought of themselves as essentially Greeks – their subjection to the

---

[95] One problem is that interests should be defined in terms of the ways that actors see that world and thus in terms of ideologies. But, according to this formulation, interest is a result of ideology and could not be the basis of the choice between different ideologies. I suspect that solid social interests and a purely symbolic system of ideology are both simplifications whose justification lies in their analytical power.

I use class here in a somewhat watered-down sense to take into account lifestyle and legal status in addition to the Marxist criteria of relationship to the mode of production. Thus the interests that influence ideology are those of Moses Finley's "statuses" more than those of G. E. M. de Ste. Croix's "classes" (Finley [1985] 35–61 *contra* Ste. Croix [1981] 91 ff). Within the field of Classics, Finley and Ste. Croix are more allied in their rooting of thought and culture in social reality than their mutual polemics would suggest.

[96] Geertz (1973b) 202.

[97] Since the harmony of mass and elite depended upon chattel slavery, even the first of these alternatives is not as innocuous as its similarity to functionalist theories of culture would suggest.

Spartans notwithstanding – who ought to unite with other Greeks to fight the Persians invaders.

The extent to which ideology wins over those who are simply oppressed tends to be exaggerated. Abercrombie, Hill and Turner in the *Dominant Ideology Thesis* and Scott in *Weapons of the Weak* present valuable correctives to such totalizing theories of ideology as those of Althusser and Foucault.[98] The ideology of the upper class does not convince lower orders of society to acquiesce in their oppression. Even in modern societies with their superior networks of communications, no unitary dominant ideology penetrates the entire society. The lower classes have their own, very different, interpretations of the way the world works. The impression of unanimity is often merely the result of the ruling class's coercive domination of the public sphere. Scott's private interviews in Malaysia made it clear that, although they were hardly closet Marxists, the poorer peasants' views were different from what their public behavior seemed to indicate.[99]

When a "dominant ideology" is accepted, it is often because it can be used against the class in whose interest it has been created. Since an ideology often idealizes social relations, it can be used to criticize the way these relations are actually practiced:[100] the classical Greek notion that citizens deserve their status by virtue of military service to the state tended to bolster the distinction between citizens and non-citizens. This ideology could threaten its creators when they allowed slaves to fight or depended on mercenaries.

Although Eagleton rightly questions Abercrombie, Hill and Turner's conclusion that the ideology of the ruling class plays no part at all in dampening revolt,[101] an overestimation of the importance of ideology lies behind one of the most common and erroneous beliefs about the use of slaves in warfare. Slaves did not fight because of any acceptance of their oppression, but because of practical inducements and constraints.

It is essential for the historian not only to compare one model of the world with another, but to judge their accuracy. For example, the view that war was a matter for citizens was common in ancient Greece. The escalation of the level of warfare in the classical period rendered it false. Arguments of this sort, that social interests can

---

[98] Abercrombie, Hill, and Turner (1980); Scott (1985) 304–351.   [99] Scott (1985) 321.
[100] Scott (1985) 336.   [101] Eagleton (1991) 36.

contribute to a image of the world that is somehow distorted or false,
lead to the dilemma known as Mannheim's paradox.[102] We can only
discuss an ideology if we know the truth that it either suppresses,
omits, or accurately represents. Since all access to truth is indirect,
we may end up comparing two ideologies and merely calling our
own the truth.[103] There may be no absolute answer to this question,
but neither ideologies nor our arguments about them are such free-
floating entities as this view seems to imply.

Symbolic systems need not only to fulfill social and political needs,
but also to provide an accurate "road map" with which to understand and act in the world.[104] This requirement ensures that much
of the interested work of ideologies is performed through categoriza-
tions, emphases, omissions, and metaphors which are not false to
social reality in any simple sense. Even when an ideology makes a
false claim, this claim often coexists with the useful knowledge which
it contradicts: the stereotype of slaves as cringing cowards rarely
prevented their use in war.

False ideologies cannot be ruled out altogether. There are many
examples of ideological beliefs that were counterproductive, but
nevertheless did determine action. To continue the metaphor,
people sometimes do use road maps that are faulty or, at least, out of
date. Geertz believes he can evade Mannheim's paradox through his
concentration on the internal workings of ideology rather than its
relation to truth: whether the "road map" is accurate is "a separate
question."[105] Geertz's approach may perhaps avoid this dilemma,
but it also lames one's historical insight without so great an addition
of scientific certainty as to justify the sacrifice.

For, notwithstanding Mannheim's paradox, the relation of an
ideological model to social reality is essential to its study. A study of
the internal structure of the ideology of American Vietnam War
movies, for example, might well be fascinating. Historians, at least,
would feel the investigation was missing something if no mention

[102] Geertz (1973b) 194.

[103] Michel Foucault distrusts the word ideology because it evokes this – to him – false contrast
between ideology and truth. Foucault ends up by attributing to truth most of the partial
and subjective qualities that are usually associated with the concept of ideology (Foucault
[1980] 118).

[104] Geertz (1973b) 216 uses the road map metaphor. Gay (1974) 198–199 conceives of the
forces that tend towards and away from distortion in terms of Freud's Reality and Pleasure
Principles.

[105] Geertz (1973b) 220.

was made of the fact that the United States was on the losing side in the Vietnam War. This background might be the well-spring of the most interesting insights that could accrue from such a study. Similarly the ideologically motivated omission of slave involvement that I find in Thucydides only exists insofar as I can argue that slaves were, in fact, important to the Peloponnesian War.

Any short treatment of the broad interpretive issues covered in this section is bound to be somewhat simplistic and thin. My main concern is that by trying to accommodate the view of ideology as an interested interpretation of the world and as a symbolic system, my approach may lose the coherence that belongs to either view. I hope rather to use the analytic power of both views while filling in the gaps of each.[106]

---

[106] Compare the approaches of Gay (1974) 198–199; Bourdieu (1977) 43; F. Jameson (1981) 82–83; Scott (1985) 321.

CHAPTER 2

Herodotus: the Persian Wars

Slaves fought then for the first time.
Pausanias on the battle of Marathon.[1]

The Greeks used every resource, including their own slaves, to counter the threat to their lives and freedom presented by the Persian invasions. Helots or slaves fought in the three great land battles of Marathon, Thermopylae, and Plataea. Slaves made up part of the crews of the Athenian navy, which was largely responsible for the victory of Salamis. Herodotus is our only source for some of these cases. Epigraphic or later evidence sometimes informs us about slave participation that Herodotus neglects.

MARATHON AND THE HELOT REVOLT

Most notoriously, Herodotus does not mention the slaves who fought for the Athenians at Marathon in 490. Pausanias refers to the grave of the slave casualties after describing that of the Athenians: "the other is for the Boeotians from Plataea and the slaves; for slaves fought then for the first time."[2] Autopsy is implied by Pausanias' admission that he was unable to find the mound covering the Persian

---

[1] Paus. 1.32.3. One tradition maintains that *douloi* and women defended Argos after the calamitous defeat at Sepeia (*FGrH* 310F6, Paus. 2.20.8–10). These slaves were probably a Helot-like class called the Gymnetes because they usually fought without heavy armor. Significantly, this battle involved a conspicuous escalation beyond the conventional hoplite battle. Rather than resting content with a victory on the battlefield, Cleomenes, the Spartan king, surrounded and massacred the Argive survivors of the battle. Herodotus relates that slaves temporarily took charge of affairs in Argos, since so many of the citizens had been killed (H. 6.83). For the obscurities of this later affair see Seymour (1922) and Tomlinson (1972) 93–100, 268; *contra* Forrest (1960). For a recent discussion with current bibliography see M. Jameson (forthcoming).

[2] Paus. 1.32.5.

dead; his description of the slaves' mound contains no such qualification.[3] In a description of a later action by the Achaean league, Pausanias reveals that the slaves had been set free before the battle: "he [Diaeus], imitating the policy of Miltiades and the Athenians before the battle of Marathon, set the slaves free."[4] Scholars have almost without exception accepted the emancipation and participation of slaves at the battle of Marathon.[5] It is hard to think of a reason for such a disgraceful incident to have been invented.

The slaves probably fought as hoplites. Why else would they have been given their freedom? An individual hoplite attendant might be freed after a battle at his master's discretion for some particular act of valor, but attendants would not have been liberated *en masse* before a battle.

The Athenian decision to arm slaves appears enigmatic in one respect. The Athenians had no significant navy at this time and so the *thetes*, the lowest category of Athenian citizens, were playing no role in the war. The Athenians could have armed *thetes* to fight the Persians. They chose the even lower status slaves instead. The *thetes*, who were to acquire progressively more power after Salamis and throughout the fifth-century naval empire, may have already been threatening hoplite and aristocratic supremacy. The use of slaves could not give any particular rights or prestige to slaves, who could never take a role in politics. The action may even have enhanced the repute of the slave owners who in effect performed a liturgy. To use *thetes*, however, would be to give added status to a more threatening social group. The battle of Marathon could never have become a rallying cry of conservatives at Athens, if the Athenian hoplites had made this mistake in 490.

This explanation will remain speculative, but Aristotle notes a tendency parallel to our putative situation: oligarchies are forced to use mercenaries because of their distrust of the common people.

---

[3] Paus. 1.32.4.

[4] Paus. 7.15.7. Paus. 10.20.2 also mentions the slaves at Marathon: he includes them among the nine thousand men, including also men who were unfit for service, who went out to Marathon.

[5] Sargent (1927) 209–211; Notopoulos (1941); *UAK* 1.22–35; Finley (1980) 99; Garlan (1988) 171; Ducat (1990) 162. Hammond (1992) 147–150 believes that a tomb excavated by Marinatos contains the remains of the slaves. From their numbers he argues that about 400 slaves were given Plataean citizenship, like the Arginusae slaves in 405, and trained as a separate unit of hoplites. On the identification of this tomb with that of the slaves and Plataeans see also Welwei (1979), Van der Veer (1982) 301–304, Lazenby (1993) 75 n. 76.

Such governments sometimes prohibit the poor from possessing heavy arms in particular.[6] Aristotle also notes several cases where changes in prestige due to participation in war had undermined a class's grip on a city.[7] Fear of such a change may have motivated the recruitment before Marathon of slaves, who like mercenaries were outsiders without their own political aspirations.[8] This will not be the last time that we will find attitudes and actions towards slaves determined by politics among the free.

It is not only these slave hoplites that Herodotus skips in his account of Marathon. Plato reports that a war with the Messenian Helots prevented the Spartans from making it to the battle in time.[9] The historicity of a Messenian revolt – the connection with Marathon is more tenuous – has met with responses ranging from trenchant skepticism to outright acceptance.[10] I believe that the well-known evidence on its own makes the revolt probable. More important, Herodotus' failure to mention the revolt is hardly decisive evidence against its occurrence. Rather, in Herodotus we see the first signs of the unease with and omission of Helot revolt that we will be tracing through Thucydides and up to Xenophon's failure to mention the founding of Messene over a century later.

To begin with, one must admit that Plato's story is suspect. Den Boer shows that Plato and his pro-Spartan sources had both the motivation and opportunity to fabricate a Messenian revolt. In the context of Spartan bitterness after the liberation of Messenia in 370, the story of a Messenian revolt would have great appeal: the Messenians had not shown themselves to be true Greeks at the moment of truth, but had rather aided the Persians by keeping the Spartans from Marathon. The existence of two Spartan kings named Leotychidas made the invention plausible: one led the Spartans in an early war against Messene, another was reigning in 490. To simplify Den Boer's complex argument, the Messenian war associated with the first Leotychidas was transferred to the second in order

---

[6] Arist. *Pol.* 1297^{z}29–32, 1306^{a}20–27, 1311^{a}12–15.

[7] Arist. *Pol.* 1274^{a}13–16, 1304^{a}20–31.

[8] The conventional explanation for the use of slave soldiers and bodyguards in medieval, Islamic states is this same distrust of the citizen and consequent preference for outsiders. See below p. 211.

[9] Pl. *Leg.* 3, 698d–e.

[10] Skeptics: Den Boer (1956); Pearson (1962) 421; Starr (1965) 26. Believers: Schwartz (1937) 42; Shero (1938) 526–530; Wallace (1954) 32; Wade-Gery (1967) 290; Forrest (1968) 92; Ducat (1990) 141–143. Cartledge (1979) 153 is undecided.

to defame the Messenians and exculpate the Spartans for tardy arrival at Marathon.[11] Nevertheless, although some of the arguments adduced for the revolt are weak, other indications support the story of a revolt – if not Plato's convenient connection of it with Marathon.[12]

Evidence indicates Helot unrest in the period before the Ithome revolt of 464. In particular, the story that Pausanias was plotting revolution with the Helots in the 470s would make better sense if there had been signs of discontent more recent than the late seventh century when the Second Messenian war was decided.[13] Indeed, the Spartans themselves blamed the earthquake that prompted the 464 revolt on their mistreatment of Helot suppliants.[14] Although we will never know for sure who these Helots were, the failure of the putative 490 outbreak would have provided an opportunity for the Spartans to respect or to abuse suppliants.

Ducat goes so far as to say that Herodotus does not suppress mention of a single revolt but rather, along with Plato, portrays a state of open war between the Helots and the Spartans throughout the period from 520 to 460.[15] Only one, however, of the three passages Ducat cites must refer the period before 464. The other two concern the prophet Tisamenus and Spartiate leader Arimnestus, both of whom were present at Plataea.[16] Both are also linked to undated struggles against the Messenians: Tisamenus assisted the Spartans in a battle near Isthmus; Arimnestus died with his three hundred men at Stenyclerus, an unsung Leonidas at a second Thermopylae. Although Herodotus' references do show how little we know about Sparta's fifth-century wars with Messenia, the battle of Plataea and the Ithome

---

[11] Den Boer (1956); *contra* Parker (1993). The Spartans, however, had no need to excuse their religious scruples, the precise nature of which Herodotus seems to have mistaken. There are plenty of fourth century cases of the Spartans changing their war plans for reasons of religion (Parker [1989], 155; Robinson [1992] 132).

[12] Two pieces of evidence in favor of the revolt are weak. First, Wallace (1954) 32 adduces Strabo's mention of four Messenian Wars before independence. However, the Naupactians' occupation of Pylos, which produced a victory dedication, could as easily count as the fourth as could the war of 490 – along with the two archaic wars and the Ithome revolt. Second, the "Rhianos Hypothesis" is a case of source criticism gone berserk. Nevertheless, Wade-Gery (1967) 290, who demolishes it, still believes in the historicity of the revolt. The existence of a revolt in 490 need not fall with this theory.

[13] Parker (1993) 45 dates the first war to 690–670, the second to 625–600.

[14] Wallace (1954) 35 on Th. 1.128.1.   [15] Ducat (1990) 141–143.

[16] H. 9.35, 9.64. Although our manuscripts have Isthmos, some editors follow a conjecture, Ithome, which links Tisamenus explicitly with the revolt of 464.

revolt were only fifteen years or so apart. Tisamenus and Arimnestus could have fought at both. We need not posit further hostilities between Sparta and Messenia based on these two passages.

A Herodotean speech set in 499, on the other hand, does refer to hostilities between Sparta and Messenia. Aristagoras, seeking Spartan support for the Ionian revolt, rebukes the Spartans for fighting on equal terms against the Messenians, and also against the Arcadians and Argives.[17] This seems to imply Messenian wars at or shortly before the time of the speech. But Herodotus wrote after the revolt of the 460s. He may be guilty of anachronism rather than presenting an argument appropriate to an earlier period.

The evidence for a specific event around 490 is stronger. The sculptor Ageladas made a statue of Zeus for the Spartans as a thank-offering for a victory over the Messenians. The lettering of the inscription could be as late as 464, but the construction of the pedestal suggests an earlier date.[18] The dating of this offering has no doubt been influenced by archaeologists' awareness of the question of a revolt in 490. Thus, the case of another dedication of tripods for a Messenian victory is more decisive: Pausanias reports that these were made by Gitiadas, a sculptor active in the 480s.[19]

Most conclusive, the tyrant Anaxilas changed the name of Zankle to Messene. Numismatic evidence confirms the dating of the name change to around 489 but does not tell us the reason for the switch. Thucydides claims that Anaxilas made the change to commemorate his Messenian ancestry.[20] Both Strabo and Pausanias report that Anaxilas changed the name since Messenian refugees from the Peloponnese made up a large proportion of the new inhabitants.[21] It is almost painful to prefer the word of Strabo and Pausanias to Thucydides. But, if the last appearance of Messenia on the historical stage had been its defeat in the seventh century, why, well over a century later, was Anaxilas suddenly inspired to celebrate his ancestry? The immigration of Messenians to Sicily seems a preferable explanation – or, at least, jogged Anaxilas' memory of his supposed descent.[22]

---

[17] H. 5.49.

[18] Jeffrey (1949) 30; *contra* Pearson (1962) 421 n 56. Meiggs and Lewis (1988) 47 give further bibliography and print "490–480 (?)".

[19] Cartledge (1979) 154 on Paus. 3.18.8.　　　　[20] Th. 6.4.6 with *HCT* ad loc.

[21] Strab. 6.2.3; Paus. 4.23.6–9.

[22] W. P. Wallace points out that the two reasons are not incompatible (Wallace (1954) 32 n. 4):

Cartledge concludes his even-handed discussion of the revolt of 490 with the caveat that "we should, I think, take a lot of convincing that Herodotus ignored, deliberately suppressed or was ignorant of so crucial an event in Spartan history."[23] Our brief discussion has contributed little to the well-known evidence for and the arguments against the revolt. I do hope, however, that, as our examples pile up, it will become clear that there is nothing surprising about Herodotus ignoring a Helot revolt. In his neglect of the Messenians, Herodotus is typical of Greek historiography.

THERMOPYLAE AND PLATAEA

The three hundred Spartans who fought to the last man at Thermopylae remain famous to this day.[24] Herodotus himself claims to know the name of every single one of these heroes.[25] Ancient historians are also aware that Thespians too met their end in the final battle in the pass. Nevertheless, in our concentration on free Greeks defending Greece's freedom, we may paradoxically end up resembling the ignorant Persians of a Herodotean anecdote. Herodotus reports that Xerxes arranged tours of the battlefield to boost his armies' morale. The Persians on these ghoulish excursions imagined that all of the dead were Thespians and Lacedaemonians. They did not realize that some of the dead men were Helots.[26] This incident presents our first case of a recurrent pattern in Greek historical treatment of Helot and slave fighters: their presence is only mentioned in passing and almost accidentally. If Herodotus had not related this story of Persian credulity, we would never have suspected that Helots fought at Thermopylae.

Consequently, neither the numbers of Helots present nor their role in the battle can be determined. Herodotus reports that there were 4,000 casualties at Thermopylae. His earlier total for the Greeks – not including the Helots – that made the final stand in the pass was 1,400.[27] Of these 1,400, 400 Thebans defected to the

---

one can imagine a variety of scenarios that would lead to both explanations of the name change.

[23] Cartledge (1979) 153.

[24] For example, "Go Tell the Spartans," from the epitaph for the three hundred, is the title of a movie about the Vietnam War.

[25] H. 7.224.   [26] H. 8.25.2.   [27] H. 7.202, 7.222.

Persians.[28] This leaves only 1,000 Greeks – 300 Spartans and 700 Thespians – but the late historian Diodorus Siculus mentions an additional 1,000 Lacedaemonians, presumably *perioeci*, who died at Thermopylae.[29] Our total would then be 2,000. In the following year seven Helots accompanied each Spartan at Plataea. If this were the proportion at Thermopylae, the famous 300 Spartans would have been accompanied by 2,100 Helots, who also fought to the death. Along with the Thespians, Spartans, and Lacedaemonians this would bring the total dead up to 4,100. Such a figure might easily be rounded off to the 4,000 casualties that Herodotus reports.[30]

Unfortunately, once we start using sources other than Herodotus to fill out his numbers, the chance of coherence – not to mention accuracy – diminishes. We could after all prefer Isocrates' total of 700 Lacedaemonians rather than Diodorus' 1000.[31] And why not add in the 80 Myceneans from Pausanias?[32] Scholars have even argued that the number 4,000 does not represent the casualties in the final debacle. Rather Herodotus misread an inscription indicating that 4,000 Peloponnesians *fought* the Persians at Thermopylae.[33] Since Herodotus is our source for the inscription, this particular argument seems hypercritical. Neither can we positively assert that 2,100 Helots were present at Thermopylae.

The most we can say is that Herodotus' story about the Persians inspecting the battlefield would have had no point unless the number of Helots was large compared to the Spartan and Thespian dead. Thus the Helots cannot have been merely shield bearers present in the usual one-to-one ratio. The bravery of the three hundred Spartans who died under Leonidas has become a by-word for patriotic courage. That greater numbers of Helots, whom the Spartans called their "slaves", also died defending Greece puts the noble struggle for freedom in a rather different light.

In contrast to his omission of the role of slaves at Marathon, of the contemporaneous Helot revolt, and his passing mention of Helots at

---

[28] Some of these Thebans seem to have been killed, but perhaps not enough to enter into Herodotus' calculations (H. 7.233).

[29] Diod. 11.4.5. Of course, Helots too could be counted as Lacedaemonians. See below 34 n. 39.

[30] Rawlinson (1880) 4.273 raises this possibility.   [31] Isoc. *Paneg.* 90.

[32] Paus. 10.20.1; cf. H. 7.202. Isocrates' total of 1,000 includes the 300 Spartiates.

[33] Macan (1908) on 8.25; cf. H. 7.228

Thermopylae, Herodotus reports repeatedly that 35,000 Helots, every one "equipped for battle," accompanied 5,000 Spartans at the battle of Plataea.[34] It is modern historians who tend to excise these Helots from their accounts of the battle. I believe, however, that the Helots did indeed fight at Plataea.[35] They made up the mass of Lacedaemonian phalanx while the Spartiates formed the front row. Herodotus' ratio of seven Helots to each Spartan, repeated several times, is derived from his knowledge that the Spartans made up the front rank of the phalanx and from the conventional assumption that a phalanx was eight men deep. The number of Helots – and indeed of Spartiates – in Herodotus' account may indeed be improbably high; the ratio between the two allows us to discern the part that Helots played at Plataea.

Three considerations lead to this conclusion. First, Herodotus insists on the presence of Helots on the battlefield but does not ascribe any independent role to them. His narrative thus suggests that the Spartans and Helots were in a single formation. Second, the proportion of seven Helots to one Spartiate reflects Herodotus' method of calculation. Third, Herodotus' account is historically plausible: the Spartan phalanx incorporated outsiders on other occasions and was often organized according to the distinction between the front rank and the mass of the phalanx.

Herodotus' account of the Helots at Plataea appears enigmatic. Although he clearly puts the Helots on the battlefield, he does not describe their actions during the battle. Herodotus not only mentions the Helots in his initial enumeration of the Greek army, but he also includes them in his number for the Lacedaemonians and Tegeans, who stood alone against the Persians after the retreat of most of the Greek forces. Herodotus later refers to a grave for the Helots who died in the battle and describes the Helots despoiling the dead after the battle.[36] Since Herodotus describes the Helots as armed, on the battlefield, dying in the battle, and active afterwards, he at least thought that they had fought.

The problem is to reconcile Herodotus' statements that the Helots were on the battlefield with the fact that he reports nothing about their participation in the battle.[37] The best explanations to date

---

[34] H. 9.10.1, 9.28.2, 9.29.1.   [35] I present here an abridged version of Hunt (1997).

[36] H. 9.61.2, 9.85.2, 9.80.1–3.

[37] See the following for representative views and bibliography: K. J. Beloch, (1916) 2.2.78; *UAK* 1.123; Garlan (1988) 169; Ducat, (1990) 158; Lazenby (1993) 228.

probably combine several approaches. If the number of Helots was less than Herodotus relates, if some Helots served as attendants, if others guarded the supply lines, if few were truly "equipped for battle," perhaps there was no separate force of Helots worthy of note. The weaknesses of even this position are significant. We end up with a picture of Helot participation which is exactly what we would have expected had we not read Herodotus at all, a picture of the Helots as non-combatant assistants. Rather than encountering a challenging text, we have eliminated everything in Herodotus that surprises us. We have lost everything in his account that might tell us something. After this cleansing operation at Plataea, it becomes easy to dismiss the Helots from later campaigns – such as that of Mantinea where the Spartans "themselves and the Helots campaigned in full force" – without asking how we became so sure about the role Helots played in the Spartan army.[38]

The hypothesis that the Helots were part of the Lacedaemonian phalanx at Plataea makes sense of Herodotus' account rather than dismissing it. Herodotus only needed to indicate what the "Lacedaemonians" did to cover the Helots also.[39] There is no need to place a large number of Helots on the borders of the battlefield, up in the passes, or to explain why they had no military weight against the light-armed Persians.

Indeed, Herodotus links the Helots intimately with the Spartiates in several ways. His assertion that seven Helots attended "each" man implies an attachment between the Helots and individual Spartiates.[40] The emphasis on the relation of seven Helots to each Spartan would be needless and confusing if the Helots operated as a separate body, either light-armed or in the supply train. Finally,

---

[38] Th. 5.57.1, 5.64.2. See below p. 60–61.

[39] In H. 9.28.2 the Lacedaemonians include only the Spartiates and *perioeci*. In his account of the final clash at Plataea, Herodotus first refers to the Lacedaemonians as being 50,000 strong (H. 9.61.2). This total includes the Helots as well as the *perioeci*. Thereafter, he alternates between using the terms Spartiate and Lacedaemonian to refer to this force with no apparent difference in meaning (Spartiates: H. 9.61.3, 9.62.3, 9.64.1; Lacedaemonians: H. 9.62.1, 9.63.1, 9.63.2, 9.65.1). Apparently, this contingent could be named according to its leaders, who were Spartiates, or more accurately, with the vague and inclusive 'Lacedaemonians'. In apportioning praise, Herodotus concludes that the 'Lacedaemonians' surpassed the other Greeks in that they defeated the strongest part of the Persian army (H. 9.71.1–2).

[40] H. 9.10.1, 9.28.2, 9.29.1: ὡς ἐόντων ἑπτὰ περὶ ἕκαστον ἄνδρα Powell (1966) 300, *vid.* περί A.I.2, lists the meaning here as "with a person"; cf. Plut. *Aristides* 10.8–9.

when Herodotus counts the light armed Greeks, he describes the
Helots as "belonging to the Spartan formation."[41]

In a short article Friedrich Cornelius argues that the Helots made
up the rear of the Spartan phalanx whereas the Spartiates fought in
the front two rows. This incorporation of the Helots would have
allowed the Spartiates to field a much larger formation against the
Persians. Although Cornelius points out that heavy armor was not
crucial to the rear ranks of a phalanx, his main argument is
connected with the accusation – vouched for by Thucydides – that
Pausanias was conspiring to make the Helots full citizens.[42] Cornelius' reconstruction is entirely plausible, but given the obscure and
puzzling career of Pausanias remains speculative. That the Helots
fought in the rear of the phalanx at Plataea can be better supported
by a consideration of the seven-to-one ratio between Helots and
Spartiates.

Beloch argued that the basis of most of Herodotus' numbers for
the Greek army is calculation from known figures or in order to
arrive at round numbers.[43] Although Beloch's arguments are not
universally accepted, Herodotus is manifestly calculating the
number of Helots. He indicates three times the basis of his calculation: there were seven Helots for every Spartan. In the decisive
passage Herodotus enumerates the light-armed soldiers in the Greek
army:

Belonging to the Spartan formation there were thirty-five thousand men, as
there were seven [Helots] attending each [Spartan] and all of these were
prepared for warfare. The light-armed soldiers of the rest of the
Lacedaemonians and Greeks, as there was one attending each man, were
thirty-four thousand and five hundred in number.[44]

The Greek phrase that I translate "as there were seven [Helots]
attending each [Spartan]" may by itself indicate the calculation that

---

[41] H. 9.29.1: τῆς μὲν Σπαρτιητικῆς τάξιος.

[42] Cornelius (1973) 503 on Th. 1.132.4.

[43] Beloch (1916) II.2.74; Munro (1904) 146. The total number of Spartans may have been
calculated on the basis of there being five *lochoi*, each of which contained a thousand men.
See also Kromayer and Veith (1928) 34; Anderson (1970) 237–239; *contra* Lazenby (1985)
50–54.

[44] H. 9.29.1–2: τῆς μὲν Σπαρτιητικῆς τάξιος πεντακισχίλιοι καὶ τρισμύριοι ἄνδρες ὡς
ἐόντων ἑπτὰ περὶ ἕκαστον ἄνδρα καὶ τούτων πᾶς τις παρήρτητο ὡς ἐς πόλεμον. οἱ δὲ
τῶν λοιπῶν Λακεδαιμονίων καὶ Ἑλλήνων ψιλοί ὡς εἷς περὶ ἕκαστον ἐὼν ἄνδρα.
πεντακόσιοι καὶ τετρακισχίλιοι καὶ τρισμύριοι ἦσαν.

Herodotus is making.[45] Our suspicion is confirmed when we consider the exactly parallel phrase: "as there was one attending each man." This is certainly a calculation. Herodotus did not have access to a separate count of the hoplite attendants and then make the observation that their numbers seemed about the same as that of the hoplites. He estimates the number of attendants to be roughly equal to the number of hoplites, because standard Greek practice was for each hoplite to have one attendant, usually a slave.[46]

Although this seven-to-one ratio is the basis for the figure of 35,000 Helots, few scholars seem to have seen its significance.[47] There was, however, a standard Greek military practice that would account for Herodotus' method of estimating the number of Helots. The most common depth of Greek – and especially Spartan – armies in the classical age was eight.[48] The proportion of seven Helots to each Spartan is neatly explained if Herodotus heard that the Lacedaemonian front row consisted of Spartiates and the remaining ranks were Helots. Herodotus simply multiplied the number of Spartans by seven to come up with the number of Helots.

The depth of the phalanx varied in practice, but a calculation based on the conventional figure of eight appears in the only other detailed, fifth-century enumeration of a Spartan army. Thucydides estimates the number of the Lacedaemonians at Mantinea by first calculating the number of front-rank men. After admitting that there were differences in the depth of the phalanx, Thucydides falls back – like Herodotus – on the conventional depth of eight men.[49] As I postulate of Herodotus, Thucydides arrives at the total number of soldiers in a Spartan army by figuring out the number in the first row and then multiplying by the standard depth of eight. Whereas Thucydides is explicit, Herodotus' calculation is

---

[45] Powell (1966) 391, *vid.* ὡς section D.2.

[46] On the one-to-one ratio see *UAK* 1.59–60 *contra HCT* 2.275. Herodotus even uses this one-to-one ratio to calculate the probable number of the Persians' support troops (H. 7.186.1).

[47] Rustow and Kochly (1852) 50 portray the Helots as standing behind the Spartiates and making up the rear ranks of a typical Spartan phalanx, eight-men deep. Unfortunately, they do not elaborate on or support their thesis. Fehling (1989) 226 lists the ratio of Helots and Spartans as an example of Herodotus' predilection for certain typical numbers. Pritchett (1993) 10–143 demolishes many of Fehling's individual arguments and his general approach, but does not treat this passage.

[48] Although he notes some exceptions, *GSW* 1.137 agrees with prior German scholarship, e.g., Kromayer and Veith (1928) 79, that the *Urtiefe* of the Greek phalanx was eight.

[49] Th. 5.68.2–3.

not, because he stresses the number of Helots and the unfamiliar seven-to-one ratio.

The hypothesis that the Helots formed the mass of the Spartan phalanx not only best explains Herodotus' account of Plataea, but is also consistent with other evidence about the Spartan army, which was not an homogeneous group of Spartiates. Men of various inferior grades were incorporated. Nevertheless, the resulting force was still referred to as the "Lacedaemonians."[50]

One of the secrets of how the Spartans were able to incorporate outsiders into their army was their distinctive practice of having an officer as the front rank man in each file.[51] Sparta's belief in the importance and superiority of these front rank men is shown by the maneuver that Spartan armies underwent when faced with an enemy in the rear. Although the rear rank was the other proverbial place for the best soldiers, the Spartans did not have each person turn around to face the enemy. Rather the Spartan army counter-marched so as to face the enemy with the front-rank officers.[52]

Two pieces of evidence from Isocrates even suggest the incorpora-tion of non-Spartiates in the Spartan army according to the distinction between the front rank and the mass of the phalanx. In Isocrates' description of the Spartans at the battle of Dipaea, he says that they fought and won even though they were only one rank deep.[53] There may be a kernel of fact within Isocrates' rhetorical extravagance: Cawkwell has suggested that the single line of Spar-tans at Dipaea was not the entire army – which is indeed improbable – but the single rank of Spartiates that led a heterogeneous army into combat.[54] So, the Spartans may have made up the front rank in a larger army in a major battle less than a decade after Plataea.

Among Isocrates' other criticisms of Sparta in the *Panathenaicus* is the statement that the Spartans station *perioeci* next to them in battle and sometimes even put them in the first line.[55] The veracity of Isocrates' claim is unknown. His argument is based on the premise that for Sparta to use non-Spartiates in the front rank of the phalanx would be much more serious than merely incorporating them into the mass of the soldiers.

---

[50] Anderson, (1970) 239 and Toynbee (1969) 382–383 point out that from 425 BC on Perioeci outnumbered Spartiates in the army.
[51] Anderson (1970) 73.   [52] Anderson, (1970) 106 on *Lac.* 11.8.
[53] Isoc. *Archidamus* 99.   [54] Cawkwell (1983) 387 n. 9; Kromayer and Veith (1928) 37 n. 6.
[55] Isoc. *Panathenaicus* 180.

Finally, Thebes provides a parallel for the Lacedaemonian army at Plataea. The mass of the Theban army consisted of citizen amateurs; the elite troops that were to become the Sacred Band were stationed in the front rank.[56] The Theban army exhibited, perhaps in imitation of the Spartans, a similar distinction between the mass of a phalanx and trained men in the front rank.[57]

Although there may never have been another Spartan army like that at Plataea in which the Spartiates made up only the first rank with only Helots behind them, the incorporation of other groups into the phalanx and the importance of the Spartan first rank make Herodotus' account plausible.

I have treated several objections to this hypothesis at length elsewhere.[58] One crucial thread runs through my arguments: our job is not to show that Herodotus was wrong given our knowledge of ancient warfare. This is only a last resort. Rather we should alter and reconsider our ideas about that warfare in the light of evidence such as Herodotus' account of Plataea.

One objection, however, is inevitable and crucial to the present investigation. I have just been arguing for the probability of a Messenian revolt around 490. There was certainly a large Helot uprising in 464. Is it plausible that the Spartans risked taking so many potential enemies with them in this critical campaign in 479?[59] Would the Spartiates arm the notoriously rebellious Helots and then station them behind themselves in battle? Two points make this objection less formidable.

First, it is unclear whether leaving Helots behind or bringing them along would have been more dangerous. Against the dangers of arming them, one must weigh the advantages of close supervision and of keeping Helot men separate from their families, who may have served as hostages for their good behavior. Throughout their history, the Spartiates were far more willing to use Helots in their

---

[56] Diod. 12.70 and Plut. *Pel.* 19.3 accepted by *GSW* 2.222 and DeVoto (1992) 6. The Sacred Band was not, however, large enough to provide front-line men for the whole Theban army.

[57] Xenophon's *Cyropaedia* provides yet another parallel for the arming of the Helots at Plataea. The Persians manufactured and gave heavy arms to men ἐκ τοῦ δήμου who were previously light armed, in order to match the numbers of the enemy (*Cyr.* 1.5.5, 2.1.8–19). The Persian nobles – ὁμότιμοι like the Spartan ὅμοιοι – were originally the only heavy armed soldiers. These officers, after the reorganization of the army, made up the front rank of the Persian formation (*Cyr.* 2.1.10–11, 3.3.57).

[58] Hunt (1997).   [59] Cartledge (1979) 175.

military than to march out of the Peloponnese leaving the Helots behind. Of course, the advantage of fielding a much larger army against the Persians was immense.

Second, the use of Helots at Plataea was not an isolated case of the apparent paradox of the Spartans using their restless Helots in the military. As we shall see, this problem has generated considerable scholarly interest and controversy without any special reference to the battle of Plataea. The strongest counter-argument to the objection that the Helots were rebellious and could not have been trusted with arms is that the Helots were rebellious and yet were often trusted with arms. Despite the obvious precariousness of fighting the Persians in a phalanx with Helots at their backs, the Spartans took similar risks on other occasions. Sparta's rule of the Helots was a dangerous affair.[60]

Several additional factors specific to the campaign of Plataea made the Spartans' use of Helots less bold than the image of a thin line of Spartiates between revolutionary Helots and the Persian army might suggest. Although Persia was threatening Greece, the previous year had seen the victory of Salamis. Sparta was the leader of most of Greece in the struggle against the invasions. Many cities, such as Athens and Aegina, had deferred their bitter quarrels to fight together against the Mede. Helots too may have felt that their fight with the Spartans could be put aside until the Persians were repelled. They also would have known that, although they outnumbered the Spartiates, they were but a part of a large Greek alliance under Spartan leadership and that their homes and families were under Spartan control.

The Helots were not kept in line by fear alone. Even if they were not promised freedom as a reward for loyal bravery,[61] Helots who fought enthusiastically or, on the other hand, gave their masters trouble could expect very different lives on the Spartiates' estates. In many ways we can easily imagine, as well as countless others we cannot, Spartiates could exercise their power over the Helots to reward or punish. The story that the Helots stole booty from the Spartiates may well conceal the first rewards they reaped for their service; usually, the Spartans exercised close supervision over the distribution of captured goods.[62]

---

[60] See below pp. 115–120 for a full discussion of this apparent paradox.
[61] Cornelius (1973) 503.   [62] *GSW* 5.415.

SALAMIS

Chattel slaves rowed in the Greek navies that fought and finally defeated the Persians. During the Ionian revolt the Chians could not have manned 100 ships with their citizens alone.[63] Themistocles' famous proposal to build up the Athenian navy with the profits from the silver mines was crucial to the defense of Greece; the slaves who worked the mines and produced the silver were also a *sine qua non* for the Athenian victory. Nor could the Athenians have manned 200 ships to fight at the battle of Salamis without their slaves.[64] Neither the Athenians nor the Chians earlier could have recruited among the Greeks of the Aegean islands and Asia Minor, who later supplied mercenary rowers for Greek navies. During the Ionian revolt, the other Ionian states were already straining to man their own over-sized navies. At the battle of Salamis, almost all of the Aegean was under Persian control and Ionian contingents were fighting for Persia.

Both Chios and Athens are known to have used slave rowers in later periods.[65] When their fates hung in the balance in the wars against Persia, these cities must have employed every available man in their navies. Indeed, Herodotus relates that the Chians manned their navy with forty selected citizens on each trireme.[66] This is parallel to the mobilization described in the Decree of Themistocles: one hundred Athenian citizens were assigned to each ship.[67] In each case the distribution of a certain number of citizens to each ship is most plausibly interpreted as implying two things. First, the navy was not filled entirely by citizens – triremes required about two hundred men as a full complement.[68] Second, the states involved

---

[63] Roebuck (1986) 81.

[64] M. Jameson (1963) 393 estimates that the Athenian navy would have required between 37,000 and 43,000 able-bodied men for a fleet of 200. This would have been impossible for Athens even at the height of its empire. Cf. Murray (1980) 265, 277. See also *UAK* 1.79. H. 8.61 has Themistocles claim that the Athenians have manned 200 ships, but in his own voice he vouches for a total of 180 (H. 8.44).

[65] See below p. 83ff.   [66] H. 6.15.

[67] M. Jameson (1963) 393–394. For an introduction to the vast bibliography on the veracity of the decree see Ewbank (1982) 182–204.

[68] A decree from the mid-fifth century set minimum numbers for launching, hauling up, and pre-campaign inspections (*IG* I³ 153 with Gabrielsen [1994] 109). These numbers were 120, 140 and 100 respectively even in circumstances when speed was not a matter of life or death – as it would be in battle. Gabrielsen (1994) 109, 249 n. 11 argues against the thesis that Athenian triremes were often incompletely manned.

wanted to be sure that every ship had a certain minimum of free, and thus loyal and energetic, sailors on board.[69] Herodotus reports a Spartan speech to the Athenians in the period between the battles of Salamis and Plataea. The Spartans wanted to be sure that Athens would stay in the war. They promised that they would take care of the women of the Athenians and those of their slaves who were useless for the war.[70] How were the other slaves, the ones who were useful in war, being used? During the battle of Salamis, the Athenians had no significant land forces. If slaves were to be useful in this campaign, they would have had to serve in the navy.[71] In the campaign of Plataea, the Athenians fielded 8,000 hoplites. Hoplite attendants, who were usually slaves, would have been needed. Large numbers of slaves are also likely to have been in the navy at the battle of Mycale, which took place at about the same time as Plataea.[72] In our passage, the Spartans may have been referring to slave rowers as well as attendants. If so, this oblique reference of the Spartans is the only hint of what was probably the case: slaves constituted part of the navy that defeated the Persians.

[69] M. Jameson (1963) 394.

[70] H. 8.142: γυναῖκάς τε καὶ ἐς πόλεμον ἄχρηστα οἰκετέων ἐχόμενα. Herodotus uses the term οἰκέτης, but he could not mean free house servants – if such a thing existed – since as citizens these would be counted among the Athenians themselves.

[71] *UAK* 1.81.

[72] Barron (1988) 593 argues that a large Athenian contingent was present at Mycale at the same time as Athenian hoplites fought at Plataea.

CHAPTER 3

Herodotus: freedom or slavery

Then young men come carrying libations of wine, jars of milk,
and pitchers of olive-oil and myrrh, free young men – for no
slave is allowed to take part in the ceremony, since the men
being honored died for freedom.

> Plutarch, *Aristides* 21 on annual ceremonies commemorating
> the battle of Plataea.

The participation of slaves seems to have fallen almost entirely out of
the historical record of the Persian Wars. Two explanations could
account for this lacuna. Either Herodotus avoided the subject or
modern historians have misinterpreted his account.

ANCIENT AND MODERN OMISSION

We hear of the slaves who fought at Marathon only from a chance
reference to their grave in Pausanias. Herodotus, for his part, had a
motive for not mentioning their role. As we shall see, the subject of
slave fighters in general clashed with Herodotus' emphasis on
freedom and on its connection with military prowess. Marathon, in
particular, was a source of Athenian pride: they had defeated the
Persians all by themselves – some accounts even skip the Plataeans'
participation.[1] Why bother bragging about the absence of other
Greeks, if foreign slaves took part in the victory?

The omission of these slaves is so striking one is tempted to call
it suppression. Their participation must have been known to
Herodotus – or to some of his informants.[2] For slaves to have been

---

[1] *UAK* 1.24. Loraux (1986) 156–158.

[2] It may always be overconfident to attribute to an individual author the omission of unfree
participation. Perhaps Herodotus' sources never mentioned the slaves at Marathon to him.
Although we could not then hold Herodotus personally responsible for suppressing evidence,

freed to fight at Marathon was unusual and important enough to have deserved mention in Herodotus' account of that famous battle. Finally, we can find sufficient motives for Herodotus to suppress the involvement of slaves.

Already we see two of the main contentions that unite this work: slaves and Helots were important to classical Greek warfare; Greek historians play down their role. The combination of these two arguments is both powerful and hazardous. Both aspects are worth some further discussion now that we have seen some concrete examples.

The power of the resulting thesis is illustrated by the striking difference between the picture of Greek warfare presented here and conventional views that allow slaves and Helots a marginal role if any. In a field studied as long and intensively as classical military history, this variance is particularly striking. The singularity of this book is neither due to new evidence, nor to radically different interpretations of individual cases. Although I have made specific, original arguments on occasion, in general, as in the case of Marathon, I adopt positions that other scholars have taken. What distinguishes this work is the interpretive framework provided by my second argument: ancient historians tended to avoid the subject of slaves in warfare.[3]

We will see ample indication that the Greeks thought that slaves should not take part in warfare. Modern historians can – and usually have – used such evidence to argue against cases of possible slave use. My hypothesis that such distaste affected Greek historiography rather than military practice leads to a contrary approach. Rather than purging the record of cases of slave involvement on the grounds that the Greeks would never do such a thing, my tendency is to accept the attested cases. I even think it likely that there was more slave involvement than is mentioned. Consequently, from the sum of dozens of different interpretations of individual cases, a sizable gap emerges between this and previous accounts of Greek warfare.

The perils of this approach are considerable. A critical reader might object that my argument is circular and thus cannot be proven: if slave soldiers are attested, I have more evidence that they were used; if slave soldiers are not attested, I have more evidence of

---

we can say that the world of Herodotus' text, regardless of the sources of its emphases and omissions, neglects the unfree.
[3] Welwei notices this tendency, but does not focus on it (*UAK* 1.3).

suppression of their role. Another way of putting this is to ask how a pattern of widespread use of slaves and the frequent historical neglect of this use can be distinguished from a pattern of rare use fairly represented.

Fortunately, this dilemma, though not negligible, presents more of a theoretical than a practical problem. In many cases, a historian describes a single incident in a way that makes clear the regularity of slave use. For example, Thucydides mentions that the crews in some Syracusan ships were more insistent on receiving their pay than the rest of the navy, "since the majority of their crews were free." The implication of regular slave use both in the Syracusan and, more important, in the rest of the Peloponnesian navy, is clear. There are many such examples where an isolated and unstressed incident reveals a submerged pattern of slave use. If, on the other hand, a classical historian refers to a case of slave use in such a way as to indicate that it is exceptional, my argument would fail.[4]

A striking contrast will illustrate another way that my thesis could be proven false and will highlight the scanty treatment of slaves by Greek historians. Slaves did not play a particularly large role in Rome's Second Punic War. Nevertheless, the historian Livy spends a fair amount of time tracing the history of a division of slave volunteers, the Volones. He describes their feelings, fears, enthusiasm, and relationships with the free troops. In pre-battle speeches, their general stresses the slaves' unique motivations. In short, Livy treats the Volones just as he would any other unit of soldiers of unusual provenance. The difference between Livy and Herodotus' account of Marathon is obvious. Not just Herodotus. Again and again, Greek historians do not give slave soldiers and rowers the same attention that they regularly lavish upon even small detachments of the free. Despite the apparent methodological quandary with which we began this digression, neither the regularity of slave use nor the reality of Greek historical neglect is an intrinsically unprovable proposition.

Modern historians, for their part, often screen out even those cases which have slipped past the ancient reticence regarding the practice. The issue of the Helots at the battle of Plataea is a case where Herodotus is explicit – one might almost say emphatic – that the Helots fought in the battle. Herodotus has seven times as many

---

[4] This particular claim is falsely made about the slaves who fought at Arginusae. See below pp. 87–95.

Helots as Spartans on the field; modern scholars with few exceptions either dismiss the Helots from the battle altogether, put them in the supply train, or merely state that they were unimportant, light-armed soldiers whose part in the battle did not require any special description. Here Herodotus most definitely places the Helots on the battlefield, but modern scholars minimize their role.

Some cases are difficult to assign definitely either to the category of ancient neglect or to that of modern dismissal. One such case is the neglect of the role of slaves in the Greek navies of the Persian Wars. Since Herodotus portrays Salamis as central to the whole Greek struggle for freedom, he may not have wanted to admit slave participation. But perhaps Herodotus assumed slaves in the Athenian fleet. He felt no need to mention what was a standard practice in his day -- making allowances for the total mobilization to meet the emergency situation.

Herodotus may even have viewed slaves as no more than extensions of their masters. The use of Athenian slaves at Salamis would then be no more of a reduction of Athenian glory than the use of Athenian ships.[5] As we have seen Herodotus does not seem to shirk referring to this use of slaves in war when it becomes relevant to the Spartan attempt to keep Athens in the war. In this view, it is modern scholars who have written slaves out of the Persian Wars by imposing modern views of personal participation on a society that viewed some people as tools.

I suspect that Herodotus was, in fact, reluctant to contaminate the glory of the Greeks at Salamis, but we need not assign each case to one category or the other. Rather ancient reticence can encourage modern neglect. Since classical historians habitually omit slave soldiers, few parallels survive when the modern scholar considers those cases that receive mention. Accordingly, these isolated reports necessarily strike modern historians as unusual or even impossible.

For example, specialized studies sometimes doubt or question their own evidence when it points to slaves in Greek navies. Roebuck observes that the one hundred Chian ships in Herodotus' account of the Ionian revolt seems too high for the number of Chian citizens.[6] He raises the possibility that the Chians used their plentiful slaves as rowers. Then he dismisses this possibility – almost a certainty I

---

[5] Cf. below p. 192.
[6] Roebuck (1986) 81 on H. 6.15.1; cf. Wilson (1987) 59–61.

would say – on the grounds that Chian slaves were rebellious during
the Peloponnesian War. Since the Chians demonstrably did use
slaves in their navy in the very period that their discontent was so
conspicuous, this argument will not stand. The evidence for this
later practice consists, however, of a short phrase in Thucydides and
the interpretation of a little-known inscription.[7] Ancient reticence is
not here an alternative to modern underestimation, but rather
contributes to it.

SLAVERY AND WARFARE

The focus of this book is, of course, ancient rather than modern
historiography. So we must turn to Herodotus to understand in
greater detail why he neglects slaves during the Persian Wars.[8] Much
recent scholarship on Herodotus concentrates on his early books
which interpret other cultures to the Greeks. In his narration of the
Persian Wars, however, the subtlety of the ethnographer falls before
Greek patriotism. For example, the simple dichotomy of Greek and
barbarian is found in Herodotus' introduction and then not until
Book 6. In his account of the Persian wars, Books 6–9, Greeks and
barbarians are bluntly contrasted again and again.[9] Although the
following depiction of Herodotus as a militaristic slave-owner does
not represent the full measure of the historian, the topic of slave
soldiers demands this focus.

Our picture of the mainstream Greek ideology will gain depth
and subtlety as we consider Thucydides and Xenophon; the main
lines are already clear in Herodotus. Rather than thinking much
about the social practice of slavery, the Greeks tended to think about
other relationships in terms of the metaphor of slavery.[10] This

---

[7] Th. 8.15.2. Robert (1935) 459.
[8] Harvey (1988) discusses slaves in Herodotus, but does not focus on the intersection of
slavery and war with which this chapter is concerned. We will reserve the topic of Helot
soldiers and rebels for treatment in Chapter 4.
[9] Weiler (1968) n. 34.
[10] Vlastos (1941) 300. Wiedemann (1987) 11. Hartog (1988) 334 points out that the analogy
between types of rule had implications for each: the relationship of master and slave could
be explained by reference to the relationship of king and subject. Although the metaphor of
slavery was used for other hierarchies far more often than the converse, there is no reason
to deny that the metaphor could be reversed; cf. Genovese's discussion of the Southern fear
of "confusing" slaves with speeches about freedom on the Fourth of July (Genovese [1979]
126–134).

metaphor lies behind the contrast between freedom and slavery, one of the most important dichotomies by which Herodotus structures his narrative.[11] Freedom is connected with toughness and martial prowess and is proven by success in war.[12] Slavish people get conquered while the truly free, most notably the mainland Greeks, are able to defend their freedom. Military necessity dictated that the Greeks use their slaves against the Persians. No such necessity required Herodotus – or his aged or second-hand informants – to emphasize or even mention this role of slaves, a role so disruptive of how he structured his world and especially the terms in which he presents the Persian Wars.

Herodotus depicts Persian expansions as the enslavement of successive peoples. He describes the subjugation of countries or cities as enslavement on many occasions. Persian conquests in particular seem to have involved a great deal of what even we would call enslavement, especially as punishment for cities in revolt.[13] But Herodotus can refer to any subjection of one state to another as slavery. So regardless of the extent to which Darius intended to actually enslave Greece – he did enslave the Eretrians – for Herodotus the Persian Wars were fought against slavery and for the freedom of Greece. This is clearly not the story of slaves on the Greek side at Marathon and Salamis.

Modern readers find no difficulty in sharing Herodotus' disapproval of Persia's arrogant conquest and enslavement – in whatever sense – of country after country. Herodotus for his part came from a slave society. Although the metaphor of slavery could serve to condemn unjust relations among the free, the brunt of opprobrium

---

[11] Pohlenz (1966) 13; Immerwahr (1966) 45, 108; Fornara (1971) 80, 87; Konstan (1987) 60; Raaflaub (1987) 225; Lateiner (1989) 226; Herington (1991) 155; Ostwald (1991) 142.

[12] Lateiner (1989) 48, 182; Herington (1991) 155.

[13] On ten occasions he uses a derivative of *andrapodon* which usually signifies slaves viewed as property (H. 1.155, 1.156, 3.25, 3.59, 4.203, 4.204, 6.9, 6.17, 6.94, 8.126.). In these cases there is a strong possibility of more than the end of political independence and imposition of tribute. On 34 occasions Herodotus uses a derivative of *douloi* to describe the fate of states (H. 1.27, 1.89, 1.94, 1.95, 1.164, 1.169, 1.170, 1.210, 3.19, 3.21, 4.93, 4.128, 5.49, 5.109, 5.116, 6.22, 6.45, 7.7, 7.8, 7.9, 7.19, 7.51, 7.102, 7.108, 7.154, 7.168, 7.235, 8.100 (twice), 8.142, 8.144, 9.45, 9.60, 9.90.). These expressions can imply either the political subjection of a state or the taking of its people into captivity. In twelve instances, Herodotus makes it clear that the peoples involved were taken away from their homes and used as chattel slaves or threatened with this fate (H. 3.39, 3.125, 3.134, 3.138, 6.9, 6.23, 6.94, 6.96, 6,101 [cf. 6.107, 6.115, 6.119], 6.102, 7.156, 7.181). Flory (1987) 119–149 and Evans (1991) 9–40 offer recent treatment of imperialism in Herodotus of greater depth than this brief excursus.

often fell upon those victims compared to slaves. For Herodotus the results of wars are often determined by the contrast between slavish and free peoples. To put it bluntly, slavish countries often get what they deserve, just as certainly as the cringing slaves of Attic comedy or the tiny slaves of the vase painters deserved their inferior position.

A despotic form of government, physical softness, and cowardice tend to characterize slavish peoples. Since in Herodotus tyranny, softness, and most obviously timidity produce bad armies, slavishness is connected with military incapacity. Herodotus emphasizes the Ionians' physical and moral softness: their good weather makes them weak.[14] Herodotus reports the Scythian characterization of the Ionians as the basest free men, but excellent slaves, "lovers of their masters and no runaways."[15] Accordingly, Herodotus regards the Ionian uprising against the Persians as a slave revolt and consequently doomed. He treats it unsympathetically and unfairly.[16] Before the crucial battle of Lade, their general reminds the Ionians of the threat of enslavement. Nevertheless, Herodotus represents the Ionians as preferring "their coming slavery" to the discomfort of training for battle.[17] So, defeated, they languish in metaphorical slavery to the Persians until the Athenians rescue them – and subject them again. The Ionians' softness and lack of martial determination keep them in the slavery for which they are suited.

The Persian defeat too was due in part to the slavish character of their empire. Narrative constraints, however, make for a more complex treatment than that of the Ionians: Herodotus' portrait of the magnificent defense of Greece required that the invaders be worthy foes not merely craven slaves. The tactic of emphasizing the multitude of the Persian force and the extent of the Persian empire to some degree obviates this dilemma. A victory over slaves can be glorious, if there are enough slaves.[18] Also, although Herodotus in general depicts the invaders as cowardly slaves, he attributes Greek victories to weapons, skill, and tactics in addition to superior moral fiber. The distinction between the Persian conquerors and their debased subjects also allows Herodotus to praise the Greeks: even the Persian elite troops, the Immortals, cannot defeat them.

Nevertheless, Herodotus on a number of occasions emphasizes

---

[14] Flory (1987) 146 on H. 1.142–3.   [15] H. 4.142.
[16] Immerwahr (1966) 230–232. See Waters (1985) 125–7 for a contrary view and bibliography.
[17] H. 6.11–12; cf. H. 5.109.   [18] Cf. Flory (1987) 87.

that the Greeks were fighting against a Persian army consisting of
slaves. He explicitly states that the Persian generals were "slaves just
like the rest of the troops."[19] The Thebans who defected to the
Persians were subjected to the pain and humiliation of being
branded as Xerxes' slaves.[20] The Persians were driven into battle
with whips.[21] Herodotus makes the connection of slavishness with
cowardice clear by stating that the Persian army contained many
people – the word he uses has derogatory connotations – but few
real men.[22]

The Persian army's slavishness derived from several sources.
Despotic rule makes a country slavish. The Persian king is like a
slave master: each "exercises his power over people's bodies,
marking them as he will, in the first place with the whip."[23] Even a
Persian noble was subject to another man: nobles and members of
the royal family could be killed at the whim of the king much as
Greek slaves.[24] The word with which the king addressed his satraps
and generals, "bandaka," means bondsman and would have been an
insult to Greek ears.[25] Herodotus was aware that Persian subjects
were not really slaves: in one place he doubts the story that Persian
nobles jumped off a ship for the sake of Xerxes; among other
objections Herodotus insists that the rowers would have been forced
to jump first.[26] The slave status of all Persian subjects can fade out of
the picture in the contrast between the rich nobles and dispensable
rowers. The slavishness of absolute rule and its connection with
military weakness are nevertheless clear: Xerxes believes that armies
fight better if they are subject to one man who can force them to be
brave beyond their natures; the Spartan king Demaratus, in exile at
the Persian court, is proven right when he says that the Greeks fear
the law and will fight better out of this fear.[27] Herodotus' earlier

---

[19] H. 7.96. Other passages imply that all Persian subjects are slaves or that even high nobles
are slaves: H. 3.83, 7.19, 7.39, 7.103–104, 7.135, 7.223, 8.68, 8.102, 8.116, 8.118.

[20] H. 7.233; see Hartog (1988) 334.   [21] H. 7.223.

[22] H. 7.210. See Dover (1974) 282–284 for the connotations of ἄνθρωπος.

[23] Hartog (1988) 332–334 cites H. 3.16, 3.29, 3.130, 3.154–155, 7.22, 7.35, 7.54, 7.56, 7.223,
7.233, 8.109, 9.78–79 for the theme of the king marking the bodies of his subjects like a
slave-master.

[24] H. 7.39, 9.111–113.

[25] Cook (1983) 249 n.3. Gould (1989) 27 believes that Herodotus may have misunderstood such
expressions as implying chattel slavery, and that this may have contributed to his treatment
of the whole Persian army as slaves.

[26] H. 9.119.   [27] H. 7.103–104.

claim about the Athenians makes the same point: they began to meet with success – he singles out military victories – as soon as they had rid themselves of their tyrants.[28]

Much of the Persian army did not come from Persia but from states subject to Persia. Although not all losers of wars are slavish, loss in battle and national subjection could create the presumption of slavishness. In fact, the particular inferiority of these troops is mentioned on several occasions.[29]

Herodotus even suggests that the Persians themselves have become soft. The History ends with an incident from early Persian history, which recalls themes, phrases, and the "entire course and tendency of Herodotus' great story."[30] An advisor has suggested that the Persians, now conquerors, should leave their rough hills and move into the fertile plains they have conquered. Cyrus replies that soft lands make soft and unwarlike men. Thus he convinces the Persians to stay as rulers in their harsh environment rather than descending to the rich low-lands and becoming slaves themselves.[31] These followers of Cyrus were manifestly not the same Persians whose silver couches, bakers, cooks, and delicacies the impoverished Greeks captured after Plataea two or three generations later.[32] Herodotus' choice of this ending throws into contrast the way the very successes of the Persians made them slavish and militarily vulnerable.

At first, this freedom whose connections with military capacity are manifest may seem distant from the question of the use of actual slaves and Helots in Greek armies. Herodotus' freedom is primarily a quality of relationships among states and between governments and their subjects: the Ionians lose their freedom when the Persians conquer them; the Greeks are free because they obey laws rather than a king. Basing his argument on the work of Finley, Pohlenz and Raaflaub, Patterson has recently argued that the ideal of freedom was not a disembodied ideal, but was inseparable from chattel slavery.[33] The Greeks based a series of dichotomies on the distinction between slaves and masters, because the actual contrast between the two was one of the most absolute and basic facts in their social world. The Greeks would not have compared the soft, despotically-

---

[28] H. 5.77–78, 5.91.   [29] H. 8.68, 8.113, 9.71, 9.102.
[30] Herington (1991) 150; cf. Immerwahr (1966) 146.
[31] H. 9.122.   [32] H. 9.80–9.83 especially 9.82.
[33] Patterson (1991) 177; Pohlenz (1966); Finley (1982a), (1982c); Raaflaub (1983), (1985).

ruled losers of wars with slaves, if they had considered actual slaves tough, independent, and warlike. As in many slave societies, Greek slaves were typed as cowardly, weak, obsequious, and irresolute.

Herodotus himself makes it clear that military incapacity characterizes actual and not just metaphorical slaves. When the Scythian men wanted to return home after a lengthy stay in Asia, they found that their wives had had relations with their slaves. The sons of these unions formed a large army, and barred their return. The Scythians tried without success to defeat in war these unworthy opponents. They only succeeded when they changed their tactics and used whips instead of the weapons of war. At this point these sons of slaves realized that they were slaves: they no longer tried to fight but ran away.[34]

Scholars usually analyze Herodotus' whole account of the Scythians in terms of his status as a proto-anthropologist either interpreting the foreign in Greek terms, or accurately relating traders' stories, whose grains of truth are confirmed by archaeology.[35] This particular story is more likely to tell us about the attitudes of Herodotus, his sources, and his readers than about any actual battle in which whips were used against armed slaves.[36]

The success of the Scythians' new tactic seems to indicate a belief that slave nature was inherited.[37] The use of whips could recall even the half-breed sons of slaves to their true slave selves. Indeed, according to the story, these sons had never had masters and could never have experienced whipping. The story's insistence on reasserting the proper places of slaves and masters either has no use for such details or implies not only an inherited slave personality, but a universal meaning for the whip. Most significant for our purpose, the nature of a slave precluded fighting bravely. The prediction proves true that when confronted with whips, the rebels will "know that they are our slaves, and realizing this will not stand up to us."

This tale begins with the world turned upside down. Slaves have sex with their masters' wives. The sons of slaves defeat the masters in open warfare. The story of the Scythians' slaves evokes some of the

---

[34] H. 4.1–4.
[35] Hartog (1988); *contra* Pritchett (1993) 191–209; cf. Redfield (1985).
[36] Finley (1980) 118.
[37] Evans (1982) 66; Cartledge (1993a) 142. This is one piece of evidence that, contrary to Williams' argument, the idea of "natural slavery" came out of Greek culture rather than being exceptional. See below p. 160 n. 85.

greatest fears of the Greeks: a half-breed servile class born of their wives, warlike slaves armed and fighting against their masters.[38] The resolution that the Scythians hit upon brings the slaves back into their proper place and out of the arena of war, in which they do not belong and where their very presence is subversive. In a similar way Herodotus for all his evocation of freedom, slavery, and slavish Persians keeps actual slaves off of the battlefield. The same unease is assuaged by the Scythian slave story and by Herodotus' neglect of slaves in the Persian Wars.[39]

[38] Macan (1895) *ad. loc.*

[39] The contrast between the slave and free served also to clarify the often hazy distinction between the Persians and the Greeks in the "Persian" wars. The Greeks who fought against the Persians were few and divided among themselves. Many Greeks fought on the Persian side; Herodotus himself was born in the Persian empire from Carian stock (Cartledge [1993a] 39, 43–45).

CHAPTER 4

Thucydides: Helots and Messenians

The Messenians and Naupactians dedicate to Olympian Zeus a
tithe of the spoils from the enemy.
A dedication at Olympia for victories over the Spartans during the
first part of the Peloponnesian War, the Archidamian War.[1]

The Peloponnesian War was a particularly long and bitter one. The
complete breakdown of traditional limits on warfare ensured that all
resources of the opposing cities would be brought to bear. Both
Sparta and Athens, as well as Syracuse, Corcyra, and Chios,
possessed large unfree classes. These were crucial to the course of
the war. On the one hand, the campaigns of Pylos and Decelea
showed how vulnerable each side was to desertion or rebellion by
their slaves. On the other hand, Brasidas won his victories with the
help of Helot soldiers. The crews of the Peloponnesian navies that
finally won the war contained a large proportion of slaves. Similar
crews manned the Athenian navy, the pride and strength of Athens.

In some of these cases unfree participation was the *sine qua non* of a
particular outcome or campaign; the importance of slaves to the
course of the Peloponnesian War is often more difficult to judge.
How many slaves in the Athenian navy would make them significant? How many in the Peloponnesian navy would make them
indispensable? Two approaches help to assess the importance of a
contingent in a larger force.

The first is to consider the reaction of an imaginary general to the
news that his force was to be deprived of the slaves. For example,
even if slaves made up only 20% of the crews of the Athenian navy,
an Athenian general would have been appalled at the prospect of
losing one fifth of his ships before a major battle. Such a situation
might well encourage a previously intimidated opponent to attack.

[1] Meiggs and Lewis (1988) 223–224 (no. 74).

53

The second approach is to take Thucydides' own account as a standard for what is significant. Thucydides often considers the presence or activities of small detachments of free soldiers important enough to narrate. When far larger numbers of the unfree can be shown to have been active, we can say that, according to Thucydides' own standard, they ought to be considered significant.

Although, by these two criteria, the involvement of slaves and Helots was crucial to the Peloponnesian War, this is not at all the impression given by Thucydides. Thucydides omits some incidents of slave participation entirely. More important, his usual technique is to marginalize slaves by not incorporating their participation into his overall view of the war. Thucydides states what slaves did and even stresses their importance on some occasions; the overview of the war which he imposes on his readers centers on his well-known concerns with the essential characters of Athens and Sparta, with land and sea power, with the amorality of international relations, and with the use and abuse of oratory. Specifically the link between planning – especially when documented in speeches – and action is a main focus of Thucydides.[2] That slaves' involvement is omitted from all of the speeches and from the discussions of war strategy keeps the subject in the background.[3]

Was this Thucydides' conscious intention? Since we have access only to his text and not to his mental processes, it is unlikely that any definite conclusions can be drawn on this question. Whether or not Thucydides was conscious in his omission of slaves, to conclude that slaves were important to the Peloponnesian War and that Thucydides overlooks their importance would be a significant departure from prior scholarship. A distinction, however, can be made between the different classes of omission, which involve different levels of conscious intention.

To omit slave involvement – or to play it down – is to give it less prominence than another view of the situation would. We could compare Thucydides' presentation with our modern view, with Thucydides' own view of important factors in history as displayed in the rest of his work, or with the view of some set of Thucydides'

---

[2] Edmunds (1975) 212 cites Luschuit, Aron, Stahl and Hunter in support of the claim that Thucydides structures his history in such a way as to bring out the relation of plans and events. Other scholars could certainly be added to this list.

[3] The only exceptions are the curt references to Peloponnesian encouragement of Athenian slave desertion in the speeches of Pericles and Alcibiades, discussed below pp. 114–115.

contemporaries. The level of Thucydides' self-consciousness is likely to have varied in these different cases.

Some cases of slave involvement would have posed no problems for Thucydides' world view. For example, each hoplite needed to have an attendant, almost invariably a slave, to function on campaign. The hoplites' heavy armor and shield made this necessary. Thus tens of thousands of slaves and Helots accompanied and were essential to the Peloponnesian army on its invasions of Attica. A modern historian could argue that the role of slaves as attendants was crucial to the Peloponnesian War. Ancient slaveholders might consider slave attendants, who did not fight, as serving in the capacity of human tools just as they did in peace time. The significance of hoplite attendants need not have occasioned any stress in Thucydides' world view. In this case his omission might well be entirely unconscious and would not be motivated by the problem of slaves acting as soldiers which is the subject of our current inquiry.[4] If he plays down their importance, it is only in comparison to a modern view of history.

Thucydides is indeed interested in discovering the true causes of events.[5] His concept of true causes is different from ours as the example of slave attendants shows. But Thucydides sometimes suppresses slave participation, when according to his own view of history, it was important. For example, from his Archaeology on, he stresses the importance of three sources of power: a navy, finances, and civic unity. This study will show that although slavery was crucial to each of these factors, Thucydides does not discuss its involvement. This observation still does not imply conscious suppression: contradictions more blatant than this can remain unconscious. Most of the slave involvement that I discuss falls into this category of cases where Thucydides' historical aims conflict with the ideology within which he operated. Since they serve an ideological function at

---

[4] A related problem is to distinguish between cases where Thucydides suppresses slave involvement and when he takes for granted a standard ancient practice. The plausible motives for omission, which I detail below, give *a priori* grounds for suspecting suppression rather than the disinterested omission of the obvious. Furthermore, the involvement of slaves influenced the course of the Peloponnesian War in ways that were not obvious, symmetrical, or predictable and can hardly be subsumed under the rubric of standard practices. We will focus on such cases, where the omission of slaves is particularly striking.

[5] Th. 1.22.4, 1.23.5–6, 1.88.

some cost to historical understanding, we can say that such omissions are motivated.

Another type of omission occurs when an issue became a matter for contemporary debate. At this point there was no longer tension within an ideology, but rather a break into two different views. The best example of this concerns Athenian support of the Messenians. We shall see that this question was debated not only on the grounds of expedience but as a moral issue. Many Athenians, including Thucydides, were uncomfortable with the idea of inciting a "slave" revolt. Other Athenians supported the Messenians on the ground that they were unjustly oppressed Greeks rather than slaves. Thucydides' text indicates that he was aware of this position, but he did not allow it any explicit exposure. If we judge the issue to have been of some importance, then we can say that he consciously suppressed it.

These chapters do not concentrate on places where Thucydides' treatment derives from the relatively unchallenged world view of slaveholders. Its main concern will be cases where the suppression of slave involvement is contrary to Thucydides' own goals in writing history and is motivated by an ideological impasse. In the case of the Messenians, Thucydides is motivated by a contemporary political controversy as well. It is in these last two cases that we can show the motivation – not necessarily conscious – that enables us to label the omission of slave participation suppression.

HELOT SOLDIERS

We begin with Sparta's use of Helots. Thucydides' account of their participation is often obscure in its brevity. Thucydidean obscurity in itself is hardly remarkable, but in this case he sometimes reveals by a chance reference a whole submerged pattern of Helot use.

During the Peloponnesian War the use of Helots was widespread and crucial to Sparta's eventual victory. The outcome of the Peloponnesian War was not decided in a single hoplite battle. It soon became a war of attrition. Pericles says – and Thucydides explicitly agrees with him – that Athens had an advantage over Sparta in material resources. This edge enabled Athens to fight distant and lengthy campaigns.[6] In the end the Spartans overcame their inability

---

[6] Th. 1.141. Thucydides vouches for Pericles' assessment (Th. 2.65.13).

to fight a protracted land war by the use of Helots and Neodamodeis. Such soldiers could be sent on extended expeditions such as Brasidas' campaign in the Thraceward region or Gylippus' crucial mission to the relief of Syracuse. The decline in the numbers of full Spartiates made this use of Helots even more attractive;[7] it strained Spartan manpower to maintain internal security in the Peloponnese while embarking on even short expeditions. The use of Helots allowed the Spartiates to stay close to Laconia and was thought to relieve the threat of revolution.[8]

From Thucydides' account of the Peloponnesian War, we can see some of the importance of Sparta's enlistment of Helots. This is despite the fact that Thucydides gives the subject little attention except when absolutely necessary. The issues of whether Athens should fight in defense of the Attic countryside and Sparta's subversion of Athens' relations with its allies receive extensive treatment in the speeches Thucydides selects or composes. The use of Helots receives none. A brief account of their importance to the course of the war will show that Thucydides' emphases are in no sense natural or inevitable.

Despite the paucity of earlier evidence, our investigation of the battles of Thermopylae and Plataea reveals precedents for the Spartan use of their unfree population.[9] In the Peloponnesian War, Thucydides reports that Helots were present as attendants of the Spartan soldiers trapped on Sphacteria.[10] The Spartans also offered rewards of money and freedom to other Helots for smuggling food to these soldiers.[11] Thucydides relates that the Spartans had almost turned the tables on the Athenians who were blockading Sphacteria. The Helot blockade-runners may have been largely responsible for the changed situation.[12]

Thucydides does not reveal the fates of either the attendants or the smugglers when the Spartan forces were captured.[13] A key feature of Thucydides' treatment of the unfree appears in this episode. Thucydides never considers the unfree important by themselves even when they had played a key role. Unlike free people

---

[7] Cartledge (1979) 307–317.   [8] Th. 4.80.2.   [9] See chapter 2.
[10] Th. 4.8.9, 4.16.1.   [11] Th. 4.26.5.   [12] Th. 4.26, 4.29.2.
[13] Th. 4.38.5. Many of the smugglers may have escaped from the island after delivering food in order to minimize the number of people who needed to be fed. Porzio (1898) 565 points out that the presence of Helots on Sphacteria is shown by the rations that were required for them (Th. 4.16.1).

whose fate or suffering Thucydides reports for its own sake, slaves
enter the narrative intermittently and only when they impinge
directly on events: Thucydides enumerates only the hoplites killed or
captured on Sphacteria as if no Helots were there.

A similar case is that of the two thousand Helots in 424 who
claimed to have been the best in serving the Spartans in the war.[14]
Thucydides gives no hint how so many Helots could have performed
distinguished service. These Helots appear in Thucydides' history
only at the very point when the Spartans "make them disappear,"
that is, kill them.

After Pylos, the most decisive campaign of the Archidamian War
was that of Brasidas in the Thraceward region. His original force of
seventeen hundred hoplites consisted of seven hundred Helots and
one thousand mercenaries from around the Peloponnese.[15] Cartledge emphasizes Sparta's caution in arming Helots to go with
Brasidas: the Brasidian Helots were not members of the regular
Spartan hoplite phalanx; the thousand mercenaries who also accompanied Brasidas outnumbered the Helot contingent; the Helots were
in a small unit in a distant theater of the war.[16]

Despite this caution, George Cawkwell rightly argues that the use
of Helots was a decisive move, which opened the way for other
unconventional attacks.[17] As long as Athens' navy controlled the sea,
Sparta could not raise revolts among the islands. The Athenian
empire was vulnerable to land attacks in the Thraceward region, but
Sparta's regular army could not go on the extended campaigns
required. Just as Pylos showed that the Spartans could be hurt
despite their superiority on land, the campaigns of Brasidas reveal
that Athens' empire could not be entirely protected with sea power.
The Helots were central figures in the two most important strategic
breakthroughs in the Archidamian War.

Nevertheless, not only do Brasidas' battle speeches ignore them,
but some of his appeals are highly inappropriate to a force that
contained few Spartans and many Helots.[18] At one point Brasidas

---

[14] Th. 4.80.3; Garlan (1988) 169; Talbert (1989) 24.   [15] Th. 4.80.5, 4.78.1.
[16] Cartledge (1987) 39.   [17] Cawkwell (1975) 57.
[18] There is an inevitable ambiguity in ascribing the suppression of the unfree either to
Thucydides or to the speakers he portrays. Nevertheless, since Thucydides' treatment of the
unfree in his speeches and in his own voice is consistent, the ambiguity causes no difficulty
for my interpretation. Thucydides' narrative can provide an ironic commentary on the
speeches he presents; in this case, it does not.

exhorts his army, abandoned by its Macedonian allies, not to fear the great numbers of the enemy: "Remember that in the cities from which you come, not the many govern the few, but the few govern the many, and have acquired their supremacy simply by successful fighting."[19] This would hardly have provided encouragement for Helots, enslaved as the result of military defeat.

In this case, one might object that the Helots were not numerous enough to be taken into account. But, in his speech before the battle of Amphipolis, Brasidas appeals to the different parts of his force separately. Clearidas is encouraged individually to show the courage that befits a Spartan.[20] Brasidas speaks to the allies about the prospect of the freedom from Athens that they could win that day and warns of the harsher servitude that defeat would bring.[21] The Peloponnesians, who might have been thought to include the Helots, are addressed as coming from a country which has always been free because of their bravery.[22] Regardless of bravery, the Helots were certainly not from a country which had always been free. They are not included in Brasidas' enumeration of the different groups who make up his army. The unfree barely make it into Thucydides' narrative; they are even more vigorously excluded from the speeches, which mold our conception of the Peloponnesian War.

Thucydides tells us that the Helots who had fought with Brasidas were given their freedom. They were eventually settled with some other Neodamodeis whose history is entirely unknown, but who also must have done something – probably military service – to earn their freedom.[23] Thucydides' failure to explain who these Neodamodeis were prompts Gomme to speculate that he may have "intended to explain, not here but at the point when the force was instituted, and never fulfilled this intention."[24] But Thucydides regularly omits or conceals Helot involvement. There is no need here to invoke the work's incompleteness.

Brasidas' Helots and the mysterious Neodamodeis resurface once

---

[19] Th. 4.126.2. Against *HCT* 3.614–615, I accept the conventional interpretation of this passage as an appeal to the oligarchic Peloponnesians and their allies. Gomme believes that the phrase οὐκ ἄλλῳ τινὶ κτησάμενοι τὴν δυναστείαν ἢ τῷ μαχόμενοι κρατεῖν is a slur against their enemies rather than a boast about their own political system. I think that a general in a tight spot would never concede that his enemies hold their power because they win when they fight, τῷ μαχόμενοι κρατεῖν. The Helots made up less than 700 of the 3,000 hoplites present on this occasion (Th. 4.124.1). The majority of the force consisted of the allies Brasidas had recently detached from Athens.

[20] Th. 5.9.9.   [21] Th. 5.9.9.   [22] Th. 5.9.1   [23] Th. 5.34.1.   [24] *HCT* 4.35.

more to fight with the Spartans at Mantinea.[25] Gylippus' relief
mission, which came just in time to prevent Syracuse from surrendering to the Athenians, contained six hundred Helots and Neodamodeis out of a force of sixteen hundred men from mainland
Greece.[26] Sparta's whole contribution consisted of Gylippus, the
Helots, and the Neodamodeis. Later, the Spartans mustered three
hundred Neodamodeis with the intention of invading Euboea –
which they never did.[27] In addition to their role in the parts of the
war described by Thucydides, Gomme argues that, since the
Neodamodeis could undertake distant and lengthy campaigns which
the regular Peloponnesian army could not, "Sparta could not have
fought the Ionian war . . . without them."[28]

Events in the Peloponnese in 419–417 included the victory of
Mantinea, which Thucydides calls "by far the greatest of Hellenic
battles which had taken place for a long time," and by which the
Spartans regained their old reputation.[29] In his narrative of the
preparations for the battle – as in his description of the previous
campaign – Thucydides states that the Spartans themselves and the
Helots went on campaign "in full force."[30] Thucydides treats the
Spartans and Helots identically as parts of this important army.
Even the expression "in full force" seems to go with the Helots just
as much as with the Spartans.[31] Nevertheless, there is no mention of
Helots in the battle order at Mantinea.

The solutions to this apparent contradiction are various.[32] Welwei
summarizes some previous views: Toynbee thought that these Helots
were light-armed soldiers and did not fight in the phalanx; Kahrstedt
thinks that "in full force" does refer to Helots, perhaps to some class
of draftable men.[33] Welwei himself believes that this large army
needed Helots for the supply train. He refers to Xenophon's description of the complexity of the Spartan supply system.[34] This solution

---

[25] Th. 5.67.1   [26] Th. 7.19.3, 7.58.3.   [27] Th. 8.5.1.   [28] *HCT* 4.35.

[29] Th. 5.74.1, 5.75.3.

[30] Th. 5.57.1 (M): ἐστράτευον αὐτοὶ καὶ οἱ Εἵλωτες πανδημεί. Thucydides 5.64.2 has the same
nouns and order but in the genitive.

[31] *Pace* Lazenby (1985) 197.

[32] Lazenby (1985) 59–60 and Garlan (1972) 47 both conclude that, when the Helots and
Spartans were mobilized, the Helots as well as the Spartans fought; they do not give their
views on what part the Helots played at the battle of Mantinea. Lazenby even infers that
Helots were probably present in other campaigns during this period when the Spartans
manned a large army such as in Th. 5.33.1.

[33] *UAK* 1.127; Kahrstedt (1922) 1.55.   [34] *Lac. 11.2.*

is as unsatisfactory here as at the battle of Plataea. In both cases we have the similar problem of Helots whom our source unequivocally includes in an ancient army. In both cases Welwei demotes them to the supply train, where the slaves ought to be, in flat contradiction to our source. On the occasions when Thucydides is interested in questions of supply, he is quite explicit about the support of ancient armies.[35] In this case, Thucydides describes the Helots exactly as he would the forces of any other city that was going on campaign: they are a subject of the verb "to campaign."

Toynbee's theory that the Helots were light-armed and did nothing during the battle is somewhat more plausible. But, as we saw at Plataea, being light armed is not the same thing as vanishing from the face of the earth. Thucydides' description of Mantinea contains no role for a large body of light-armed troops. Andrewes speculates that perhaps Thucydides is referring to the Brasidian Helots and the Neodamodeis.[36] This theory is possible. At least these Helots are actually at the battle. But Thucydides usually distinguishes the Brasidians and Neodamodeis by name.[37]

Gomme believed, as did Kahrstedt, that these Helots were a special fighting force in addition to the Helot attendants;[38] Ducat has recently expressed a similar view. He adduces Thucydides' reference to six hundred picked Helots and Neodamodeis who were sent to Sicily.[39] Not only the Neodamodeis, but also the Helots, are described as hoplites; Sparta could arm Helots without freeing them. Even more startling is the possibility that the Spartans picked the best men out of a larger force of Helot hoplites; accordingly, this passage raises the possibility that Helots fought as hoplites at Mantinea. Neither Ducat nor Gomme make it clear where this hoplite force could have been during the battle. We saw above that the Helots who fought with the Spartans at the battle of Plataea were incorporated into the rear ranks of the Spartan phalanx. This may well also have been the case at Mantinea. What is most important to stress is that the rare occasions when Thucydides reveals slave participation in war need to be pursued, not excised, by modern scholars.

At this point some readers may object that Thucydides' emphasis

---

[35] E.g., Th. 2.78.3, 6.31.5.   [36] *HCT* 4.79 (Andrewes in square brackets).
[37] Th. 7.19.3 treats the Helots and Neodamodeis as providing separate groups of hoplites.
[38] *HCT* 4.79.   [39] Ducat (1990) 166 with Th. 7.19.3, 7.58.3.

is natural: the relation of Sparta and Athens to the Athenian allies was a central issue of the war while the presence of Helots in Brasidas' army or in the rear ranks at Mantinea was a special circumstance, important, but not part of a larger pattern. Yet when the role of the slaves in the campaigns of Pylos, of Brasidas, the Sicilian expedition, Decelea, the revolt of Chios, Arginusae and the whole Ionian war is reviewed, the lack of any mention of the issue in Thucydides will begin to appear less and less natural. Athens' treatment of her allies was certainly important. So was Sparta's policy towards its Helots and the relationships of Chios, of Syracuse and of Athens with their numerous slaves. We cannot blame Thucydides for selecting or composing speeches only on topics that he thought consequential. Once it is allowed that his interests are not the only or the natural ones, questions arise as to the reasons for his interests and how they affect his presentation and thus our conception of the Peloponnesian War.

ATHENIANS AND MESSENIANS

The Helots did not merely provide a benign source of manpower for Sparta.[40] The rebelliousness of the Helots, especially the Messenian Helots, was notorious. When Athens initiated a deliberate policy of inciting revolution among them, the Helots became central actors in the Peloponnesian War. The incitement of slave revolts was often considered an ignoble and divisive tactic. Its use was primarily recommended by expedience. The Athenian support of the Messenians was different and particularly awkward.

The Messenians justified their cause by the claim – backed by a national mythology – that they were actually free Greeks. Since some of them were free and they were manifestly Greek, their assertions found supporters. In Athens rivalry with Sparta bred sympathy for the Messenians. On its own, the Messenian avowal that they were unjustly enslaved might have implied nothing about slavery, but only about their specific position. Sparta's insistence that the Helots were slaves inevitably connected the Messenian question with the subject of slavery. The Messenians had been slaves of the

---

[40] In this section I will be dealing mainly with the Messenian Helots. The position of the Laconian Helots was different, but J. Chambers (1977/78) overdraws the contrast between the two. See below pp. 119–120.

most prestigious and powerful state in Greece for generations. If the Spartans' "most slavish of slaves" were not slaves, then whose were?[41] The Messenians' ambivalent position as Spartan "slaves" and aspirant Greeks did not fit a world view which divided the world into slave and free. Like slave soldiers the Messenians were not good slaves. The very fact of debate about and change, actual and potential, in the status of the Messenians was subversive of the boundary between slave and free. Since, as we shall see, the system of slavery was not only a prerogative of the rich, but a necessary lubricant of democratic harmony, this threat to slave ideology was a threat also to Athenian unity.

Thucydides puts the Messenians and Athens' support of them in the background as he does all slave involvement in the Peloponnesian War. The subject of alliance with these rebels was a matter of public controversy, which Thucydides chooses not to report. At several points this omission vitiates Thucydides' treatment of Athenian goals and strategies in the Peloponnesian War.

Our first subject is the rebelliousness of the Messenians and Athens' relation with them. Then we examine Thucydides' treatment of the Messenians both in Messenia and Naupactus, of the Ithome revolt, of the strategy of the Archidamian War, and of the fortification of Pylos. Finally, I show that there was controversy at Athens about the position of the Messenians. Thucydides entirely omits this contention. In this chapter our focus is on the unique aspects of the Messenian revolts. The topic of why Thucydides plays down the support of slave revolts in general will be reserved for later treatment after the discussions of Syracuse, Decelea, and Chios.

The Messenians have been aptly described as a "human volcano" waiting for a chance to rise up and destroy Sparta.[42] Paul Cartledge has analyzed Messenian rebelliousness in terms derived from E. D. Genovese's exploration of the relative lack of revolts in the American South. As his treatment is concise and sound, I follow it closely in the following discussion.[43]

The Helots wanted to revolt because they were being held against their will in a brutal system of bondage and exploitation. Their

---

[41] Critias, fr. 37 Diels.   [42] Ste. Croix (1972) 90; Arist. *Pol.* 1269ᵃ36–39.

[43] Cartledge (1985); Genovese (1979). Cartledge's originality lies in the application of categories from comparative slave history; almost all of the factors Cartledge identifies as contributing to Helot unrest are well known; e.g., Ste. Croix (1972) 89ff.; Cartledge (1979) 177ff.

desire to rebel requires no explanation; their occasional successes do. Unlike most slaves the Messenians were subjugated within their own country. They maintained their families, culture, common language, and local organization. These differences between Helotage and slavery rendered the Helots more dangerous than the slaves in most Greek cities: their national consciousness was a large factor in their desire and ability to revolt. Plato and Aristotle advise against a city purchasing too many slaves from the same area in order to avoid the problems caused by Messenian solidarity.[44]

The Spartiate custom of eating in common dining halls ensured that the Spartan owners of estates in Messenia were absent most of the time. The distance between Messenia and Sparta further reduced Spartans' ability to maintain strict control over the Helots there.[45] That the Helots vastly outnumbered the Spartans was also a factor.[46]

Autonomous colonies of runaways have often proved indispensable for the maintenance of slave revolts.[47] The Messenian rebels from Ithome, settled at Naupactus from the 450s to the end of the century, did not exactly fulfill this function; they were too far from Messenia.[48] But Naupactus, as a free city, had resources, material and ideological, far beyond those of a typical Maroon tucked away in the inaccessible backlands. The Naupactus Messenians once fielded 500 hoplites; their population has been estimated at 4,000–5,000.[49] Their walls, built on an ambitious scale, could have protected a larger population.[50] Accepted as free Greeks, the Naupactus Messenians had the resources of a autonomous city in alliance with Athens. These former Helots had not freed their country, but had obtained their own freedom. This set a very bad precedent – from the Spartans' point of view – to the Helots that had remained in bondage. The Spartans had good reasons to insist

---

[44] Plato is explicitly thinking about the Helots (*Leg.* 6, 776c, 6, 777c-d). Aristotle probably has the Helots in mind, but is giving more general advice (*Pol.* 1330a25–8).

[45] Cartledge (1985) 41.   [46] Cartledge (1985) 41.   [47] Cartledge (1985) 46.

[48] Cartledge (1985) 46.   [49] Th. 3.75.1; Lewis (1992a) 118.

[50] Lewis (1992a) 118. The Messenians were wall enthusiasts. The later city of Messene had some of the most impressive walls in Greece. In contrast Sparta was the city without walls: the Spartans had even suggested that all Greek cities pull down their walls (Th. 1.90.2). For the Messenians walls may have meant not only defense – defeat need never again bring slavery – but membership in the community of Greek states, which unlike Messenia before Epaminondas, normally possessed walls.

on the enslavement of any Ithome refugee who returned to the Peloponnese.[51]

Divisions within the ruling class are also linked to slave rebellions. A sense of this may have provided much of the impetus for the ideology of equality among the Spartiates. Despite this ideal, there were large differences among the Spartiates in terms of birth and wealth as well as differences accruing to merit and seniority.[52] Furthermore, the Spartan reputation for settled government was ill deserved: open *stasis* broke out on several occasions in the fifth and fourth century and sometimes even threatened to involve the Helots.[53] W. P. Wallace suggests that Cleomenes was involved both in the formation of the Arcadian League and the rebellion of 490.[54] Pausanias was accused – and Thucydides vouches for the accusation – of inciting the Helots to revolt and even of promising them freedom and citizenship.[55] Cartledge tentatively suggests a causal connection between this accusation and the Ithome uprising in 464.[56] Cinadon, the anti-Spartiate conspirator, included Helots among the discontented groups he had hoped would join his cause.[57] Even when Helots were not directly involved in Spartan faction fights, the lack of harmony within the ruling class left the Spartans vulnerable.

It was dissension between Sparta and other slaveholding states that gave the Helots the best chance to rebel. On two occasions Aristotle contrasts Spartan and Cretan control of their serfs: the Cretans have had more success. Sparta is surrounded by enemies eager to take advantage of its Helot problems; Cretan cities never ally themselves with the serfs of their enemies.[58] Aristotle may have been thinking about contemporary, fourth-century, Sparta, but the history of foreign subversion of the Helots began with Athens in the fifth century.

---

[51] Th. 1.103.1.   [52] Finley (1982b) 27–29; Hodkinson (1983) 243.

[53] Cartledge (1985) 44; Arist. *Pol.* 1306b28–1307a6.   [54] Wallace (1954) 32.

[55] Th. 1.132.4. See Cawkwell (1970) 51–52, Lotze (1970) 272, Cornelius (1973), and Cartledge (1985) 44 for interpretations and appraisals of this story.

[56] Cartledge (1985) 44. Lysander also planned a conspiracy against the state, but this did not involve the Helots (Plut. *Lys.* 26.).

[57] *HG* 3.3.6. Cinadon was not a full Spartiate. Disunity among different free statuses also gave opportunities to the Helots. Perioeci joined the Ithome revolt and helped the Thebans during the invasion in which Messene was established (Th. 1.101.2; *HG* 6.5.32).

[58] Cartledge (1985) 44 on Arist. *Pol.* 1269a37–b7. Arist. *Pol.* 1272b18–20 also connects trouble with serf classes with interference by foreign enemies.

The Athenians under Cimon, along with several other Greek states, came to Sparta's aid during the Ithome revolt. Thucydides tells us that the Athenians were asked to leave because the Spartans suspected their radicalism: the Spartans were even afraid that the Athenians might be won over by the rebels in Ithome.[59] Badian dismisses Thucydides' account as Athenian propaganda: Cimon's men, conservative hoplites, were hardly revolutionaries; the real reason for Cimon's dismissal was that the Athenians were useless and Sparta did not want to continue paying them.[60] Badian's argument is not conclusive: Athenian hoplites need not have been revolutionaries to sympathize with soldiers claiming to be restoring their *polis*.

Cimon's expedition did precipitate a breakdown in relations between Sparta and Athens, but the existence of Spartan suspicions – a fortiori their correctness – is now unknowable. The story of Athenian wavering and Spartan distrust at Ithome would naturally have developed in pro-Spartan circles after the Athenians established the Messenians at Naupactus. Perhaps it is in response that Thucydides specifies that the Athenians settled the Messenian rebels, "because of their hatred by that time of the Peloponnesians."[61] The word translated "by that time" emphasizes that the Athenians had not previously hated the Spartans enough to help their rebel slaves. Thucydides thus implies that the Spartans' earlier suspicions were unfounded and minimizes Athens' connection with the Messenians by portraying the Naupactus settlement as a simple act of hostility.

Naupactus was a port of vital strategic importance which presumably could have been colonized with Athenian citizens.[62] Athens' generous bestowal of this prize on the Messenian rebels was similar to the way Sparta and Athens later compensated their loyal allies, the Aeginetans and Plataeans.[63] Both of these peoples had lost their cities in part because of loyalty to their respective hegemons. In none of these three cases is it useful to distinguish between good will towards friends and self-interested beneficence to allies. That

---

[59] Th. 1.102.3.   [60] Badian (1993) 95 *contra* Ste. Croix (1972) 180.
[61] Th. 1.103.2 (M): κατ' ἔχθος ἤδη τὸ Λακεδαιμονίων.
[62] Grundy (1911) 184, 347; Holladay (1978) 411. Naupactus may have been a dangerous outpost. Athens was willing to take such risks on occasion, such as around Amphipolis, but potential threats and a paucity of fertile land in the immediate vicinity may have made Naupactus less of a prize.
[63] Th. 2.27.1–2, 5.32.1.

helping the Messenians hurt Sparta probably encouraged warm feelings for the Messenians and sympathy for their cause.[64] Their possession of a key naval base also gave Athens cause to keep the affections of the Naupactus Messenians. It was at their urging that Demosthenes made his disastrous invasion of Aetolia.[65] Demosthenes had developed close ties in Naupactus and remained there rather than face the wrath of the Athenians.[66] Finally, Athenian navies operated out of Naupactus from the beginning of the war. This ensured that contact between the Athenians and the Naupactus Messenians was not confined to just a few leaders. Years after the Peloponnesian War was over and Naupactus had been captured by the Spartans, an over-enthusiastic bodyguard of Messenians provided an escort for the Athenian general Conon.[67]

Cartledge calls Athenian support for the Messenians in the Peloponnesian War "well short of wholehearted": he points out that, in the Peace of Nicias, Athens agreed to help Sparta if its slaves, the Helots, revolted.[68] But even in the period of the Peace of Nicias, the Athenians settled at Cranii the Messenians who had joined the garrison at Pylos.[69] They had at least gained their freedom. In practice the Athenians' treatment of their Messenian allies compares favorably with the way the Spartans abandoned to their fate the Athenian subject cities they had incited to revolt.[70] Athens' policy certainly has the appearance of inconsistency – reflecting the internal divisions we shall discuss below: the occupation of Pylos was long in coming and the Peace of Nicias halted Athenian efforts.[71] There may have not been much more that Athens could have done

---

[64] These Messenians were independent allies of Athens who did not have to pay tribute. The Plataeans, the Acarnians, and the Cephallenians were in the same category (Ste. Croix [1972] 104). A fragment of an inscription has been found which specifies the terms under which the Messenians and the native Naupactians were to live together (Lewis [1992b],118).

[65] Th. 3.94.3, 3.97.1.   [66] Th. 3.94.3, 3.95.1, 3.97.1, 3.98.5, 3.107.1, 3.108.1, 3.112.4.

[67] *Hell. Oxy.* XX (XV) 3.   [68] Cartledge (1985) 44 n. 86; Th. 5.23.3.

[69] Th. 5.35.7. Probably the Naupactus Messenians just went home to Naupactus. Thus it was primarily a new group of rebellious Messenians who were established at Cranii.

[70] Th. 5.18.7; Gomme terms the arrangement the Spartans made about Scione a "base betrayal" (*HCT* 3.674).

[71] The use of the best Naupactus Messenians to man the fort at Pylos (Th. 4.41.2) was the most effective policy rather than an indication of luke-warm support. Naupactus Messenians, who spoke the same Doric dialect as the Helots, would be superior instigators of revolt than the Athenians, foreigners as well as notorious imperialists. The Spartans seem also to have thought that this was the case (Th. 5.35.6).

without the superiority on land that enabled Epaminondas to free Messenia after the battle of Leuctra.

THUCYDIDES' ATTITUDE

Thucydides' own attitude toward the Messenians and other Helots is difficult to ascertain: he never makes an editorial comment about their rebellions. More subtle clues indicate that his attitude is ambivalent. When the Helots are slaves in revolt they are regarded with hostility. In contrast, the Messenians from Naupactus, who were once Helots in revolt, appear in a favorable light as loyal and brave allies of Athens: they are then described as helping the Athenians on many occasions and particularly distinguishing themselves on several.[72]

Thucydides' view of the Helots is revealed first in his use of vocabulary. Thucydides uses the expression "the land which once was Messenia" to designate Messenia.[73] This usage denies the state's contemporary existence. This is confirmed in a strange contradiction. Thucydides explains that all the Helots are called "Messenians" because of the descent of most of them from the Messenians who were conquered by the Spartans.[74] Nevertheless, even after explaining this usage, Thucydides never once uses the term "Messenians" for the Helots.[75] He reserves this term for the inhabitants of Naupactus. They are "Messenians" because they are free Greeks; the actual inhabitants of Messenia are Helots because they are not. Being slaves, they cannot name themselves. They have only the name given by their Spartan masters.[76] By revealing a usage which he is not to follow, Thucydides reveals the contested nature of the word Messenian and his acceptance of the Spartan characterization of the Helots as slaves.[77] The dichotomy between slave and free led many Greeks to categorize all Helots as slaves; it led Thucydides sharply to divide the Naupactus Messenians from the Helots in

---

[72] They act with particular bravery or shrewdness in Th. 2.90.6, 3.108.1, 4.36.1.

[73] Th. 4.3.2 (M): τῇ Μεσσηνίᾳ ποτὲ οὔσῃ γῇ.   [74] Th. 1.101.2; cf. Th. 7.57.8.

[75] *HCT* 4.435. E.g., Th. 1.28.1, 1.132.4, 2.27.2, 3.54.5, 4.56.2, 4.80.2, 5.14.3. In Th. 5.35.6–7 the Messenians and Helots are linked in ways that make it impossible to determine what distinction is being made between the two groups.

[76] Patterson (1982) 55 points out the significance of the naming of slaves: "In every slave society one of the first acts of the master has been to change the name of his new slave."

[77] Ducat (1990) 14 also infers that Thucydides conforms to the Spartan view of the Helots.

Messenia with barely a hint that the status of both was ambiguous and controversial.

The Ithome revolt was not ancient history to Thucydides.[78] Some members of the Athenian hoplite force that the Spartans had sent away must still have been alive in 431 when Thucydides began his history. Despite – or perhaps because of – the closeness of the event, Thucydides' account is unsatisfactory. I will not attempt the problems of chronology and history that have vexed the interpretation of this passage.[79] Instead I will consider several minor points which indicate that Thucydides is relating a pro-Spartan version of the events.

Thucydides presents the Spartans as in control of the situation when they appealed to their allies for help: the Spartans asked the Athenians for help in taking Ithome, since "they were reputed to be skillful in siege operations."[80] But Gomme concludes that "Diodorus' account ([XI] 64.1) is nearer the truth." The Spartans were on the defensive when they first called upon their allies.[81] In particular, the lasting obligation, which Sparta felt toward the states which helped her at this juncture, points to aid in a difficult situation.[82]

The terms of the Messenians' surrender also raise doubts about Thucydides' account. Sparta's usual treatment of the Helots would incline even the least cynical historian to imagine that, if the Messenians "were unable to hold out any longer," they would have been slaughtered or at least re-enslaved.[83] In fact, although they abandoned the liberation of Messenia, the rebels gained freedom for themselves and their families.[84] Thucydides cites an oracle as the

---

[78] Ducat (1990) 138 points out that Thucydides treats the revolt at Ithome as more of a secession than a true war. In contrast the tradition from Ephorus, written after the liberation of Messenia, treats the Ithome revolt as a regular war. Ducat tends to minimize the goals of Helot insurrections. I would argue that the events of 369 helped Ephorus perceive more, rather than less, clearly the nature of previous Helot struggles.

[79] *HCT* 1.298ff. Many of the facts in my treatment of the Ithome revolt derive from the *HCT.* See most recently Badian (1993) 89ff.

[80] Th. 1.102.2.

[81] *HCT* 1.301. One might object that Diodorus' account may have been from a positively anti-Spartan source, but Xenophon, fair enough to Sparta, also has them on the defensive in his account of an embassy to Athens (*HG* 6.5.33).

[82] Sparta's obligations to Aegina: Th. 2.27.2, 4.56.2. To Plataea: Th. 3.54.5. To Mantinea: *HG* 5.2.3.

[83] Th. 1.103.1. But see the terms for the surrender of Pylos below p. 178.   [84] Th. 1.103.3.

reason that the Spartans let the Messenians go.[85] Perhaps, this oracle served not to encourage mercy, but to conceal the weakness which forced Sparta to let its "slaves" go free.

Several conclusions emerge from this discussion. Thucydides admitted the *de facto* freedom of the Naupactus Messenians, but regarded the Messenians in their own land as slaves; accordingly, Thucydides follows a version of the Ithome revolt favorable to the Spartans. Thucydides' attitude towards the Messenians leaves admittedly faint traces. His omissions on the subject are more obvious, but their interpretation is more difficult.

Thucydides plays down the importance of Athenian support of Messenia in the Peloponnesian war. His treatment is parallel to Herodotus' failure to mention the Helot uprising of 490 and Xenophon's startling refusal to report the founding of Messene by Epaminondas.[86] Nonetheless, I cannot argue that Thucydides is entirely unwilling to mention this tactic; he is, after all, our main source for it. This makes my argument more complex and subtle but not, I hope, any less compelling.

A greater awareness of the degree to which Thucydides structures his account has replaced the portrait of Thucydides as an impartial reporter of facts. Key themes are traced throughout the work, highlighted in the speeches, and are occasionally the subjects of Thucydides' rare editorial comments.[87] A careful reader of the

---

[85] Th. 1.103.2. The story of the curse of Taenarus can cut both ways (Th. 1.128.1). Since the Spartans believed that the earthquake of 464 was the result of their killing Helot suppliants to Poseidon, perhaps they would be more scrupulous at Ithome. On the other hand, if they tore Helots from an altar at Taenarus, what was there at Ithome that they would respect? Cf. Robinson (1992) 132.

[86] See pp. 28–31 and pp. 179–184.

[87] Investigations of these themes will be found in almost every major work on Thucydides. For example, De Romilly (1963) traces the development of Athenian imperialism throughout the history. Westlake, (1968) investigates Thucydides' conception of the importance of individuals in history. Hunter (1973) and Cogan (1981) address Thucydides' conception of the nature of history throughout the work. Edmunds (1975) details Thucydides' pervasive investigations of predictability and chance in history. The recent works of Connor (1984) and Hornblower (1987 and 1994) deal with a variety of Thucydidean preoccupations; both emphasize his deliberate structuring of the narrative. Although these examples could easily be multiplied, no studies of Thucydides' views of inciting slave revolts are likely to attain the depth, complexity and detail of studies of other themes in Thucydides. Even Losada's *The Fifth Column in the Peloponnesian War* (1972) gives only cursory treatment of the incitement of Helot revolt. Thucydides' coverage of the issue is so brief that the present study will no doubt risk over-interpretation of the few clues Thucydides lets drop on this subject, albeit one so essential to the course of the war.

History can discern the importance of Helot discontent, but the subject is denied the attention that other important issues receive. Thucydides' reticence about Helot revolts is particularly conspicuous in three places: his treatment of the war strategies of both sides at the beginning of the war, his failure to provide background to the Pylos landing of 425, and his omission of speeches against the Spartan peace proposal during the blockade of Sphacteria.

Pericles' strategy in the Archidamian War was basically conservative. It could not possibly have defeated Sparta except in that a return to the *status quo ante* would damage the credibility of the "liberators" of Greece and jeopardize the Peloponnesian League.[88] Nevertheless, Thucydides is intent on defending Pericles' decision to enter an unwinnable war that ended in disaster. His emphasis on the inevitability of the war and his exaggeration of Athenian resources are two places where Thucydides' agenda is obvious.[89]

It is thus strange that he should not mention the great and well-known weakness of Sparta, Helot unrest. Thebes would later humble Sparta by victory in a land battle and by liberating Messenia. Of these two methods of attacking Sparta, Thucydides devotes a great deal of attention to fighting a land battle, an option which the Athenians rejected, but little to raising up the Helots, even though this was actually attempted. He does not mention why the Athenians did not attempt to incite revolt at the beginning of the war. Nor does he reveal the considerations that prompted their eventual attempt in 425 at Pylos.[90]

Like risking a land battle, the campaign of Pylos involved a direct and telling attack on Sparta in contrast to Pericles' strategy.[91] Although the capture of the Spartans on Sphacteria during the initial campaign was serendipitous, the subsequent raids, and unrest among the Messenians were also spectacularly successful. On four

---

[88] Detailed argument on the subject of Pericles' strategy is beyond the scope of this book. The key passages are Th. 1.143.3–1.144.1 and 2.65.7. In general I agree with the thorough and clear arguments of Holladay (1978), who tries to draw the fine line between the tactics Pericles' strategy allowed and those it did not, as well as the probable outcome of such a strategy. I shall cite Holladay alone even though his opinions are shared – and sometimes preceded – by a number of scholars. See Hunt (1994) 105 n. 375ff. for fuller bibliography.

[89] E.g., Th. 1.23.5, 1.88. Hornblower (1991) 341 on Th. 2.65.5 points out that we know from inscriptions that Athens was facing serious financial difficulties early in the war: thus "This appreciation [of Pericles' foresight] is one of Th.'s most serious misjudgments." *Contra* Kallet-Marx (1993).

[90] Holladay (1978) 414.   [91] Holladay (1978) 400–402, 414.

occasions Thucydides stresses Spartan fear and consternation at the prospect of revolution.[92]

Spartan diplomacy during the Peace of Nicias centered on getting Pylos back.[93] Significantly, Sparta asked that Athens at least remove the Messenians from Pylos.[94] A Messenian garrison was even more of a threat than an Athenian one; the Messenians were fighting for different motives and were irreconcilable enemies of Sparta. Later, after the Athenians had replaced the Messenians – acceding to Sparta's request – the Argives, who wanted more support from Athens in their war against Sparta, asked that the Athenians reinstall the Messenian garrison in Pylos.[95]

Pylos was a major Athenian success; it was important both for the war and in Thucydides' account. Symphorien Van de Maele points out that scholars agree that Pylos was the most important campaign in the Archidamian War.[96] John H. Finley notes that the Spartan peace offer in response to the initial Athenian success is the first great climax of Thucydides' history and is the "dead center" of his narrative.[97] But if historians agree that Pylos was important they also agree that Thucydides' account is strange and abbreviated. The details of the campaign have been analyzed closely and will not concern us. Rather I will try to characterize Thucydides' attitude.[98]

Scholars agree that the salient feature of Thucydides' description of the fortification of Pylos is his suppression of the importance of planning and his focus on the role of luck.[99] The most striking example of this emphasis is Thucydides' claim that a ship from the Naupactus Messenians, which brought crucial supplies and reinforcements, "happened to be present." Since Athenian ships based in

---

[92] Th. 4.41.3, 4.55.1, 4.80.2, 5.14.3.   [93] Th. 5.36.2, 5.39.2, 5.39.3.   [94] Th. 5.35.6.
[95] Th. 5.56.2.   [96] Van de Maele (1980) 119.   [97] J. Finley (1963) 188.
[98] Since every scholar who has treated Thucydides at length has wrestled with the problems of the Pylos campaign, a bibliography on the subject would approximate one on Thucydides. Cornford (1907), Hunter (1973), and *HCT ad loc.* emphasize the Pylos episode. I have also found Kagan (1974), J. Finley (1963), Connor (1984), and de Romilly (1963) particularly useful. Strassler (1990) and Wilson (1979) concentrate on the military history of the campaign.
[99] Van de Maele (1980) 123 cites De Romilly, Westlake, Edmunds, Stahl, and Kagan as agreeing that Demosthenes is portrayed as succeeding at Pylos more through luck than through skill or planning. To these scholars one could add Cornford (1907) 88ff., B. Henderson (1927) 193, Connor (1984) 108ff., and Hunter (1973) 63ff. On the other side, Lamb (1914) 53–55 defends Thucydides' treatment of the Pylos incident. Gomme in *HCT* 3.438, 456, 460, 488–489 argues against an emphasis on luck, but even he concedes some points and his arguments have manifestly not carried the field.

Naupactus joined the Athenian fleet after it left Pylos, there must have been communication between the main fleet and Naupactus. The Messenian ship came because word had reached Naupactus about the fortification.[100] Thucydides is a deliberate writer and his omissions are not unmotivated.[101] The gaps in his account of the Pylos campaign have evoked a battery of explanations.

Some are textual and apolitical. Connor points out that Thucydides is as elliptic about the beginning of Brasidas' campaign as he is about Pylos, but nobody claims that Thucydides had a grudge against Brasidas.[102] Of course not. Brasidas is given more speeches than any other person in Thucydides.[103] In addition, the strategy of detaching Athenian allies had been pursued, however lamely, since the beginning of the war.[104] The issues involved in this strategy are explored in the speech of Brasidas at Acanthus and are a major concern of the entire history.[105] Demosthenes' tactic of using *epiteichismos* to incite the Messenians never gets this treatment. One can fairly say that, in Thucydides' account of the Pylos incident, Demosthenes does not get treatment equal to that of Brasidas.

Connor further argues that Thucydides structures the Pylos affair in order to emphasize surprise and paradox. He points out that Thucydides puts off any discussion of planning in the case of the attack on Plataea to evoke the surprise of the event.[106] The idea of inciting Helot revolt, however, was in the air before Pylos. Athens had been raiding politically sensitive areas of the Peloponnese since the war began.[107] No doubt the Messenians in Naupactus, some of Athens' staunchest allies, had been advocating a Messenian fort since the outbreak of hostilities. Indeed, Demosthenes, the instigator of the Pylos landing, had conducted several campaigns over a year with the Naupactus Messenians.[108]

At Athens, Aristophanes' *Achamians* was produced in January of

---

[100] Th. 4.9.1 (M): ἔτυχον παραγενόμενοι. Gomme argues that the force of ἔτυχον is not that the boat just happened to be there, but that it happened to come just when it was needed. Nevertheless, he admits that "it remains notable that Thucydides does not say that an immediate message had been sent to Naupaktos to send Messenians to Pylos" (*HCT* 3.444–445).

[101] De Romilly (1956) 299 exclaims that "il semble qu'aucun mot n'y soit mis au hasard."

[102] Connor (1984) 128.   [103] Tigerstedt (1965) 129.

[104] E.g., Th. 3.29–33, the abortive relief mission to Mytilene.   [105] Th. 4.85–87.

[106] Connor (1984) 110–113.   [107] Westlake (1945) 81–84; De Wet (1969) 106.

[108] Demosthenes had remained around Naupactus for a year after his initial failures (Th. 3.94–98, 3.102). When he won a subsequent series of battles in which the Naupactus

425, before the Pylos expedition. In it the protagonist, Dicaeopolis, wishes that Poseidon would punish the Spartans: "I hope Poseidon, who watches Taenarus, shakes the earth and knocks their houses down on them all."[109] Why does he wish this particular evil upon the Spartans? The Spartans had previously suffered an earthquake, most notorious as the occasion for the great Helot revolt of the sixties. The identification with the Helot revolt is strengthened by the allusion to Taenarus. The curse of Taenarus, to which the Spartans attributed their earthquake, resulted from the killing of Helot suppliants at this temple.[110] Aristophanes is not just wishing for an earthquake out of the blue, but wants one which, like the last one, would result in a Helot revolt.

In such an atmosphere, the fortification of Pylos could not have been that startling. Rather the shock of the Pylos episode is a result of Thucydides' treatment, which ignores the obvious tactic of inciting Helot revolt as long as possible.[111] In a telling contrast, the part of the Pylos campaign that was a complete surprise was the isolation of the Spartans on Sphacteria. Thucydides' account of this is utterly unproblematic and historians are not bothered by the Spartan decision, however stupid, to put hoplites on Sphacteria.

The plan to fortify Pylos certainly required secrecy.[112] So did the plans of the Athenian generals in Sicily, the campaign against Delium, the escape of the Plataeans, and the Athenian attack on Megara.[113] Thucydides relates the planning behind all these actions, but as much as possible, he suppresses Demosthenes' plans and aims in fortifying Pylos.

The converse of Thucydides' neglect of planning is his emphasis on the importance of luck. Virginia Hunter argues that the foresight involved in a carefully planned campaign is suppressed in favor of ridiculous coincidences.[114] The objection of Francis Cornford still stands: the war provided Thucydides with plenty of opportunities to show the importance of luck without distorting his account of a

---

Messenians distinguished themselves, he felt secure enough to return to Athens (Th. 3.105–3.114).

[109] Ar. *Ach.* 510–511.   [110] Th. 1.128.1.

[111] This can be described as a case of narrative displacement: an event described outside of its expected place in the narrative. Hornblower (1994) 166 notes that Thucydides often uses narrative displacement to diminish the impact of a fact rather than, as in modern novelists, to emphasize it.

[112] Kagan (1974) 221; Strassler (1990) 110–112; *contra* Roisman (1993) 34.

[113] Th. 7.47–49, 4.89, 3.20, 4.66.3.   [114] Hunter (1973) 66–74.

victory which did not, in fact, depend on luck. Cornford's own explanation is that Thucydides had recourse to a pre-rational tragic view of the world: he could not understand the commercial policy of Athens. Such outright mercantilism, however, seems improbable in a society where much trade was in the hands of non-citizens. Although elements of Thucydides' history resemble Attic tragedy, he need not have been so tightly constrained by the Cornford schema: fortune at Pylos and nemesis at Syracuse.[115] Thucydides could have been satisfied with the actual luck of Athens – there was a fair amount – that contributed to the capture of the Spartans on Sphacteria.

Several theories regarding Thucydides' Pylos episode link his brevity with a personal dislike for Cleon or Demosthenes or both of them.[116] Policy differences could also have alienated Thucydides from these two generals. Both went beyond the conservative Periclean war strategy that Thucydides endorses. Demosthenes was involved in four of the five major departures from a conservative war policy during the Archidamian War. Cogent, though not detailed, evidence links Cleon also with the more aggressive war policies of 427–424.[117]

An awareness of Thucydides' reluctance to dwell upon the incitement of slave revolts intersects with and reinforces explanations linking Pylos to riskier, un-Periclean war strategies and their proponents. An advantage of this approach is that Pylos is located in a pattern of Thucydidean uneasiness about the incitement of slave revolt. The reticence of Thucydides that we will see in the cases of Chios and Syracuse, as well as his portrayal of the Ithome rebellion, supports the hypothesis that it is the subject of inciting slaves that distorts Thucydides' Pylos episode. In contrast, theories based on Thucydides' fixation on luck, his evocation of surprise, an ignorance of mercantile policy, respect for the secrecy of plans, or a dislike of Demosthenes fail to find support in a consideration of Thucydides' work as a whole. Although it would be simplistic to argue that Thucydides' reluctance to discuss the incitement of slave revolts is the sole cause of his strange narrative of Pylos, it probably did contribute.

---

[115] Cornford (1907) 95ff., 244.
[116] E.g., Woodcock (1928); Holladay (1978) 424; Van De Maele (1980).
[117] Th. 2.65; Van De Maele (1980) 123; Holladay (1978) 421–426.

THE MESSENIAN QUESTION

The possibility that some Athenians justified their actions within a framework of opinions about the Messenians opposite to that of the Spartans is *a priori* likely. Indeed, there is evidence of support for the Messenians at Athens. On the other side, the Spartans' strategic equation of Helots and slaves also found a receptive audience. Although Thucydides had ample opportunity to mention this debate, he omits this awkward issue entirely.

The description of the Helots as slaves served Spartan interests. The Second Messenian War was a bitter one. The revolts of 490, of 464, and the Pylos base exacerbated Spartan anxieties. Low-level resistance and even violence may well have been a constant irritant to Spartan suspicions. Sparta's entire foreign policy was influenced by fear of Helot insurrection.[118] One purpose of the Peloponnesian League was to procure aid in the event of a rebellion. For this end, the equation of Helots with slaves, however sociologically inept, was a useful strategy. Sparta could ask the slave-owning states of Greece to help it put down her "slaves" when they were in revolt. Conversely, no state led by slaveholders – as all Greek states were – would rush to ally itself with the "slaves" of Sparta.

The predominant attitude at Athens, at least among our elite sources, was acceptance of Sparta's domination of the Messenians. Most classical writers refer to the Messenians as "slaves."[119] Many Greek states, including Athens, helped Sparta during the Ithome revolt. Unity among the slave-owning classes in Greece encouraged such support. Admiration for Greece's strongest state and its military elite must also have alienated people from the Messenians' cause. Inertia too favored the acceptance of a long-standing system whose details were little known to the Greek world at large and then primarily through Spartan informants, a state of affairs due in part to Sparta's deliberate policy of keeping foreigners out.

Aristides, the Athenian paragon of civic and military virtue, was an admirer of Sparta.[120] Before the first Peloponnesian War, the great general Cimon – who named his son Lacedaemonius – argued that Athens should help the Spartans crush the Ithome revolt.[121] At

---

[118] Grundy (1908); Ste. Croix (1972) 90ff.   [119] See above p. 16.

[120] Plut. *Aristides* 2.1.

[121] Henderson (1987) 201; Plut. *Cim.* 16. Alcibiades had a Laconian nurse (Plut. *Alc.* 1).

the time of Pylos some Athenian oligarchs may already have preferred the Spartan rule to the democracy. Probably more numerous were Athenians such as Nicias, who served their country loyally in the war, but who would rather peace and harmony prevail among the two great Greek powers.[122] For such men the tactic of inciting the Helots would make the regrettable antagonism between Sparta and Athens far more bitter. In contrast, aggressive strategists may have been hoping for a complete defeat of Sparta such as that accomplished by Epaminondas in the next century.

For, already in the fifth century, we find an anti-Spartan tradition: the Helots were Messenians and thus Greeks, unjustly enslaved. Many of the factors that led to the invention of a detailed Messenian past after Epaminondas established the city of Messene in 369 were operative and attested by 490. At issue is not the veracity of early Messenian history, but only when its stories began to be told and believed.[123] Lionel Pearson may have shown how little was actually known about early Messenian history and how much was invented after the liberation of Messenia.[124] Nevertheless, even Pearson allows that the settlement at Naupactus and the Pylos campaign probably heightened Athenian interest in Messenia.[125] Piero Treves more correctly argues that it was not the founding of Messene which led to the formation of a national tradition but rather the national consciousness that inspired and allowed Epaminondas' success.[126]

The concept of Messenian unity may well have grown out of the long and bitter second Messenian War in the seventh century. Messenian exiles are attested as early as 550 B.C.[127] They were unlikely to have called themselves runaway slaves. By 490, exiles in Sicily referred to themselves as Messenians and changed the name of Zankle to Messene.[128] Merely by naming themselves Messenians they proclaimed that they were not Spartan Helots.[129] This is again confirmed during the Peloponnesian War when the "Messenians

---

Depending on the original status and feelings of such nurses, their presence could either bind or alienate aristocrats from Sparta.

[122] De Romilly (1963) 176–188.   [123] Treves (1944) 103; Cartledge (1985) 41.
[124] Pearson (1962). See also Den Boer (1956). See Pritchett (1985) for a defense of the veracity of Messenian history.
[125] Pearson (1962) 403–404.   [126] Treves (1944) 104
[127] Miller (1970) 233; Wade-Gery (1967) 297.   [128] See above p. 30.
[129] Schwartz (1937) 35–36.nt

and Naupactians" made a dedication for a victory over the
Spartans.[130]

Even if some early Messenian history was invented after Epaminondas, it is hard to believe that no stories of their struggles with the
Spartans survived in Messenia itself and among the exiles from
Helotage who were so proud of their name. The mythical hero
Aristomenes is not attested until the 4th Century.[131] This may
merely reflect the fact that, until the establishment of Messene, his
reputation was confined to western Arcadia and Messenia.[132]
Arcadia was rarely a subject of history or a producer of historians. It
may be granted that the Livyesque battles and lengthy sieges of the
later tradition are the products of Hellenistic embellishment; some of
the stories preserved in Polyaenus and Pausanias are the types told
about bandit heroes rather than mythic warriors: Aristomenes
evades execution; he escapes from prison; and he takes advantage of
a festival to kill Spartans.[133] Again the veracity of the tales is not the
issue. The point is that they are more likely to have arisen among an
oppressed, resentful, and powerless class like the Helots than in the
context of a new city trying to gain acceptance among the Greeks by
the invention of mythic and heroic forebears.

Was the subjugation of Messenia an issue at Athens? *A priori*
considerations suggest that it was. The Athenian squadrons stationed
for long periods at Naupactus would have exposed many Athenians
to Messenian opinions. Since the Messenians were Greeks, not to
mention brave allies complaining about Athens' arch enemy, their
account was probably persuasive. Any benevolence that may have
contributed to Athens' decision to settle the Messenians at Naupactus in the first place was probably reinforced during this fresh
acquaintance under conditions likely to breed sympathy.

Euripides' *Cresphontes* was probably produced at Athens in the
years before 421.[134] The fragments of this play indicate that, already
in the fifth century, the story of the Messenian royal house had taken

---

[130] Meiggs and Lewis (1988) 223–224 (no. 74); Roebuck (1941) 27.
[131] Pearson (1962) 409.   [132] Wade-Gery (1967) 295.
[133] Polyaenus *Strat.* 2.31.2–4. Paus. 4.16.9, 4.17.1, 4.18.4–5, 4.19.5–6 presents folklore-type
stories about Aristomenes; see also Paus. 4.27.1. Eduard Schwartz (1937) 44 rightly
characterizes some of these tales as "zeitlosen Räubergeschichten." Pausanias has
Aristomenes die of an illness in exile (Paus. 4.24.3). This seems more like history than
either national myth or legendary brigandage.
[134] Pearson (1962) 403 n. 15; Schwartz (1899) 449; Treves (1944) 103. Harder (1985) 4 argues
convincingly for 430–424 for the production.

shape and that "Sparta's right to Messenia was disputed."[135] In the fourth century, Plato and Isocrates follow a version of Messenian history that justified Spartan rule.[136] In this account the sons of Cresphontes fled to Sparta. They received Spartan support in exchange for the right to rule Messenia.[137] In Euripides' version the son of Cresphontes grew up in Aetolia or Arcadia and returned from there to Messenia.[138] Such a version cuts out the episode on which the Spartan claim to Messenia was based. In the context of the Athenian fortification of Pylos and alliance with the Naupactus Messenians, Euripides' play shows that Messenian independence was supported at Athens on ideological – that is, mythological – grounds as well as out of considerations of military advantage.

Thucydides could have discussed this issue when Demosthenes' commission was first mentioned, when he tried to convince the generals or soldiers that the fortification was a good idea, or at any number of other occasions. The place where the absence of discussion is most noticeable is when the Spartan peace offer was rejected during the blockade of Pylos. Cleon could have argued exclusively on the basis of the expediency of refusing peace at that juncture and of pursuing a policy of fomenting Helot unrest. But even in the debate about Mytilene, where an emotional and moral issue is presented in Thucydides as a pragmatic one, the humane considerations motivating the Athenians' change of heart are at least referred to: the motivation for reopening the issue at a second assembly is described in moral and emotional terms; the speakers have at least to mention the moral arguments that could be made.[139] Thucydides never lets the ideological issues surrounding Athens' Messenian policy surface even to that extent.[140]

In his fascinating and comprehensive *Les Hilotes*, Ducat reaches a conclusion opposite to mine concerning Thucydides' treatment of

---

[135] Pearson (1962) 403; Schwartz (1899) 449. Poole (1994) 16 agrees that the Cresphontes was "a play in favor of Messenian independence." The document relief with inscription IG I³ 148 may commemorate a treaty between Athens and the Messenians, either around the middle of the fifth century or in the 420s. Unfortunately, not only is the dating controversial, but the inscription could also refer to an Athenian alliance with Messene in Sicily. See Lawton (1995) 114 (#66) for a recent discussion and bibliography.

[136] Morrow (1960) 67; Schwartz (1899) 449.   [137] Isoc. *Archidamus* 22–24; Pl. *Leg.* 3, 683cff.

[138] Schwartz (1899) 448; Harder (1985) 51.

[139] Th. 3.36.4, 3.37.2. These points are well known.

[140] Compare Thucydides' silence about the ideological justifications offered for the oligarchic coup of 411 (Hornblower [1987] 141ff.).

the Messenians in the Peloponnesian War. Ducat believes that, by the Peloponnesian War, the once rebellious Messenians had been reduced to the status of obsequious Helots. Rather than playing down the Messenian problem, Thucydides overestimates the possibility of the revolt.[141]

Surprisingly, this contrary conclusion can actually be used to bolster my argument. Ducat makes a sharp distinction between the hostility of the Messenians during the time described by Herodotus, 520–460, and their passivity during the Peloponnesian War described by Thucydides.[142] Once the weakness of Ducat's historical argument is revealed, it becomes obvious that the real difference is between Herodotus and Thucydides.

Ducat believes that by 460 Sparta's policy of treating the Messenians like Helots succeeded.[143] From this time on the Messenians, like the Helots in Laconia, did not revolt because they accepted their inferiority.[144] Two considerations argue against this rewriting of Spartan-Messenian relations.

First, the wholesale imposition of a dominant ideology is improbable in general.[145] This is especially the case when the process is hypothesized of a class of absentees, the Spartiates, fooling a people, the Messenians, already possessed of their own national, anti-Spartan traditions.

Second, Ducat does indeed show that evidence for Spartan fear of the Helots was exaggerated in some sources: the Spartans were not much more suspicious than other Greek slave-owners.[146] During the Peloponnesian War, however, the Spartans sent out hoplite garrisons and raised a special force of 400 cavalry as well as archers. These innovations aimed at suppressing revolts due to the Pylos occupation.[147] Such a cavalry force seems excessive to waste on unnecessary policing of contented Helots as Ducat's account would have it; at the height of their power, the Lacedaemonians only fielded 600 horsemen for the battle of Nemea.[148] Furthermore, far from being disheartened by their lack of complete success at Pylos, the Athenians established another base across from Cythera after the breakdown of the peace of Nicias.[149] On what evidence are we to dismiss

---

[141] Ducat (1990)137, 144–45, 81ff. *HCT* 3.481 makes a similar argument.
[142] Ducat (1990) 15, 137.   [143] Ducat (1990) 83, 137.   [144] Ducat (1990) 143–150.
[145] See page 23.   [146] Ducat (1990) 146–151.   [147] Th. 4.55.2.
[148] *HG* 4.2.16.   [149] Th. 7.26.

Spartan fears or Athenian hopes as groundless?[150] Especially given Ducat's case for large scale and bitter warfare from 520 to 460 and the stout defense of Messene after 369, Messenian unrest must be considered a real threat during the Peloponnesian War.

Since the contrast between Thucydides and Herodotus on the Messenians does not reflect a historical reversal, could it not reflect the different points of view of the two historians? As Ducat emphasizes, Thucydides views the Messenians as mere slaves or Helots. He portrays the revolt of the 460s as a slave revolt. Ducat also admits that this corresponds to the Spartan point of view.[151] The Messenian problem had not disappeared by the time of the Peloponnesian War, but Thucydides accepts the Spartan erasure of the Messenian name. He is occasionally forced to mention the restlessness of those he calls Helots because he could not avoid the subject in a history of the Peloponnesian War.

Imagine the difference in our conception of the Peloponnesian War if Thucydides had included a speech to justify inciting the Messenians to revolt. Consider Cleon speaking at length on something like the following lines:

The Messenians are Greeks like ourselves. We must free the unjustly enslaved. What difference is there between the Messenians in Messenia and our brave allies in Naupactus? We need not fear reprisals. Our slaves are barbarians and naturally servile. They may be able to desert, but will certainly not try to revolt. On the other hand, Sparta, with the aid of much of Greece, was barely able to put down the revolt at Ithome. With our active support the Messenians will either regain their freedom or at least force Sparta to come to terms with us. The Spartans have been killing all the prisoners they take, Plataean and Athenian. The time for foolish scruples is over.

Some of these arguments must have been urged when Demosthenes, with the close cooperation of the Messenians at Naupactus, got permission to build a fort in Messenia or when Cleon rejected the Spartan peace offer after the Sphacteria campaign.

Was the abandonment of the Messenians an issue among the

---

[150] There seem to be three reasons for Ducat's mistaken position. He makes too sharp a distinction between the acquiescent Helots and the independent Messenians (Ducat [1990] 143, 145) – see below p. 119. He puts too much faith in the systematic and almost ritual humiliation of the Helots (Ducat [1990] 110–118). He makes the common mistake of considering military service a test of loyalty (Ducat [1990] 144 n. 46) – see pp. 115–120.

[151] Ducat (1990) 138, 14.

Athenians opposed to the Peace of Nicias? We shall never know; Thucydides gives short shrift to the Messenians in his account of Ithome and the Peloponnesian War and never reveals that Athenians existed who considered aiding the Messenians the good as well as the smart thing to do.

CHAPTER 5

Thucydides: manning the navies

The slaves went out and defeated the Lacedaemonians near
Arginusae and recovered the bodies of the slain. As a result they
were freed and nobody was allowed to hit slaves.
A garbled account of Arginusae in the scholia to Aristophanes' *Clouds*.[1]

This book concentrates on the ideological problems caused by the
use of slaves in war; there were practical difficulties as well. If a city
entrusted slaves with weapons but not with their freedom, they
might well use the weapons against their masters. Besides the
Spartan Helots, we find no cases of this potentially dangerous
practice. In other states, slave recruitment was of two types.

On the one hand, some slaves earned their freedom in return for
their service. This method of recruitment was rare because it meant
that slave owners permanently lost their property: you can only free
a slave once. Once freed, slaves might leave and deprive the city of
even their military service.[2]

The second and most significant way that a city could use its slaves
was in the navy. Slaves could serve in the navy without obtaining
their freedom, since the possession of oars did not make slaves more
dangerous. Additionally, it seems that in all Greek fleets the marines,
who did have weapons, were recruited from the citizens. Aristotle
points out that the marines make it possible for a city to have a navy
without including too many people among its citizens: "[Warship

---

[1] Holwerda (1977) 9 on Ar. *Nub.* 6: οἱ δοῦλοι ἐξελθόντες ἐνίκησαν τοὺς Λακεδαιμονίους περὶ
Ἀργενούσας καὶ τὰ σώματα τῶν ἀποθανόντων ἐκόμισαν. καὶ διὰ τοῦτο ἐλευθερώθησαν
καὶ οὐκ ἐξῆν οὐδενὶ τύπτειν δοῦλον. This account gives the slaves sole credit for the victory,
but it seems more likely to derive from a mangling of traditional sources than from an
independent tradition.
[2] After a long captivity, freed slaves might not have had a home to which they could return.
For example, the fleet at Aegospotami probably contained many of the same rowers as had
been freed for Arginusae the year before.

crews] need not be part of the city, since the marines are free and from the [city's] infantry class. They are the ones in charge and control the crew."[3] Since the marines commanded the ship, the provenance of the crew was not important – though their skill and experience certainly were. In many navies there were probably plenty of other free men in the crew itself, often including the masters of the slave rowers. They would also help keep the slaves in line.

NON-ATHENIAN NAVIES

Slaves played a important part in the navies of all the combatants in the Peloponnesian War. From the beginning of the war, the use of slaves enabled the Peloponnesians to man ships against Athens, whose power depended on its naval superiority. We do not know how large a percentage of the navy was unfree, nor how great a financial or other gain the use of slaves provided. Some considerable advantage must have justified this widespread practice. Perhaps, the use of slaves increased the manpower pool from which crews could be selected. Since a city would not have wanted to hazard a large percentage of its free population, the use of slaves made the manning of a large navy against the superior Athenians more palatable.[4]

Since Pericles, whose insight Thucydides emphasizes, stated that the Peloponnesians would not be able to man a navy, we might expect some treatment of how they did, even if unsuccessfully at first.[5] But Thucydides refers only in passing to slaves in the Peloponnesian navy and in no way incorporates their presence into his overall view of the Peloponnesian War.

To begin with an egregious example, the Corinthians took more than one thousand Corcyraean prisoners after a large naval battle near Sybota. The eight hundred of these who were slaves constituted about eighty percent of the total, but Thucydides makes no comment.[6] Perhaps this proportion was not that unusual.

---

[3] Arist. *Pol.* 1327b8–11. The same distinction between crew and marines is explicit in *HG* 7.1.12–13.

[4] This is not to deny the importance of free mercenary rowers to the Peloponnesian navy. In the last years of the war, the opposing navies were more equal and the Peloponnesians could attract mercenaries by higher pay, which the Persian king provided.

[5] See Kelly (1979) on Peloponnesian naval potential.

[6] Th. 1.55.1. Obviously, the Corcyraeans were not Peloponnesians. See Morrison and Coates (1986) 62–71 and Wilson (1987) 58–60.

A fragment of Myron may refer to Helots, called *desposionautai,* "slave sailors," freed because of service in Peloponnesian War navies.[7] The largest Spartan contingent in the Peloponnesian War consisted of ten ships of which nine sank so the Spartans did not have to reward very many rowers.[8] Far more important were the navies of Sparta's most important naval allies: Corinth, Chios, and Syracuse.

In 429/428 Phormio fought two successful actions against a Peloponnesian navy, which was mainly composed of Corinthian ships. He captured twelve ships with their crews in the first battle and six with some crew members in the second.[9] He brought back to Athens "the free men out of the captives from the naval battles."[10] This implies that not all of these prisoners were free. Nevertheless, when we look back to see how Peloponnesian commanders addressed their crews before the second battle there is no hint that any slaves were part of the force.[11]

This passage also makes it likely that the fleet of Corinthians and their allies that had fought the Corcyraeans at Sybota also contained slaves. Both navies contained a large contingent of Corinthian ships with allies.[12] In fact, the navy that fought Phormio was smaller than the one at Sybota. The latter is likely to have contained slaves since the former did.[13]

Thucydides states that Chios had more slaves than any other Greek city except for Sparta.[14] Archaeological evidence about Chios is consistent with a system of mixed agriculture on large estates. Such a system of intensive farming could employ many slaves.[15] When Chios revolted from Athens after the Athenian debacle in Sicily, it quickly became the most important Peloponnesian ally in the Ionian campaign which was to decide the outcome of the entire war.[16] By itself Chios supplied close to fifty ships to the Peloponnesian navy.[17] Henderson points out that, if Athens had kept Chios, it

---

[7] Myron *FGrH* 106F1; *UAK* 1.160; Cawkwell (1983) 392 n. 30.

[8] Lazenby (1985) 60.   [9] Th. 2.84.4, 2.92.2.

[10] Th. 2.103.1 (M).   [11] Th. 2.87.

[12] Both navies are referred to by the same expression (Th. 1.30.2, 2.83.3).

[13] Th. 1.46.1 (90 Corinthian ships out of 150 total), 2.86.4 (77 total). Salmon (1984) 168 believes that there were fewer than 20,000 slaves at Corinth to 50,000 free inhabitants.

[14] Th. 8.40.2. Cf. *HCT* 5.86–87 on Theopompus *FGrH.* 115F122.

[15] M. Jameson (1992) 140.   [16] Westlake (1989) 129.

[17] *HCT* 5.29 counts "very possibly" 44 Chian ships in addition to the full crews Chios supplied for five Spartan vessels.

would have easily maintained control of the sea.[18] Thucydides notes Chian energy, wealth and power on several occasions.[19]

Chios used slaves on the crews of her ships. In 411, after the defection of Chios to the Peloponnesians, the Athenians imprisoned the crews of seven Chian ships serving with the Athenian fleet. Thucydides reports that the slave members of the crew were set free.[20] Since these slaves crewed a regular squadron, there is no reason to think that this practice was anything but routine.

For Chios to man fifty ships, after the loss of considerable contingents in Sicily and of the seven crews mentioned, required special measures: the most probable explanation of a Chian list of slaves in "decades" is that the inscription records the names of slaves who had been freed for their service in Chios' large navy.[21] The desertion and disaffection of many Chian slaves may also have induced Chios to reward – and ensure – loyalty with freedom.[22]

In 411, the crews of the Thurian and Syracusan contingents fighting in the Ionian war are described as demanding their pay more vigorously, since they "were for the most part free men."[23] The *Historical Commentary on Thucydides* concludes that this passage not only indicates that the Thurian and Syracusan ships had slaves among their crews, but that the rest of the Peloponnesian fleet had an even larger proportion of slave sailors.[24] This conclusion may still be too conservative. Thucydides states that most of the Thurian and Syracusan crews were free.[25] He implies that this statement was not true of the rest of the Peloponnesian navy. In the rest of the Peloponnesian navy, a majority of the crew may have been slaves. Taken literally, Thucydides' text implies that in this navy of 112 ships, with about 20,000 rowers, over fifty percent of the sailors were slaves.[26]

Two years earlier Syracuse itself was in peril, manning a large fleet, and fielding substantial land forces at the same time.[27] It is a

---

[18] B. Henderson (1927) 408.   [19] Th. 8.15.1, 8.22.1, 8.40.2, 8.45.4.

[20] Th. 8.15.2.   [21] Robert (1935) 459.   [22] Th. 8.40.2.

[23] Th. 8.84.2: ὅσῳ μάλιστα καὶ ἐλεύθεροι ἦσαν τὸ πλῆθος οἱ ναῦται. The textual variants do not effect my case.

[24] *HCT* 5.279; oddly Garlan (1988) 168 only draws the first conclusion. Syracuse and Thurii were democracies and, like Athens, seem not to have had slaves making up a majority of their naval crews.

[25] Betant (1961) 328 gives the meaning *maior pars* for τὸ πλῆθος in this passage.

[26] Th. 8.79.1, 8.87.4.   [27] Th. 7.37.1, 7.39, 7.50.3, 7.53.

fair assumption that the crews of this navy included at least as many slaves as the Syracusan contingents in the Ionian war. In the naval battle that sealed the fate of the Athenian expedition, the Syracusans manned about 76 ships against the 110 of the Athenians.[28] We do not know what percentage of the crews of this navy were slaves. Diodorus reports that, fifteen years later, Dionysius I of Syracuse manned 60 ships entirely from slaves he had freed.[29] This report may well be exaggerated, but Syracuse probably used every possible resource against the Athenian attack.

The exact role of slave rowers in what Thucydides describes as the greatest action in Greek history will never be known. Although Thucydides lists every city that helped Syracuse regardless of its size, he does not mention the ratio of free and slave in the navy that first defeated Athens.[30] There is no hint of slave rowers in the appeals to crush the Athenians who had come to enslave Sicily and inflict "the worst indignities upon our wives and children."[31]

In the absence of any evidence to the contrary, we must conclude that slaves were routinely used in the crews of non-Athenian navies in the Peloponnesian War. The only cases where we have any numbers to work with suggest that slaves may have made up from fifty to eighty percent of these crews. Even if these percentages are too high, it is hard to deny the importance of slaves to the navies that eventually defeated Athens. Nevertheless, Thucydides only refers to slaves in passing and completely excludes them from speeches. In two instances their existence can be detected solely by his use of "free" for only part of the crew.

ARGINUSAE

This use of slave rowers in non-Athenian navies has excited relatively little controversy and is generally accepted. Given that slaves rowed in the Syracusan, Corcyraean, Corinthian, and Chian navies, we should demand strong evidence before concluding that they did not serve in the Athenian navy. Many scholars believe they have this

---

[28] Th. 7.60.4, 7.70.1 with 7.52.1. [29] Diod. 14.58.1.

[30] Th. 7.58. Thucydides mentions free contingents as small as 20 cavalry or 200 hoplites (Th. 6.67, 7.19).

[31] Th. 7.68.2.

evidence and deny the participation of slaves in the Athenian navy.[32] In fact, our sources make it clear that, at least during the Peloponnesian War, a portion – perhaps something like the 20–40% of *IG* i³ 1032 – of the crews of Athenian triremes consisted of slaves.[33]

A detailed treatment of all the positive evidence is beyond the scope of this book and is unnecessary because of Welwei's comprehensive work and Graham's recent article.[34] Accordingly this section will treat three subjects. First, two pieces of evidence, which some scholars believe preclude the employment of slaves in the Athenian navy, require treatment. These are the exceptional nature of the Arginusae fleet and Thucydides' statement that the Athenians could and did raise navies "by themselves." Second, scholarship that denies the use of slaves in the Athenian navy often consists of the citation of good evidence for the practice followed by diverse rationales for ignoring it. The real reasons for skepticism derive not from the unambiguous evidence, but from false preconceptions about the difficulties of the use of slaves as rowers. Third, Thucydides gives slaves in the Athenian navy no emphasis and only mentions them in passing. A pointed contrast can be made: Thucydides is consistently concerned with the importance of finance for naval power, but virtually ignores one of the ways in which the war

---

[32] Sargent's treatment (1927) is largely based on incorrect *a priori* arguments and does not consider all of the available evidence. Although frequently cited as a standard work, it is also marred with factual errors, some of them important to the argument. For example, there are four errors on page 277 alone. The Athenians did not free the slaves of the Chians (Th. 8.15.2 not 7.15.2) on the ground that they felt that those who helped her at sea ought to be free. In fact, Athens imprisoned all of the free crew members of these same Chian ships. It was only the revolt of Chios that motivated the emancipation. If the Athenians had gone about freeing their allies' slaves every time an allied contingent helped them, their empire would have been even less popular than it was. The Corinthians did not free the slaves among their Corcyraean prisoners, they sold them, ἀπέδοντο (Th. 1.55.1 not 1.55.5; see Betant [1961] 123–124). Less relevant for our purposes is Dionysius I making an appearance a century late. Casson (1966) 36–37 seems to think that an activity that required skill and hard work could not be performed by slaves. If slaves could help build the Erechtheum and mine for silver at Laurium, they most certainly could learn to row. Jordan (1975) thinks that public slaves rowed for Athens. He identifies them with the *hyperesia*. *UAK* 1.67–70, Morrison (1984) and Ruschenbusch (1979) make important criticisms of this theory, cf. Dover (1993) 49 n.14. Nevertheless, in squarely facing the evidence for slave rowers in Athens, Jordan's treatment is nearer to the mark than those of Sargent and Casson.

[33] Laing (1966) 93. *IG* ii² 1951 (now *IG* i³ 1032).

[34] *UAK* 1.65–104; Graham (1992). See also Gabrielsen (1994) 108. The main evidence consists of the following: H. 8.142 (see above pp. 40–41); "Decree of Themistocles" with M. Jameson (1963) 393–394; [Xen.] 1.11; Th. 7.13.2, 8.73.5; *HG* 1.6.24; Isoc. 8.48; Dem. 4.36; *IG* i³ 1032.

potential of money made itself manifest, the use of slaves to help fight a state's wars.

Although Xenophon rather than Thucydides relates the battle of Arginusae, the subject of slaves in the Athenian navy requires its discussion here. Arginusae is often trotted out as the exception that proves the rule that slaves did not serve in the Athenian navy.[35] This cannot be the case. The consensus of scholars, regardless of their opinions about usual Athenian practice, is that Athens used slaves as rowers on several occasions from the Sicilian expedition until the end of the war.[36] Their participation is clear both from Thucydides' description of the desertion of slaves from the crews of Athenian triremes in Sicily and from the roughly contemporary *IG* I³ 1032 – which cannot, however, refer to Arginusae.[37]

Nevertheless, scholars consider Arginusae an exception for two reasons. First, Xenophon may mention the enlistment of slaves for the battle only because this was an unprecedented action. Second, the Athenians gave the slaves who fought at Arginusae their freedom and even enrolled them as citizens. If the freeing of naval slaves was a regular practice, their use cannot have been. For, in that case, to use slaves as rowers would have been an expensive and unrepeatable action.

In response to these two arguments, this section makes a historiographic and then a historical argument. First an examination of Xenophon's account will show that it does not imply that the use of slaves was exceptional. I will then put the freeing and enfranchisement of the Arginusae slaves – which was indeed unique – in the context of the usual use of slaves in the navy and the unusual conditions of the final period of the Peloponnesian War.

In 406 the news reached Athens that Conon's fleet had been defeated and the surviving ships were under blockade at Mytilene.

---

[35] Sargent (1927) 266; Amit (1965) 33; Casson (1966) 36.

[36] *UAK* 1.95–96; Garlan (1988) 167.

[37] Th. 7.13.2 with Graham (1992). Laing (1966) 104 summarizes the cogent objections to the theory that *IG* II² 1951 (now *IG* I³ 1032) records the casualties of Arginusae: "the epigraphic dating of these fragments is inconclusive and cannot be used to support only one occasion within the 20-year period from 410–390; no explanation is given for the predominance of members of the tribe Erechtheis in these lists . . .; there are enough men on these stones who seem to reappear in later documents to make us uneasy about reckoning them as dead in 406; and finally, in a casualty list that does not look like a casualty list . . . we are given no explanation as to why there should be only eight ships commemorated when twenty-five were lost." Garlan (1988) 166 and *UAK* 1.81ff. are similarly skeptical.

The Athenians were in financial trouble and had already suffered the loss of the Sicilian expedition as well as Conon's navy. In order to raise a relief force, they took emergency measures:

They voted to go to the rescue with one hundred and ten ships, putting aboard all who were of military age, both slave and free: and within thirty days they manned the one hundred and ten ships and set forth. Even the knights went aboard in considerable numbers.[38]

This fleet won a great victory at Arginusae at what may have been the largest battle between Greek navies up to this date. In immediate terms the battle was particularly decisive. The Peloponnesian navy lost 64% of its ships at Arginusae whereas the battles of Abydos, Notium and Cynossema had only cost the losers an average of 28% of their fleets.[39]

Two features of Xenophon's account require comment. First, he stresses the completeness of the Athenian effort rather than drawing attention to slave use as special. Xenophon first states that everybody was enlisted. He amplifies this by the expression "both slave and free." The words "slave" and "free" are exactly parallel. If his account does not imply that the enlistment of free men was exceptional, then neither does it identify slave use as unusual. In contrast, the information that the members of the cavalry embarked forms a separate sentence and does indicate that their participation was unusual. Second, Xenophon never mentions the notorious fact that the slaves who fought at Arginusae were freed and given Athenian citizenship.

Both features of Xenophon's treatment can be explained by the hypothesis that he wanted to show the generals, who were later condemned by the *demos*, in the best light. The use of slaves in the Athenian navy was normal, but the complete mobilization of Athenian manpower deserved special praise. On the other hand, the emancipation and enfranchisement of slaves was a disturbing and tyrannical practice, which would have detracted from Xenophon's tale of efficient and patriotic generals in a rabid democracy.

Peter Krentz points out that "Xenophon credits the generals with winning in a desperate situation so they appear all the more

---

[38] *HG* 1.6.24 (A).: ἐψηφίσαντο βοηθεῖν ναυσὶν ἑκατὸν καὶ δέκα, εἰσβιβάζοντες τοὺς ἐν τῇ ἡλικίᾳ ὄντας ἅπαντας καὶ δούλους καὶ ἐλευθέρους. καὶ πληρώσαντες τὰς δέκα καὶ ἑκάτον ἐν τριάκοντα ἡμέραις ἀπῆραν. εἰσέβησαν δὲ καὶ τῶν ἱππέων πολλοί.

[39] Kagan (1987) 352.

wronged when they are summarily condemned and executed for events they could not control."[40] Several details in his account of the preparations and battle corroborate this hypothesis. The inferior seamanship and slower speed of the Athenian ships was probably a result of less experienced and inferior crews made up of those whom Conon had left behind.[41] Xenophon may emphasize the deficiency of Athenian seamanship because it makes the generals' accomplishment more impressive.[42] According to Diodorus and Plato the Athenians manned only 60 ships at the Piraeus. Here too Xenophon may be exaggerating the generals' accomplishment by blurring the details of the relief navy's provenance.[43]

Since Athenian slaves regularly served in the navy during this period, Xenophon would consider it laudable that the generals conscripted all of them who were of military age in this emergency. In contrast the freeing and enfranchising of the slaves who fought was a blemish in the Arginusae campaign. Xenophon's *Hiero* lists, along with other unnatural acts or desires which reveal the tyrant's fearful soul, "to long to keep free men slaves, and yet be forced to make slaves free."[44] It was even worse that the Athenians gave the slaves citizenship. In Xenophon's *Hellenica*, an assassin justifies his murder of the tyrant Euphron with just this argument: "was he not beyond question a tyrant, when he not only freed slaves, but made them citizens?"[45] Xenophon's interest in praising the generals explains both his emphasis on the completeness of the Athenian effort and his omission of any mention of rewarding the slaves.

---

[40] Krentz (1989) 151; cf. Delebecque (1957) 69.

[41] *HG* 1.6.31 and again 1.6.32 mention the Athenian's inferior seamanship. Krentz (1989) 155 cites *HG* 1.6.16 which shows that Conon's crews consisted of picked men.

[42] Krentz (1989) 155 points out that even after the Sicilian expedition the Athenian navy generally retained its edge in naval skill.

[43] Diod. 13.97.1 has the Athenians pick up 80 more ships from the islands. This may include those enlisted from the allies as well as an Athenian squadron of between 32 and 52 ships which was at Samos (Krentz [1989] 151). Pl. *Mx.* 243 c has the Athenians man 60 ships from the citizens – and then apparently win the Peloponnesian War.

[44] *Hier.* 6.5. This was a *topos* in ancient political theory (*UAK* 1.3) but also reflected the practice of fourth-century tyrants such as Dionysius I and Jason of Pherae (Garlan [1972] 41). Of particular interest is Aristotle's version of this *topos* in which the tyrant disarms the citizens and frees the slaves (Arist. *Pol.* 1315a38–39). Enslaving the citizens – as in Xenophon – and disarming them – as in Aristotle – are parallel actions.

[45] *HG.* 7.3.8 (A): καὶ μὴν πῶς οὐκ ἀπροφασίστως τύραννος ἦν, ὃς δούλους μὲν οὐ μόνον ἐλευθέρους ἀλλὰ καὶ πολίτας ἐποίει. The second phrase is often mistranslated (Whitehead [1980]; Cartledge [1980]).

My historical argument is also twofold. First, the Athenians did indeed take the unprecedented step not only of freeing but even of enfranchising the slaves who fought at Arginusae. Second, this need not have been the result of unprecedented slave enlistment, but was rather aimed at keeping these victorious slaves in the Athenian navy. Although slaves usually rowed in the navy without even the promise of liberty, exceptional conditions led the Athenians to reward the Arginusae slaves even with citizenship.

The unambiguous, contemporary evidence of Aristophanes and Hellanicus attests to this emancipation and enfranchisement.[46] Most historians accept that the Athenians freed the slaves, but given Athenian exclusiveness, exemplified by Pericles' citizenship law, many doubt that they would have allowed a large group of slaves to become citizens *en masse*.

The evidence, however, indicates that this was exactly what happened. Early in the *Frogs*, the slave Xanthias complains "Woe is me, why didn't I fight in the naval battle?"[47] The scholia inform us that this is a reference to the freeing of the slaves who fought at Arginusae the previous year: "[he means] that in the previous year . . . the Athenians had won a naval battle with their slaves fighting along with them . . . whom they freed."[48] Later Aristophanes addresses the audience, "For it's shameful for people who have fought in one naval battle immediately to be Plataeans and masters instead of slaves."[49] We know from Demosthenes' quotation of the law in question that the survivors of Plataea were given Athenian citizenship.[50] From this evidence alone, it would be a fair assumption

---

[46] The tradition based on Ephorus also mentions the naturalization of metics (Diod. 13.97.1; Krentz [1989], 152).

[47] Ar. *Ran.* 33.

[48] Scholia to Ar. *Ran.* 33 in *UAK* 1.99: ὅτι τῷ προτέρῳ ἔτει . . . .ἐνίκων ναυμαχίαν οἱ Ἀθηναῖοι συμμαχούντων δούλων . . . .οὖστινας ἠλευθέρωσαν.

[49] Ar. *Ran.* 693–694: Καὶ γὰρ αἰσχρόν ἐστι τοὺς μὲν ναυμαχήσαντας μίαν / καὶ Πλαταιᾶς εὐθὺς εἶναι κἀντὶ δούλων δεσπότας.

[50] Dem. 59.104: It is decreed "that the Plataeans are to be Athenians from this day on, with full rights just as the other Athenians, and they are to have a share in all the things that Athenians share in both sacred and profane, except if some priesthood or rite is hereditary, nor are they eligible for the nine archonships, but their descendants are. The Plataeans are to be assigned to *demes* and tribes." Πλαταιέας εἶναι Ἀθηναίους ἀπὸ τῆσδε τῆς ἡμέρας, ἐπιτίμους καθάπερ οἱ ἄλλοι Ἀθηναῖοι, καὶ μετεῖναι αὐτοῖς ὧνπερ Ἀθηναίοις μέτεστι πάντων, καὶ ἱερῶν καὶ ὁσίων, πλὴν εἴ τις ἱερωσύνη ἢ τελετή ἐστιν ἐκ γένους, μηδὲ τῶν ἐννέα ἀρχόντων. τοῖς δ' ἐκ τούτων. κατανεῖμαι δὲ τοὺς Πλαταιέας εἰς τοὺς δήμους καὶ τὰς φυλάς.

that the slaves who fought at Arginusae became citizens just as the Plataeans did. A further piece of evidence amply confirms this impression. The scholiast to line 694 cites the historian Hellanicus: "Hellanicus says that the slaves who fought with them in the naval battle were freed and, enrolled as Plataeans, shared political rights with the Athenians."[51]

Nevertheless, Welwei argues that neither Aristophanes nor Hellanicus says "expressis verbis" that every slave who fought was given Athenian citizenship.[52] Although one may grant that neither specifies that "every" slave was so rewarded, Hellanicus' expression that they "enrolled as Plataeans, shared political rights with the Athenians," is much too close to "expressis verbis" for this argument to carry much conviction. Welwei further argues that the enfranchisement of thousands of slaves is unlikely given Athenian citizenship policies.[53] Connor, however, details the cases when non-Athenians entered the citizen body and argues that actual diversity was masked by an ideology of civic identity.[54] The final period of the Peloponnesian war, in particular, saw several innovations: a law of 406 made previously illegitimate children legitimate; after the Athenian loss at Aegospotami, the Samians were given Athenian citizenship.[55] Perhaps these measures were less distasteful than making slaves citizens, but they were equally breaches in the usual practice of requiring two Athenian parents for citizenship.

Welwei further suggests that the slaves were settled at Scione with the Plataeans who had previously been given this city.[56] This hypothesis strays even further from the evidence of Aristophanes and Hellanicus. Osborne in his study of *Naturalization at Athens* correctly rejects this suggestion: the Athenians in 406/405 needed men at Athens not at Scione – not to mention the Plataeans' feelings on the matter. To deny that the slaves who fought at Arginusae received citizenship flies in the face of the evidence.[57]

The Arginusae relief mission was exceptional because all able-

---

[51] Hellanicus *FGrH* 323a F25: τοὺς συνναυμαχήσαντας δούλους Ἑλλάνικός φησιν ἐλευθερωθῆναι καὶ ἐγγραφέντας ὡς Πλαταιεῖς συμπολιτεύσασθαι αὐτοῖς.

[52] *UAK* 1.101. Garlan (1972) 36 cites problems with the scholiast's citation of Hellanicus; *contra* *UAK* 1.99.

[53] *UAK* 1.1.   [54] Connor (1994) 35–37, 39, 41.

[55] Osborne (1981) 35; Meiggs and Lewis (1988) 283–287 (no. 94).

[56] *UAK* 1.101.

[57] Osborne (1981) 36. Tucker (1906) 174; Stanford (1958) 132; Dover (1993) 279 and Cartledge (1993a) 133 also believe that slaves were given citizenship.

bodied males were drafted and notoriously exceptional because the slaves who fought were given their freedom and Athenian citizenship. As our other evidence suggests, slaves often rowed in the Athenian navy. They were routinely paid just as the slaves who helped to build the Erechtheum were. At the discretion of the trierarch any member of the crew could bring along slaves and receive wages for them as long as they performed a useful function.[58] Slaves in the navy might save whatever portion of their wages their master allowed and eventually buy their freedom; this possibility was unrelated to the fact that they had served in the military.

Athens' reasons for making an exception and freeing and naturalizing the Arginusae slaves were several. Freeing the slaves may have been necessary to gain their loyalty, since the crews of the Arginusae fleet included a larger proportion than usual of slaves. For rather than ships being manned by the slaves of the officers and some crew members, the Arginusae sailors may have included large numbers of slaves from the mines – to whose operation the recruitment of the Arginusae fleet seems finally to have put an end[59] – and the more numerous slaves of the cavalry class, who, contrary to usual practice, served in this navy themselves. These two classes of slaves were not only more numerous. They were also less likely to be known by their masters or to be in any way attached to them or to Athens.

The motivations for the grant of citizenship may have included gratitude towards the slaves who saved Conon's navy and defeated the Peloponnesians. More concrete factors also entered into the decision. At this late stage of the Peloponnesian War, both sides were competing for rowers: Xenophon rightly emphasizes Cyrus' decision to pay the Peloponnesian rowers an *obol* per day more than the Athenians were paying.[60] By the next spring, Conon was only able to man 70 ships instead of the more than 100 the Athenians had had the year before. The Peloponnesian fleet had grown from 90 ships to

---

[58] Laing (1966) 134–148 seems to be the only scholar who has thoroughly thought out the practical details of how privately owned slaves were used in the Athenian navy. Graham (1992) 262 adds the possibility that ordinary crew members, just like the *thetes* of the Erechtheum work records, may have owned slaves who worked next to them on triremes. If men from the hoplite class sometimes rowed in the fleet, as Rosivach (1985) 55 argues, they might also bring slaves and receive pay for them.

[59] Lauffer (1979) 224–225.

[60] *HG* 1.5.4–1.5.8; see also Plut. *Lys.* 4.

140 and then to 170.[61] Desertion from the Athenians almost certainly contributed to this stunning reversal.

Although Xenophon's focus on wages makes the rowers seem like mercenaries, one imagines that sailors generally preferred to fight on the side to which their cities were adhering. In fact, rowers from states within the Athenian empire could be banished for fighting against Athens.[62]

In contrast, slaves might prefer to desert and take up service for the enemy; this course could bring freedom with it. Many of the Athenian slaves who deserted to Decelea may have ended up in the Peloponnesian navy. For these reasons, the pool of slave rowers was likely to be particularly volatile – although the practical difficulties of deserting should not be minimized. Giving freedom to the Arginusae slaves would at least give Athens an even chance to keep this subset of its rowers. The grant of citizenship might even give Athens a decisive edge; the liberty of slaves who deserted to the Peloponnesians was probably not secure. The knowledge that they had an official, secure status in the imperial city of Athens would have been a strong inducement for such ex-slaves to earn their wages there.[63]

In the end, the Arginusae slaves probably stayed with the fleet and died or were captured at the battle of Aegospotami in the following year. Some, however, were perhaps among the worthless people that the Thirty first murdered. Others may have been among those men who were obviously slaves and did not get – or in this case retain – citizenship for helping to reestablish the democracy.[64]

The contemporary case of slaves in the Chian navy – discussed above – provides an apt conclusion to our discussion of Arginusae. As at Athens, slaves served regularly in the Chian navy. It was only at times of crisis that they were given their freedom in return. In both Athens and Chios the war led to a situation where slaves' options expanded and their support had to be courted. Athens freed the slaves of Arginusae after the fort at Decelea opened the way to mass desertion. So too, the freeing of Chian slaves was as much in response to their desertion and rebelliousness as to the extremely high manpower demands of the Ionian War.

---

[61] *HG* 1.5.4–8, 1.5.10, 1.5.15, 1.5.20, 1.6.3, 1.6.16.   [62] Th. 1.143.2.
[63] See Chapter 6 for the fates of slaves who fled to Decelea.
[64] Arist. *Ath. Pol.* 40.2.

OTHER OBJECTIONS

Sargent makes the argument that Thucydides describes the manning even of especially large fleets with citizens and metics.[65] But even in his far more detailed description of the preparations for the Sicilian expedition, there is no reference to the recruitment of slaves; they are only mentioned later in the letter of Nicias.[66] Clearly the recruitment of slaves for the Athenian navy was not a congenial topic for Thucydides.

Sargent also misrepresents Thucydides when she says that he specifies Athenian citizens. In fact Thucydides merely uses the word for "themselves."[67] Thucydides' wording can include Athenian slaves as the following parallels make clear.

After the Persian Wars Themistocles urged the Athenians to quickly rebuild their walls: "all those in the city, they themselves, their women, and their children" should help.[68] Diodorus and Nepos add the detail that the Athenian slaves also took part.[69] If all of the Athenians, even their women, were building the walls, their slaves were not likely to have been exempted. For Thucydides, this went without saying or, according to a different formulation, the "Athenians themselves" included their slaves.

An even closer parallel for the elision of slaves is in the Corcyraean speech asking for Athenian help against Corinth. The Corcyraeans pointed out that they defeated the Corinthians in the previous naval battle, "we ourselves repelled the Corinthians single-handed."[70] As we have already seen the Corcyraean navy may have contained an extraordinarily high proportion of slaves. It certainly contained some. Nevertheless, the Corcyraeans did not think that anybody other than themselves won the naval battle. No deductions about the

---

[65] Sargent (1927) 266 on Th. 1.143.1, 3.16.1, 8.95.2.

[66] _UAK_ 1.92; Th. 6.24–26, 6.30–31, 7.13.2.

[67] Th. 1.143.1, 3.16.1: αὐτοί. In 3.16.1 Thucydides notes that the Athenians embarked πλὴν ἱππέων καὶ πεντακοσιομεδίμνων. The exclusion of two classes of citizens does not imply the exclusion of slaves or imply that only citizens are included in αὐτοί. In 8.95.2 Thucydides says nothing whatsoever about the source of the ill-trained crews that were raised on the spur of the moment.

[68] Th. 1.90.3 (M): τειχίζειν δὲ πάντας πανδημεὶ τοὺς ἐν τῇ πόλει καὶ αὐτοὺς καὶ γυναῖκας καὶ παῖδας; _HCT_ 1.258 decisively defends the text as I have printed it.

[69] Diod. 11.40; Nepos _Themistocles_ 6.

[70] Th. 1.32.5 (A): αὐτοὶ κατὰ μόνας ἀπεωσάμεθα Κορινθίους.

crews of Thucydides 1.143.1 and 3.16.1 can be made except, perhaps, that they included only sailors resident in Athens.[71]

Most objections to the use of slaves in the Athenian navy do not depend on any particular piece of evidence. They spring rather from preconceptions about the functioning of Athenian society, about slavery, and about the use of slaves in war. If it were not for these general arguments, the evidence for slaves in the Athenian navy would have convinced historians.

In one view, service on a trireme was a sought-after job that would not have been taken away from a citizen for the sake of a slave. Considerations of manpower did indeed play a part in what classes would be enrolled in the Athenian navy, but it will soon become apparent that this argument cuts two ways. Considerations such as the size of the required navy, the speed with which it needed to be launched, and the availability of experienced rowers determined the composition of a crew. A ship's officers and marines were always attended by slaves who by themselves probably made up 10% of the total complement.[72] This precluded any absolute ban on slaves on triremes. The single exception, noted as such by Thucydides, was the state ship Paralus – and presumably the Salaminia.[73]

Trierarchs were responsible for having a competent crew, not concerned with giving jobs to citizens; they could dismiss on the spot citizens whom they judged incompetent and seek rowers else-where.[74] Insofar as the sum of Athens' financial interest was concerned it was irrelevant whether citizen slave-owners or *thetes* received the wages paid for rowing. For a non-citizen, either a metic or islander, to be paid out of the Athenian treasury was perhaps a loss for the Athenians. But there is no debate about the use of metics and foreigners in the Athenian navy. One is forced to conclude either that civic status was not the determining factor in hiring rowers, or that the job was not so lucrative after all, or that there were often not enough qualified rowers.

---

[71] Hansen (1985) 23–24 on [Dem.] 50.6, 50.16 discusses a similar problem with the related phrase αὐτοὺς ἐμβαίνειν in the fourth century. This is the technical term for conscription but "the assumption that the phrase αὐτοὶ ἐνέβησαν implies 200 Athenians on board every trireme are undermined by the only reliable piece of evidence we have."

[72] Laing (1966) 93.

[73] Th. 8.73.5. In contrast, if a slave or metic tried to speak in an Athenian assembly he risked execution (Hansen [1991] 62).

[74] Sargent (1927) 269 on [Dem.] 50.7.

In fact, all three explanations have some validity. In times of peace or unthreatened supremacy, the active navy would have been small and jobs hard to get. In such cases, trierarchs may have had their choice of qualified citizens and perhaps were expected to hire citizens as rowers. Of course, such navies were historically inconsequential. When Athens was threatened, as during the Mytilenian revolt and during the entire period of and following the Sicilian expedition, the situation was entirely different. A job in the navy was a risky one with mediocre pay; the casualties in naval battles dwarfed the worst hoplite clashes. The manpower demands of a two-hundred ship navy – or of a hundred and fifty ship navy after the loss of at least 130 ships in Sicily – were beyond the capacity of Athens' citizens.[75] Not only did Athens employ metics, islanders, and slaves, but citizens had to be drafted.[76] Worries about bitter competition for jobs rowing in the navy can safely be put to rest.

Another argument admits that there were slaves on board, but relegates them to the category of servants for the ship's officers.[77] This explanation for the indisputable presence of slaves on Athenian triremes is refuted by the only piece of evidence that gives us the numbers required: in *IG* I^3 1032 the numbers of slaves on some ships is more than the officers could possibly require.[78] Furthermore, triremes were compact and efficient ships. They did not even have space for cooking facilities. There was no room for unnecessary people to sit around on board.[79] If slaves were present, they were not "given a chance at the oars,"[80] but served some vital function in assisting the officers, or – as is clear in *IG* I^3 1032 and in the letter of Nicias – rowed.

There may have been all sorts of practical problems with the use of privately owned slaves in the navy. Discipline, desertion, recruitment, and the property rights of owners are some of them.[81] The

---

[75] See above p. 40.   [76] Hansen (1985) 22 on *IG* I^2 897–901 (now *IG* I^3 1127–1131).

[77] Sargent (1927) 274; Casson (1966) 36. Garlan (1988) 164 is correct that only slaves beyond those needed to serve the officers would present the ideological problem of slave participation in war.

[78] Laing (1966) 93.   [79] Laing (1966) 134; *UAK* 1.89.   [80] Sargent (1927) 274.

[81] Sargent (1927) 272–273; Amit (1965) 37. We know that the navy did indeed have trouble with desertion: half of each sailor's pay was held back until the ship arrived home at Piraeus to keep sailors from leaving early (Morrison and Coates [1986] 119). Casson (1966) 35 n.1 notes that sometimes the whole crew of merchant ships were slaves. If traders managed the problem of maintaining discipline and preventing desertion, why could not navies which certainly contained some free citizens?

decisive rebuttal to all such arguments, however, derives from the accepted use of slaves in other contemporary navies. There must have been some solution to the problems that some historians find so baffling. Of the five largest navies in the Greek world during the Peloponnesian War, it is generally admitted that four, the Corinthian, the Corcyraean, the Syracusan, and the Chian, used slaves in their crews. It cannot have been impossible or impractical for Athens also to use slaves.

Two arguments against the use of slaves in the Athenian navy invoke the high status of the navy. Sargent argues that rowing in the Athenian navy was not a menial task, but was recognized as "an honorable profession."[82] She is arguing against those who believed that rowing was a contemptible task for which only slaves and riff-raff were used. There is some truth to her argument: Aristophanes, for one, treats rowing in the navy as a respectable way to serve one's country.[83] Farming too was a perfectly respectable profession; this does not mean that slaves took no part in farming. In another place, she regards it as improbable that slaves and free could have sat next to each other and been subject to similar discipline. But the laborers and craftsmen of the Erechtheum, slave and free, seem often to have worked next to each other on apparently equivalent tasks.[84]

A related argument is that the *demos* of the Athenians gained its power largely from the prestige attached to the navy.[85] Nobody denies that *thetes* rowed in the Athenian navy and gained power thereby. But just as the *thetes* could gain by service in the navy despite the presence of metics and foreigners, slave participation would not deprive them of the political advantages of manning the navy on which Athens depended.

After this lengthy investigation of slaves in the Athenian navy, the consideration of Thucydides' treatment will be brief. We have already mentioned that Thucydides elides slaves when he describes the manning of Athenian fleets: the letter of Nicias reveals that slave desertion was crippling the crews of the Athenian navy besieging Syracuse, but we had no hint of their presence in the lavish narrative

---

[82] Sargent (1927) 264–265; *contra* Böckh (1886) 328–330.

[83] Sargent (1927) 265 on Ar. *Vesp.* 1118–1119; cf. Ehrenberg (1951) 213–214. Ar. *Vesp.* 1093–1101, Ar. *Av.* 108, Ar. *Ach.* 162–163. See below pp. 123–126 for a full discussion.

[84] Randall (1953) 209. Since Sargent's work was done before the publication of the Erechtheum work records, she cannot be held responsible for their implications.

[85] Sargent (1927) 269; B. Strauss (1986) 71–72.

of the preparations for the expedition.[86] Thucydides' description of the crew of the Paralus as being "all free Athenians" is similar to those cases where the presence of slaves is revealed only by the use of "free" for a part of a force.[87]

Thucydides' extremely spare treatment of slaves in the Athenian navy bears some responsibility for the erroneous views of modern scholars on the subject. The combination of an ideology that did not admit that slaves could fight and a reluctance to mention when they did served effectively to conceal Athenian use of slaves in the navy. Only the survival of *IG* i^3 1032 and a few off-hand remarks in all of extant Greek literature have made it possible to discern slave participation.

Lisa Kallet-Marx's recent book reveals Thucydides' constant awareness of the importance of money in naval warfare.[88] But why was money so important? It was not because triremes were so expensive. It cost less to build a trireme than to outfit two hundred hoplites.[89] Naval warfare was in fact less capital intensive than hoplite warfare. On the other hand, to pay the wages of a trireme crew cost up to a talent each month.[90] Money was crucial for the crews that often exceeded the total number of a city's citizens. With the severing of the link between citizenship and military service, a

---

[86] Th. 6.24–26, 6.30–31, 7.13.2. On Thucydides 7.13.2 in general see Graham (1992) 257–262 and *UAK* 1.93; *contra HCT* 4.388–389. Graham (1992) 258–259 shows decisively that the deserting slaves must be part of the active crews of the Athenian triremes. Graham (1992) 260–263 also discusses several possible interpretations of the phrase ἐπ' αὐτομολίας προφάσει. He argues that it refers to free sailors deserting by claiming that they are pursuing their own runaway slaves. This is the best option suggested to date since it picks up on αὐτομολοῦσι used to describe the slaves just a few lines earlier.

[87] Th. 8.73.5 (A): ἄνδρας Ἀθηναίους τε καὶ ἐλευθέρους πάντας. Graham (1992) 259 correctly describes Dover's attempt (*HCT* 4.388) to evade the natural implication of this line as "special pleading."

[88] Kallet-Marx (1993). Reflecting Thucydides' focus, the book does not have "slave" in the index, but see p. 64, 95 n.54.

[89] Pritchett uses a figure of one talent for a trireme and summarizes the scholarship and evidence (*GSW* 5.473 n.704, 5.484), but Gabrielsen (1994) 142 emphasizes variations in price. In the fourth century a good set of armor could cost 300 dr. (Jackson [1991] 229). If we assume mediocre sets of armor cost 100 dr. each, then 200 of them would cost 20,000 dr. (3 1/3 talents).

[90] 200 (crew members) × 30 (days) × 1 (drachma/day) = 6000 drachmas = one talent. This could be reduced by up to two-thirds if the crew was only given subsistence wages, but even impressed slaves – if such people existed in non-Athenian navies – could not be kept alive for less. Gabrielsen (1994) 115 gives examples of the enormous sums expended on naval campaigns.

city's navy was limited only by how many sailors – be they citizens, slaves, metics or foreigners – it could pay for. Although Thucydides demystifies war to the extent that he reduces it from being a matter of skill and courage to one of ships and money and mercenary crews, he balks at fully acknowledging the key role slaves play in the war he expected to be "great and memorable above any previous war."[91]

[91] Kallet-Marx (1993) 13; Th. 1.1.1.

CHAPTER 6

Thucydides: encouraging slave desertion

To hell with this war; I can't even punish my slaves anymore.
Aristophanes, *Clouds* 6–7.

Chattel slaves, as well as Helots, took part in war to the detriment as well as for the benefit of their masters. Their detrimental actions ranged from simple desertion to aiding the enemy to opportunistic revolts. Only a few cases, such as the flight of slaves to Decelea, made it into the historical record, but evidence suggests that slave desertion at least was a constant problem for warring Greek states. Ancient historians had little interest in these forgotten victors – or victims as the case may be – of classical warfare. Thucydides was particularly uncomfortable about free cities encouraging slave desertion. Perhaps as a result modern historians tend to underestimate both the extent of slave desertion and the active role Greek cities played in inciting it.

DESERTION AND REVOLT

Athens' infamous decrees against Megara exacerbated relations between Athens and the Peloponnesian League in the years before the war. Thucydides reports that one of the grievances that provoked the Megarian decrees was that Megara was harboring runaway Athenian slaves.[1] Badian considers this the most important Megarian offense.[2] It was indeed this grievance that Aristophanes parodied, but this may be more a function of the subject's comic potential than of Aristophanes' judgment of the issue's importance.[3]

Gomme points out that it was neither illegal nor immoral to

[1] Th. 1.139.2.   [2] Badian (1993) 156.
[3] *HCT* 1.449; Ste. Croix (1972) 240 on Ar. *Ach.* 524ff.

receive escaped slaves but to encourage them would be "unneighborly conduct."[4] It was probably hard to ascertain a person's status away from his or her home city. This difficulty would have given the Megarians enough leeway to prevent, or at least hinder, the recapture of Athenian slaves without overt breaches of commercial agreements.[5] Nevertheless, the degree and nature of the help which the Megarians provided remains obscure. What is significant for our purposes is that, even before the war began, Megara's antagonism towards Athens manifested itself in the encouragement of slave desertion.

Sources other than Thucydides regard the Megarian decrees as one of the chief causes of the Peloponnesian War. They blame Pericles for not rescinding them to avert war.[6] Perhaps the base nature of some of Athens' complaints contributed to Thucydides' reticence on the subject of the Megarian decrees. Athenian anger about runaway slaves was hardly a fitting start to a great and tragic war. Although slave involvement was probably not the main reason that Thucydides minimized the significance of the Megarian decree, this episode prefigures Thucydides' sketchy treatment or omission of slave desertion in the Peloponnesian War.[7]

Chios' trouble with its slaves extended beyond the Peloponnesian War. Even before the war, Chian slaves seem to have caused trouble: Thucydides reports that because of their great numbers these slaves were punished more severely when they misbehaved.[8] Polyaenus reports that, two decades later in 389, Iphicrates again took advan-

---

[4] *HCT* 1.449.

[5] E. Cohen (1973) 62ff. argues that throughout the Greek world, cases involving foreigners, including the mysterious δίκαι ἀνδραπόδων (18), were judged on the basis of supranationality: the national status of the litigants was irrelevant. In a hostile city such as Megara, an Athenian slave-owner who managed to find his fugitive slave could have been forced to bring him to court to prove his status. This could involve great expense, long delays, and perhaps an unfriendly hearing.

[6] Despite Ste. Croix (1972) 245ff., the consensus of scholars remains that many Athenians believed that the refusal to rescind the Megarian decree was a principal cause of the Peloponnesian War: e.g., Cornford (1907) 25; *HCT* 1.447; J. Finley (1963) 119; Dover (1972) 86; Rhodes (1987) 157 n. 5; Hornblower (1991) 111.

[7] The bibliography on the Megarian decrees is extensive. Ste. Croix (1972) and Kagan (1969) contain lengthy discussions. Badian (1993), Hornblower (1991), Rhodes (1987), and Lewis (1992a) provide more up-to-date references.

[8] Th. 8.40.2. Could Chios' caution about revolting and its long-standing loyalty to Athens (Quinn [1981], 41–44, Barron [1986] 103) be due in part – like Sparta's distaste for distant campaigns – to its awareness of its vulnerability to slave revolts?

tage of this vulnerability of Chios: he spread the report that he was gathering weapons with which to arm the slaves of the Chians. The Chians feared a repetition of the events of the Peloponnesian War and submitted to Iphicrates' demands.[9] Later, in the first half of the third century, Chios may have experienced one of the few chattel slave revolts of Greek antiquity.[10]

Chios revolted from Athens in 411 after the failure of the Sicilian expedition. In the subsequent campaign the Athenians erected a fort to harass the Chians.[11] Slaves not only deserted to the stronghold but even helped the Athenians lay waste the country. In fact, with their knowledge of the country, the slaves did the most damage.[12] Thucydides emphasizes how hard pressed the Chians were as a result.[13] The numbers of slave deserters may have been quite large: a Peloponnesian fleet of something less than one hundred ships, about seventeen thousand men, helped support itself by working for hire in Chios during the summer of 406.[14] The Chians may have needed this extra labor because of the loss of so many of their slaves.

In Thucydides' account of the Chian campaign, the Athenians' role seems to be passive. After they have firmly established their camp, the slaves desert to them and cause trouble for the Chians. Thucydides does not even say that the Athenians on the spot cooperated with the slaves. A single detail from the earlier narrative indicates that Athens intended from the beginning to make use of the slaves of the Chians. When the Athenians arrested the Chians on the triremes serving with Athens' navy, they set the slaves on board free.[15] But why? The Athenians could have made money, which they certainly needed, by selling the slaves. It was hardly standard practice to set slave captives free. In his work on the treatment of prisoners of war, Pierre Ducrey concludes that slaves could not anticipate any improvement in their status upon capture.[16] In fact, Ducrey mentions no other case of slave prisoners being set free. The

---

[9] Polyaenus *Strat.* 3.9.23.   [10] Garlan (1988) 181ff.; Fuks (1984).
[11] Delphinium in Chios has been excavated and the remains were found of what are believed to be the Athenian walls. These had been erected hastily with small stones and were probably no more than three meters in height (Boardman [1956], 47).
[12] Th. 8.40.2.   [13] Th. 8.40.1. See also 8.56.1.
[14] *HG* 2.1.1; Krentz (1989) 172.   [15] Th. 8.15.2; cf. Th. 3.3.4.
[16] Ducrey (1968) 284. I take issue below with the extension of this generalization to the case of slaves who desert to the enemy. In this case the Chian slave rowers were prisoners of war as surely as their free peers.

Athenians, anticipating a long struggle, were probably planning to use the slaves of the Chians against them from the very beginning of the revolt.[17] Their success at Pylos and their own suffering at the hands of the Peloponnesians at Decelea is likely to have suggested this plan to the Athenians.

The damage inflicted by the slaves of the Chians was not merely a result of their numbers and poor treatment in the past but was a success of Athenian policy. It is this fact that Thucydides' account ignores. Thus Thucydides' account of affairs at Chios closely parallels his treatment of the Pylos campaign. Again, Athens deliberately makes effective use of unrest among her enemy's unfree population. Again, Thucydides plays down Athenian participation in and responsibility for this practice.

In his catalogue of military stratagems, Polyaenus describes the repression of a slave revolt within Syracuse during the Athenian campaign. He recounts that twenty of the revolt's leaders were tricked into negotiating by a promise of freedom, of enrollment among the hoplites, and of an equal food ration. These slaves did not want to help the Athenians. They wanted to fight for Syracuse as high status hoplites – rather than in the navy perhaps. After seizing their leaders at the conference, the Syracusan commander Hermocrates attacked the remaining slaves. By a promise of amnesty he induced the slaves to return to their individual masters. Three hundred, however, deserted to the Athenians.

The authority of Polyaenus is minimal, but there is no reason to reject this story. Thucydides' omission of the story is consistent with his typical treatment of slave participation in war and does not speak against it. Some aspects of Polyaenus' account argue for authenticity.

The passage contains the same type of internal contradiction that appeared in Thucydides' account of the Helot revolt centered at Ithome. After Hermocrates had attacked and captured the slaves, he promised that they would suffer nothing dreadful, if they returned to their masters.[18] Why did Hermocrates promise the slaves anything if he had already attacked and taken them prisoner? Could he not have just handed them over to their masters? How did the three hundred slaves whom Hermocrates did not persuade desert to the

---

[17] Ducrey (1968) 288 also implies that this was the motive for the emancipation.

[18] Polyaenus, *Strat.* 1.43.1.

Athenians if he had already captured them? Usually inconsistencies discredit a historical account; in this case, the problems with the story fit the pattern of the description of slave revolts exemplified by Thucydides' account of the fate of the Ithome rebellion.[19] In both cases slaves, described as completely defeated, are given generous terms more appropriate to enemies still in arms. The very faults of the story are consistent with its derivation from a contemporary account and hard to square with outright creation.

Polyaenus says that Hermocrates attacked with six hundred hoplites. This is another realistic detail. We know from Thucydides that the Syracusans assigned a special detachment of six hundred soldiers to the generals to deal with crises.[20] If the story were invented, its author must have been subtle, for Polyaenus does not name the detachment as such, as well as erudite.

Several scholars agree that such a strange tale is unlikely to have been made up entirely.[21] If we accept the account of Polyaenus, we have a dramatic example of Thucydides' omission of slave activity. Even in his vivid and detailed account of the Sicilian campaign a slave revolt that had twenty leaders, was put down by six hundred hoplites, and produced three hundred deserters merits no mention.

In addition to these specific cases of disaffection, slave desertion formed an ubiquitous backdrop to classical warfare. Slaves often ran away during times of peace; in war they could count on hostilities to impede pursuit and recapture. Let us follow the fates of these slaves, for whom classical warfare was not a test of manhood and a matter of civic duty, but whose victories must have been just as sweet.

Greek slaves could run away even when there was no war to prevent pursuit nor an enemy to desert to. Runaway slaves appear often in Xenophon's writings, either in similes or in off-hand comments. For example, the future king Cyrus, as he is sneaking off

---

[19] See above pp. 69–70. Peter Green (1970) 206 believes that the original source of the story was the slaves who are reported to have fled to the Athenians. Even if this were the case the story would have been retold by slave-owners before reaching Polyaenus.

[20] Th. 6.96.3. Six hundred seems to be the traditional number for Syracusan elite guards since another such division is attested by Diodorus (11.76.2) a half century before the Peloponnesian War.

[21] Freeman (1892) 674; Westermann (1955) 17; Green (1970) 205–6; Westlake (1969a) 189. Ducat (1990) 162 withholds judgment. Garlan (1988) 180 has a brief discussion which seems to be the fullest treatment.

to go hunting, compares himself with a fugitive slave, who will be beaten and chained.[22] Socrates attacks Aristippus' avoidance of rule by pointing out what happens to disobedient slaves: punished in many ways, their masters put them in irons to prevent escape.[23] In another place Xenophon mentions the steps taken to catch fugitive slaves.[24] Finally, Xenophon insists that good methods of rule will prevent the common household situation where nearly all slaves are in fetters but try to escape anyway.[25] It may be the case that slaves in Xenophon run away more often than they perform any other action.

Such desertion could become even more of a problem in times of war. In Xenophon's *Cyropaedia* Cyrus takes special precautions to prevent the flight of his newly captured attendants.[26] In the *Ways and Means* Xenophon's claim that Athens could use mine slaves in the army and navy is a response to the objection that they will desert in the event of war and that the Athenians will lose their investment.[27] The best evidence for the ubiquity of slave desertion in war is that spies could disguise themselves as runaway slaves. Reference to this trick occur both in the *Cyropaedia* and in the practical *Cavalry Commander.*[28]

Thucydides does not mention the problem of slave desertion in his account of the Archidamian War.[29] During this period there was no Peloponnesian fort in Attica to which slaves could flee. Nevertheless, the pursuit of a fugitive slave would have been impossible during the Peloponnesians' annual invasions. Throughout the war the Athenians would not have been able to recover their slaves from nearby, hostile cities such as Thebes or Megara.[30] In fact, four plays of

---

[22] *Cyr. 1.4.13.* Other examples: *Cyr. 4.2.21, Mem. 1.6.2.* Plutarch knows of an Athenian sanctuary for runaway slaves (Plut. *Thes.* 36).

[23] *Mem.* 2.1.16.   [24] *Mem.* 2.10.1–2.   [25] *Oec.* 3.4.   [26] *Cyr.* 4.5.3, 5.2.1.

[27] *Vect.* 4.42. Aeneas Tacticus 10.1 advises cities that anticipate a siege to remove their slaves and draft animals to an allied city for safekeeping. Fear of slave desertion is probably one reason for this measure. Since both slaves and draft animals would consume food during a siege, Aeneas' advice is already motivated and does not provide independent evidence for slave desertion. See also *An.* 6.6.1.

[28] *Eq. Mag.* 4.7. *Cyr.* 6.2.2, 6.2.11. A similar stratagem is attested as early as Hom. *Od.* 4.244ff. Odysseus shamefully whips himself and dresses poorly to impersonate a disgruntled household servant. In this disguise he sneaks into Troy. He fools the Trojans and returns to the Greeks after killing many Trojans and finding out a large amount of information.

[29] Th. 2.57.1 does mention that some sort of deserters informed the Peloponnesians about the plague in 430.

[30] In a similar fashion the city of Catana later became a refuge for members of the Athenian expedition who had been enslaved in Sicily (Th. 7.85.4, Lys. 20.24, Paus. 7.16.4).

Aristophanes produced during the Archidamian War mention slave desertion.[31] In a mock tragic scene of the *Acharnians*, a slave describes Lamachus' fight with runaway slaves who had turned to banditry in the Attic countryside of 425. In the *Knights*, produced in 424, Demosthenes and Nicias, the "slaves" of *Demos*, find their lot intolerable and think of running away, but are afraid of getting whipped if they are caught.

These two plays do not mention the war as conducive to escape. But in the *Clouds*, produced in 423, Strepsiades is afraid to beat his lazy slaves. He blames the war for this. Presumably, Strepsiades fears that his slaves will desert to the enemy. In 421, the *Peace* listed a slave ready to run away among the people who benefit from the war. Just as Thucydides did not emphasize the role of the Megarian decree, provoked in part by the harboring of runaway slaves, so he skips this side of the war almost entirely.

THE FATE OF FUGITIVE SLAVES

Slaves could escape in wartime, as in peace, with no intention of deserting to an enemy's camp. Many runaway slaves would merely count on hostilities to prevent pursuit. Their destinations and prospects would be the same as that of fugitives in peacetime except that their masters could not come after them. In peace even escape to another city would not guarantee freedom. The Athenian complaint that the Megarians were receiving their fugitive slaves implies that the return of such slaves was part of truly peaceful relations.

Runaway slaves from outside of the Greek world would be in a precarious and difficult position without family or subsistence, hoping to find a place as a alien in a Greek city or to attain an unknown reception in a distant homeland. The ability to speak Greek was no doubt an advantage: an ex-slave with a Boeotian accent appears as a mercenary officer with the army of Cyrus in

---

[31] Ar. *Nub.* 5–7, *Peace* 451, *Eq.* 20–30, *Ach.* 1187–88. The authenticity of the *Acharnians* passage is defended by Sommerstein (1978) 390. Sommerstein mistakenly argues against the interpretation of δραπέτης as meaning a runaway slave (390 n. 51). He adduces only Sophocles *Ajax* 1285 as a use of δραπέτης to denote a non-slave coward. However, even there the word carries the meaning slave as lines 1289ff. make abundantly clear. The evidence from Aristophanes belongs to the period after the annual invasions of Attica had stopped. Perhaps, it was primarily the reception in cities hostile to Athens, rather than the proximity of enemy forces, that made flight a more attractive option during war.

Xenophon's *Anabasis*.[32] Actual Greek slaves would be even more likely to prosper or to regain their homes and prior citizenship.

A fugitive slave's chances may have been better in a city than in the countryside.[33] A basic requirement of trade is some assurance of the personal safety of foreigners. Coastal cities in particular, such as Corinth and Megara, cannot have permitted citizens to seize upon and enslave any strangers they came upon. Although a fugitive in a strange city was in a weak position and might even be enslaved, there is no evidence that this was the regular fate of foreigners in Greek cities. In the countryside runaway slaves would have had to depend on individual kindness or caprice. But all this was true in peace as well as in war; some slaves took their chances. The manpower demands of large navies, however, may have given able-bodied, male slaves more options than during a period of peace when a rootless person's situation could quickly become desperate.

The fates of slaves who fell into the power of a hostile army varied depending upon the circumstances: slaves could be captured in the same sense as free soldiers; they could desert to the enemy during a siege; or slaves might choose to flee to a fort, such as Decelea, instead of trying to escape on their own.

In the standard work on prisoners of war, Pierre Ducrey empha-sizes that slaves could not expect any improvement in their lot upon capture.[34] Captured slaves had only the choice of surrender or death. Their captors had no reason to forgo the money their sale could bring. This situation needs to be sharply distinguished from that of deserting slaves who had at least the option of remaining in their former captivity. If their only prospects were unknown and different masters, many might exercise that option. Would slaves risk everything merely in order to switch masters? In the American South running away to join family members was common. In contrast, the ties of family and locale were a strongly felt disincentive even when freedom would be the result of flight.[35]

---

[32] *An.* 3.1.26, 3.1.31.

[33] In times of peace it is more likely that a master would have been able to track down a slave living in a large, accessible city.

[34] Ducrey (1968) 284.

[35] Gutman (1976) 264–265; M. Johnson (1989) 230. Greek slaves could have families too: Xenophon observes that wives make good slaves better and rascals worse (*Oec.* 9.5). [Arist.] *Oec. 1.5.6* advises allowing slaves to raise families to serve as hostages for their good behavior: δεῖ δὲ καὶ ἐξομηρεύειν ταῖς τεκνοποίαις.

During sieges shortages of food could provide additional impetus for slaves to desert. One might expect that, when famine threatened, masters would cut their slaves' food. This seems to be the case. As we have seen in Polyaenus' account of the Syracusan revolt, one of the slaves' demands was for equal food rations.[36] A later source notes one advantage of promising freedom to the slaves of a besieged city: the owners will be forced to feed their slaves better to prevent desertion. Thus the city's food will run out sooner.[37]

Other evidence lends credence to my hypothesis that the treatment of fugitive slaves differed from that of captured slaves. Spies disguised as slave deserters cannot have anticipated being immediately fettered and sold off. Aristophanes' *Peace* cannot list slaves about to run away as beneficiaries of war, if they were merely to change masters. The deserting slaves of the Chians could have done little harm to Chios, if they had been sold by the Athenians. The Megarians provided refuge for Athenian runaways before the war; they did not enslave them.

Xenophon's account of an attack on Corcyra in 373 illustrates the variety of treatment slaves might experience at the hands of a hostile force. When Mnasippus, the Spartan general, invaded, he captured many slaves of the Corcyraeans. One assumes these were eventually sold.[38] During the subsequent siege many people, including slaves, fled from the starving city. At a certain point Mnasippus announced that these deserters would be sold into slavery.[39] That Mnasippus had to make a special proclamation to this effect shows that enslaving deserters was not the assumed practice. In fact, it cannot even have been Mnasippus' original policy.

Slaves who deserted had no legal or other recourse if an army or an individual soldier captured and enslaved them. Practices varied considerably depending upon the circumstances and the extent to which any one policy could be imposed upon an army.[40] The desire for immediate material gain would argue for selling deserters. The wish to injure the enemy and to discover the enemy's plans might favor milder treatment or an attitude of *laisser faire*. All of these

---

[36] Polyaenus *Strat.* 1.43.   [37] Philon of Byzantium 5.4.14–15.

[38] *HG* 6.2.6., 6.2.23, 6.2.25 refer to the slaves Mnasippus' army had with it later.

[39] *HG* 6.2.15 for this whole episode. Xenophon's grim story makes it clear that some portion – and probably a large one – of the deserters were slaves; cf. Caes. *BGall.* 7.78.

[40] Note the different fates of the Athenians captured in Sicily (Th. 7.85.2); cf. Plut. *Tim.* 29.

complexities were present in the crucial yet ill-attested case of Decelea.

The Spartan alliance established a fort at Decelea, but did not besiege Athens itself. This fortification had a different purpose than the earlier Athenian occupation of Pylos. There is no indication that the Spartans hoped or tried to stir up a slave revolt against Athens. They merely hoped to hurt Athens, largely by providing a haven for escaped slaves. Thucydides treats the occupation of Decelea and the consequent slave desertion as a major setback for the Athenians: over twenty thousand slaves, mostly skilled workers, ran away.[41] Given his focus on the material basis of military capacity in the Archeology and in the speeches of Archidamus and Pericles, this emphasis is not surprising.

But, just as in the case of Pylos and Chios, Thucydides' account plays down the most unsavory aspects of the Spartans' success. The Messenians had a national self-consciousness and had raised major rebellions on their own. The Chian slaves deserted because they were given their freedom and were previously discontented. Why did the Athenian slaves desert in such numbers? Athenian slaves had the option of staying with their masters or of trying to escape on their own. I would like to argue that so many went to Decelea, because the Peloponnesians had promised runaway slaves their freedom. The Peloponnesians' goal was to hurt the Athenians as much as possible and probably to obtain manpower for their navy.

Some slaves were so badly treated that the dangerous and uncertain journey to Decelea was worthwhile just for a change of masters. Although there is no report of famine at Athens until after Aegospotami in 404, mine slaves in particular might have cared little what happened to them at Decelea as long as they escaped the Athenian Gulag. Preventive measures taken at the Laurium mines around 409 indicate that escape before this period was possible and must indeed have occurred.[42] Work at the mines, however, declined only gradually during this period of the war until ceasing in 406/5 – probably due to the recruitment of slaves for the Arginusae fleet.[43] The proportion of deserting slaves that came from the mines is obviously unknowable, but mine slaves cannot have made up the

---

[41] Th. 7.27.5, 7.28.4, 7.47.4.

[42] B. Strauss (1986) 46. Hanson (1992) 216 n.16 argues that most of the deserting slaves were not from the mines and gives bibliography on the topic.

[43] Gauthier (1976) 159; Lauffer (1979) 224–225.

whole number: the same non-mine slaves who run away in Aristophanes' earlier plays must have taken advantage of Decelea; the mines could not have lost so many slaves without a precipitate end of production.

Not only did slaves have the choice of remaining where they were, but they could also have fled to somewhere other than Decelea – just as the runaway slaves in Aristophanes' Archidamian War plays. The mines in particular were over fifty kilometers from Decelea. If mine slaves could cover that distance in what was admittedly a dangerous countryside, they could have continued south to Megara or up to Boeotia. Slaves in the city of Athens or the countryside would in general have had shorter escape routes from Attica.

On the one hand, a slave with information to relate might desert to Decelea in hopes of reward. Slaves in the city must often have known about Athenian military plans and preparations. Slaves from the countryside would have been able to guide the Spartans or at least to tell them about hidden valuables or the most lucrative places to plunder. On the other hand, there was no need for a deserter to check in with anybody.[44] The whole countryside cannot have been patrolled by either the Spartans or the Athenians. Slaves could merely have depended on the Spartan presence in Decelea to hinder pursuit.

When Alcibiades proposes the fortification of Decelea, he implies not merely that slaves would desert to other places using Decelea as a screen, but that they would go to the Peloponnesians at the fort.[45] Thucydides seems to connect the desertion of twenty thousand slaves – in contrast to the escape of slaves in the Archidamian War which he does not mention – to the fortification of Decelea too closely for the fort merely to have hindered the pursuit of slaves making off on their own.

A promise of freedom would explain the Peloponnesians' success at inciting slaves to come to Decelea.[46] Historians have suggested that slaves came to Decelea expecting freedom and help with their escape but were duped.[47] One piece of evidence suggests that some slave deserters ended up as slaves in Boeotia. The *Hellenica Oxyrhynchia* explains how the Thebans profited when they helped the

---

[44] Peloponnesian allies escaping from Athens usually went straight to Decelea where they would be safe (*HG* 1.2.14, 1.3.22; Diod. 13.103.2); some, however, fled from Athens straight to Megara (*HG* 1.2.14).

[45] Th. 6.91.7.   [46] *HCT* 4.406.   [47] *UAK* 1.178.

Spartans fortify and man Decelea: they acquired slaves and all the other things captured in the war at bargain prices.[48] Bruce takes this as an indication that the "Athenian slaves who deserted to Decelea received no better fate than to be sold by the Spartans."[49]

We should note, however, that there is no indication in this text of the source of these slaves. Pritchett shows that the prices of slaves sold *en masse* directly after capture could be much lower than the usual market price.[50] Some of the slaves the Thebans bought could have been captured Athenian cavalrymen or farmers caught by unexpected raids: Demosthenes refers to an Athenian citizen enslaved during the Decelean War.[51] If we stray from Decelea itself, the enormous number of captives that resulted from Peloponnesian naval victories during the Ionian War probably provided Thebes with many cheap slaves.[52] It must be admitted, however, that a large number may have been slaves attempting to leave Attica.

The further conclusion that all of the slaves who deserted dutifully went to Decelea and were immediately sold off is considerably more dubious. The position of slaves deserting Athens, as of fugitive slaves in general, was varied and complex. Statements concerning the desertion are best couched in terms such as *some, others* and *probably* rather than *the slaves*.

Slaves had poor sources of information about what was happening at Decelea. If all of the fugitives, however, were immediately sold back into slavery, the word would get out and slaves would not continue over a period of years to show up at Decelea. Some slaves would escape back to Athens and bring word of the treatment received at Decelea. Merchants and metics, many of whom were ex-slaves, would also bring word in from outside. In the navy Athenians and their slaves served with men from throughout the empire and would hear reports from them. The Athenians themselves are likely to have used the common practice of sending spies disguised as deserting slaves to find out about Peloponnesian activities. Since they had an interest in keeping their slaves, they would have publicized poor treatment of slaves at Decelea.

---

[48] *Hell. Oxy. XVII.*4 (Frag. Lond.); cf. Plut. *Lys.* 27.   [49] Bruce (1967) 115.
[50] *GSW* 5.242 does, however, emphasize the insufficiency of the evidence.
[51] Dem. 57.18.
[52] In another passage, the *Hellenica Oxyrhynchia* uses Decelea merely to denote the last part of the Peloponnesian War: the Persian king did not pay his sailors well during the Decelean War (*Hell. Oxy. XIX.*2 [Frag. Lond.]).

It was in the interest of the Spartan alliance for Athens to lose its slaves, who were valuable and useful possessions. Helping them escape was one way of inflicting damage on Athens. An additional point seems to have escaped scholarly notice: both the Athenians and the Peloponnesians were manning – and losing and remanning – huge navies during this period. Manpower was likely to have been very short and thus in demand. There is evidence of competition for crews between Athens and Sparta which implies that desertion to the enemy for a higher wage was a possibility.[53] Deserters from Decelea might be most welcome additions to Sparta's navy. The exact terms of their service and their eventual fate, whether free or slave, is unclear to us – as it may have been to them. We do know that Cyrus paid wages for the entire complement of each ship; somebody was getting the wages even for slave rowers.[54]

Sparta's treatment of deserting slaves may have changed over time. After the naval war ended with the battle of Aegospotami, Sparta was no longer interested in rowers and Lysander pursued a policy of forcing as many people into Athens as possible.[55] The close siege of Athens meant that deserting slaves could not avoid the Peloponnesians, who no longer had reasons to treat them well.

Although some slaves who fled to Decelea may have not gained their liberty, it was probably the promise of freedom that led Athenian slaves to desert in such numbers. Thucydides does not discuss this key to the effectiveness of Decelea nor does he discuss the eventual fate of the slaves. Unlike the refugees from Plataea and Aegina whose destinies Thucydides tracks, the motivations and story of twenty thousand deserting Athenian slaves do not make it into his history. If my treatment of these slaves, hardly fewer in number than Athens' whole citizen body, is admittedly tenuous, it is because Thucydides does not outline the most basic facts of their flight.

The reticence of Thucydides is mirrored in the speeches that he presents on the subject. When Pericles mentions the possibility that a Peloponnesian fort in Attica could hurt Athens with raids and desertion, he does not specify that slaves were the most likely and by far, the most important deserters.[56] When Alcibiades addresses the arch-conservative Spartans about the deliberate subversion of the Athenian social structure, he is extremely vague. His formulation

---

[53] Krentz (1989) 136 on *HG* 1.5.4.   [54] Krentz (1989) 136 on *HG* 1.5.5.
[55] *HG* 2.2.2.   [56] Th. 1.142.4.

sidesteps the problematic issues connected with slave desertion. Although Greek contains words for desertion and specifically for runaway slaves, Alcibiades describes them as if they were merely the second subset of the property that Sparta will get: "most of the property in the countryside will fall into your hands, some of it when you take it, some of it on its own."[57] The escalation of the conflict to the final stage of undermining the opponent's system of exploitation is concealed. The Spartans are only going to assert a victor's right to the vanquished's property. Yet again Thucydides is capable of discussing slave desertion as a factor in the Peloponnesian War, but he is brief and conceals the active role that the antagonists took in encouraging slaves to desert or rebel.

RECRUITMENT AND REBELLION

Conventional views of Greek slave recruitment assume that war revealed the true feelings of slaves towards their masters.[58] Much as the Greeks felt that war showed the true worth of a person, modern scholars seem to think that war was an X-ray to reveal the inner structure of or breaks in the social skeleton. Under the pressure of war slaves would revolt, if they were unhappy, or fight to show their love of their masters.

True, the prior feeling of the slaves was one factor determining their actions. The Helots hated the Spartans and wanted their freedom. It was easy to predict that they would require little incentive to revolt. The Chian slaves were held in restless bondage. Consequently they were responsive to Athenian inducements to desert and harm their masters.

Nevertheless, war is not a state of pure nature that reveals the ultimate social reality. The mere possession of arms did not put a slave in a position of unlimited power and choice. Slaves were usually in armies or navies in which they made up only a minority. Even if their city was in jeopardy, there was always the strong chance that it might win through or make a treaty. In such cases the fates of a loyal and a rebellious slave could differ greatly. The high stakes involved made it imperative for slaves carefully to consider their

---

[57] Th. 6.91.7.

[58] E.g., *UAK* 1.81; Garlan (1988) 174. However, Patterson (1982) 287 argues that, in general, slaves benefit from all sides in times of war. His conception is nearer the "bidding war" model that I advocate.

options taking into account the concessions their masters might make to them, who was winning the war, their chance of successful flight, and their probable fate after escape. For the Messenians, whose homes and families were under Spartan control, there were terrible risks in case of an unsuccessful revolt, a general Athenian defeat, or a peace treaty that would enable Sparta to reassert control. Slaves could not reveal their true feelings as soon as they had a spear in hand or a chance to run.

The treatment of slave recruitment as a "loyalty test" breaks down utterly with even a cursory consideration of the time and places that slaves were recruited. If there was any time that a master would not want to test his slaves' loyalty, it was when slaves were already deserting and revolting. But this is precisely the time that slaves were most likely to be recruited. After the mass desertions to Decelea, Athens embarked slaves to fight at Arginusae.[59] Contrary to usual practice the slaves were freed and received almost all of the rights of Athenian citizenship. Chian slaves deserted, helped the enemy, but served in the navy as well. At Syracuse there were probably both slaves in the navy and a slave revolt during the Athenian siege. The case of the rebel slaves at Syracuse is telling: if promised their freedom, they would have agreed to become hoplites for Syracuse rather than rebels against it.[60]

The most striking example of the connection between recruitment and insurrection is in Thucydides. He states that, after Pylos, the Spartans feared a Helot revolt. They took a twofold approach to prevent it. They massacred two thousand Helots who claimed to have previously distinguished themselves in war, but they also enlisted seven hundred Helots to accompany Brasidas.[61] The Spartans did not recruit the Brasidian Helots in hopes that they harbored warm feelings for Spartan rule. Their treatment of the two thousand Helots, who had already fought for them, showed just how far the Spartans trusted Helot sentiment. Neither did their service in the Thraceward area reveal the feelings of the Helots with Brasidas. Rather the separation from families who were still under Spartan control,[62] the distance from known allies or territory, and the hope for freedom and advancement produced the practical loyalty which

---

[59] *HG* 1.6.24.   [60] Polyaenus *Strat.* 1.43.1.

[61] Th. 4.80.2–3. See Jordan (1990).

[62] On the other hand Helot recruits serving on distant campaigns could provide hostages for the good behavior of Messenia (*UAK* 1.110).

was all the Spartans needed or hoped for. After the Brasidians were established in their superior rights, loyalty may have followed interest: they fought for the Spartans even in the Peloponnese.

In general service in the military was a boon to those slaves recruited. The physical hardships were often less severe than those of slavery: the Peloponnesian War was not a matter of decisive Hoplite battles, but it was still a far cry from modern war.[63] Slave fighters might also have endured less supervision than under their masters since discipline in Greek armies was generally not very strict.[64] The hope of reward must also have been an inducement for good service. Athenian slaves making a wage in the navy may have been happy to get some of the money for themselves or for an eventual purchase of freedom.[65]

For a group that was despised as cowardly and unmanly, the chance to prove themselves would have been welcome.[66] The opportunity to carry arms in itself may have brought a huge gain in self esteem. At Sparta Neodamodeis, like other hoplites, may have had their own attendants.[67] Slaves in general may have expected to be treated differently when they had proved their worth in war. To what extent this hope was disappointed is unknown.[68]

---

[63] In the West Indies, in the late 18th and early 19th century, slave regiments fought well for the British even though the French promised to end slavery. Officers commonly encouraged them by reminders of how their lot compared with that of the field hands (Buckley [1979], 65).

[64] Anderson (1970) 99; *GSW* 2.244.

[65] The slave's master would certainly take some portion of the wages and had the legal right to all of it. See Chapter 5.

[66] The experience of complete dislocation and powerlessness of newly captured chattel slaves may have made them particularly eager to please their masters, even after their dependence was eased; they may even have identified with their captors as in the case of hostages who experience the "Stockholm Syndrome"; see Ochberg (1978). The articles collected in Lane (1971) are a prophylactic against taking too extreme a view of the effect of slavery on personality.

[67] *UAK* 1.134.

[68] McNeill (1995) argues that "muscular bonding" takes place among people who repeat the same movements together. This "muscular bonding" accounts for the way that throughout history soldiers recruited from the dangerous fringes of society "were swiftly and reliably transformed into pillars of the establishment"(McNeill [1995] 131–132). Such a process could help us understand how Greek cities could trust their slaves to fight for them even at difficult periods. As McNeill notes, rowers on triremes and the highly-trained Spartan army, who marched into battle to music, must have experienced "muscular bonding" (McNeill [1995] 117). As we have seen, these were the two places where the participation of the unfree was historically most significant.

For all these reasons, to place arms in the hands of slaves was not a test of their feelings. It was an excellent way to co-opt them. But before we consider making harsh judgments about the Helots who helped bail out the Spartans while their compatriots were fighting and dying for freedom, one last point should be remembered. The reason that slaves could be won over so easily was that their prior lives were so wretched. Escape from the poverty and terror of Helotage, release from a closely supervised solitary life under a hated master, or rescue from a short life in the silver mines at Laurium could provide compelling pressure upon a slave who had little hope that slavery or even Helotage would ever end.

In contrast to the "loyalty test" interpretation of slave recruitment I would suggest that more can be explained by a "bidding war" model. In wartime the support of slaves became important both to their masters and to determined enemies. This was especially true in the Peloponnesian War in which both sides possessed large slave populations, the contest was even, and only new tactics could break the deadlock. In this situation both sides tried to win over the slaves. According to this model, both the opportunity to rebel or desert and the recruitment of slaves were concessions that gained slaves' support. Of course, neither could be counted on to win over the inner sympathies of the slaves, but the antagonists cared little about their "hearts and minds" as long as slaves fought on their side.

A few examples from modern scholarship will show how pervasive is the assumption that slaves' conduct in war reveals their inner feelings. Garlan criticizes Jordan's thesis concerning the way that Athenian triremes were manned. He then postulates that Jordan argues for slave rowers in the Athenian navy in order to minimize the divide between free and slave.[69] Garlan suspects the same aim behind Welwei's argument that necessity dictated when and how slaves were used in war: the gap between free and slave cannot be that great if circumstances can alter it.[70] This suspicion is justified since Welwei says that the service of slaves in war does tell us about their feelings towards their states. Welwei contrasts the Argive slaves who overthrew their city when given arms and the Helots who loyally served the Spartans at Plataea.[71] Both of Garlan's arguments as well as the positions which he criticizes are based on the assumption that a slave's good will is a prerequisite for him to serve

---

[69] Garlan (1972) 27.   [70] Garlan (1988) 174.   [71] *UAK* 1.181.

in war. Wretched conditions and few options can also make for good soldiers.

The case of the Spartan Helots is striking. Sparta suffered more revolts and resistance than other Greek states, but also used its Helots in the military most often.[72] If military service proves one's loyalty, then the Helots cannot have been as discontent as their rebellions and Spartan precautions seemed to indicate. R. J. A. Talbert takes exactly this tack: how could rebels be instantly made into loyal Neodamodeis? Talbert decides that the Helots were not really unhappy and rebellious, but is left with the insoluble problem of trying to explain away patent indications of unrest.[73]

Several other scholars have attempted to explain the contrast between Helot recruitment and rebellion by positing differences within the Helot population. Thus some Helots sometimes were the recruits and others at other times were the rebels.[74] James T. Chambers, for example, sharply distinguishes between the Laconian and Messenian Helots. The Helots who served at Plataea were Laconian whereas the revolt of 464 was one of Messenians. The arming of Helots for Brasidas was an effective precaution since it was Laconian Helots that were armed. This freed Spartans to deal with Messenia.[75] There are several problems with this theory. The first is that Chambers has to admit that Thucydides knows nothing of the Laconian/Messenian split: Thucydides even claims that *all of the Helots* are called Messenians.[76] No ancient source explicitly makes Chambers' strong contrast between the Helots in Messenia and Laconia. In fact, Laconian Helots were not as tranquil as Chambers' dichotomy would have it: the 464 revolt may have begun in Laconia; the Athenian base across from Cythera was aimed at inciting Laconian Helots; Cinadon's conspiracy may have been primarily Laconian; and it was a generation after the liberation of Messenia that Aristotle said that the Helots were enemies waiting to attack the Spartans.[77] Nevertheless, I find it plausible that there were real differences in attitude between the Laconian Helots, the origins of

---

[72] Garlan (1975) 79; Garlan (1972) 47; *UAK* 1.180.

[73] Talbert (1989) 33 rebutted by Cartledge (1991). Ducat (1990) 144 n. 46 agrees with Talbert.

[74] Burn (1984) 379.

[75] J. Chambers (1977/78) 275, 278, 280, 283.   [76] Th. 1.101.2.

[77] Cartledge (1979) 177. Aristotle even names Messenians among the *foreign* enemies that cause trouble among the Helots (Arist. *Pol.* 1269a37–1269b7). The two thousand loyal Helots who were killed by the Spartans are hard to place in Chambers' schema (Th. 4.80).

their servitude lost in the past, and the Messenians with their national myths; these differences do not entirely explain the supposed contradiction in Helot attitudes.

Another explanation posits differences among the Helot population caused by the recruitment of some into the relatively elite Neodamodeis. George Cawkwell emphasizes that the creation of the Neodamodeis contributed to social stability by allowing an avenue for Helot advancement: "the very people once most likely to join in a revolt had been won over by the prospect of promotion and the enjoyment of their new status."[78] This explanation is sound in that recruitment is recognized as a grant to the Helots which changes their position rather than an opportunity for them to show their "true" feelings. Some Helots may have been won over by their promotion, but not all of them. Xenophon, who served in the same army as the Neodamodeis for many years, portrays Cinadon as counting on the support of the Neodamodeis for his conspiracy against the Spartiates.[79]

Slave recruitment and the incitement of revolt were not the results of opposite dispositions among slaves. They are rather intimately linked as tactics demanded by the deadlock and subsequent escalation of the Peloponnesian War. When slaves exercised either of the options, they trespassed into the citizen's realm of war and presented similar, though not identical, ideological problems. Thucydides treated both phenomena with concealment, omission, or brevity. The ideological reasons for his treatment provide the material for our next investigation.

[78] Cawkwell (1983) 392–393; Cartledge (1987) 176; Cartledge (1991) 381; Whitby (1994) 109; *contra UAK* 1.179.
[79] *HG* 3.3.6.

CHAPTER 7

Thucydides: the ideology of citizen unity

They did not think it right to slaughter slaves with their free swords.

Euripides, *Melanippe Desmotis.*[1]

As we explore Thucydides' reticence about slaves and Helots from a variety of angles, we will paint an increasingly complex picture of Athenian ideologies and of Thucydides' place within them. Nevertheless, the basic argument is straightforward. There were appropriate roles for citizens and for slaves. Slaves who fought trespassed upon the realm of the citizen. Such a blurring of categories could not be fully acknowledged because of the ideological function of the dichotomy between slave and citizen. All Athenian men, rich or poor, could think of themselves as united by the fact that they were not slaves and were indeed the very opposite of slaves. As wartime pressures led to acrimonious politics and even periods of civil war, the maintenance of the boundary between slaves and citizens became ever more critical. By glossing over slave participation Thucydides defended a threatened boundary and the increasingly shaky civic unity to which it was linked.

Before beginning we should mention one factor contributing to Thucydides' silences, which, however probable, cannot be pursued as it deserves: Greek slave owners, like masters in other slave societies, tended to adopt a stereotype of slave personality hardly consistent with their participation in war: slaves were feminine, cowardly, lazy, soft, and childish. As a rich Athenian with interests in Thracian gold mines, Thucydides almost certainly owned many slaves.[2] Unfortunately, the very absence of slaves from Thucydides' history – what we are hoping to explain – ensures that we have little

---

[1] von Arnim (1913) 31 line 38: οὐκ ἠξίουν/ [δούλους φονε]ύειν φασγάνοις ἐλευθέροις.
[2] Th. 4.105.1; Davies (1971) 237.

evidence for his view of slave personality; Xenophon will be a richer source for Greek attitudes towards actual slaves. We need to explain Thucydides' silences from oblique sources. A wide variety of texts give evidence about Athenian attitudes in general. Thucydides' own use of the metaphor of slavery, his emphasis on civic unity, and his redefinition of historical writing can be brought to bear.

Such an explanation – whose details we shall elaborate presently – also explains Thucydides' reluctance to discuss the encouragement of slave or Helot revolts. To incite slave revolts transgressed the boundary between slave and citizen. Athenian citizens, defined in opposition to slaves, ought not to choose them as allies. In the world of drama slaves were not even fit enemies for the free: two heroes in Euripides allow some enemies, who are slaves, to escape so as not to defile their "free swords."[3] For free citizens to fight against other free citizens, but in alliance with slaves, threatened the centrality of the contrast between slaves and citizens. It is to this division, its basis and function, that we now must turn.

MILITARY PREROGATIVES

In Herodotus' linking of freedom with martial prowess, we have already seen the general Greek tendency to connect military and civic responsibility. Fighting for a city gave one a claim to be included in its politics. Part of the claim consisted of having weapons in one's hands and knowing how to use them; military service also bestowed a moral right to citizenship. Just as Homer's Sarpedon claimed that his right to rule was based on valor, so Athenian citizens collectively ruled by virtue of their military service.[4] Conversely, Athenian citizens could suffer *atimia*, loss of civic rights, for cowardice in battle.[5] For slaves to fight was for them to usurp a citizen role.[6]

---

[3] Dover (1974) 284 on Eur. *Mel. Desm.* 38 (in von Arnim [1913]).   [4] Hom. *Il.* 12.310–321.

[5] Lys. 10.1. Throwing away one's shield was typically the mark of cowardice (Ar. *Vesp.* 19–24 and Ar. *Au* 289).

[6] In the classical period Athens bought public slaves, "the Scythian archers," to perform functions we associate with the police (Jacob [1928] 53–79). The Scythian archers, however, did not present an ideological impasse. In contrast with military service, police functions were emphatically not associated with citizenship. Imber even argues that the purpose of buying Scythian archers for police duties was to prevent a situation in which certain citizens could legally use physical force against others (Imber [1995]). So the role of the Scythian archers harmonized perfectly with Athenian notions of appropriate and inappropriate roles for citizens.

Although this argument is unexceptionable when applied to hoplites and cavalry, we need more carefully to consider the navy and its status. One strain in Greek thinking despised the navy: naval service was most appropriately done by slaves and lower-class people.[7] It was with this background in mind that earlier scholars such as Böckh posited a navy manned almost entirely by slaves.[8] Sargent, in contrast, insisted on a high-status navy from which slaves would be entirely banned. Both fall into the same trap of making a harmonious and organic world out of Athens. If slaves fought in a low status navy, there would be no stress in Athenian ideology. If slaves were barred from a high status navy, we could also picture a world in which ideals and reality meshed. The actual situation was more complex. Rowing in the navy was not so high class and respected – as hoplite service was – that slaves could not take part. It was neither so lowly and disconnected from Athenian self-definition that slave participation was unproblematic.

The self-regard and high morale of the navy first suggest the prestige and claims that naval service bestowed. Pericles expressed pride at the quality of Athenian steersmen and crews and emphasized the difficulty of acquiring naval skill.[9] The navy of Phormio vaunted its ability to defeat any number of Peloponnesian ships.[10] Even Xenophon, usually contemptuous, admires naval discipline and order.[11]

There were regular trireme races at Sunium and near the Piraeus.[12] These suggest public enthusiasm and a competitive spirit among the rowers. Thucydides himself effusively describes the high hopes, impressive spectacle, and solemn sacrifice with which the Sicilian expedition set off.[13] Again, the triremes raced to Aegina to start their voyage.[14] Such self-confidence, high spirits, and pride in ability were hardly desirable attributes for slaves.

The moral claims that naval service bestowed became evident during the oligarchic coup of 411. In its opposition to the oligarchs at Athens, the navy at Samos conducted itself as the legitimate Athenian government: it declared its independence from the oligarchy at Athens; the navy selected new captains and generals and seems even to have minted its own coins.[15]

[7] Amit (1965) 58–59.   [8] Böckh (1886) 328–330.   [9] Th. 1.142.6–143.2.
[10] Th. 2.88.2.   [11] *Mem.* 3.5.6, 3.5.18, 3.5.21; cf. Th. 2.89.9.
[12] Lys. 21.5; Plut. *Them.* 32.5.   [13] Th. 6.32.1–2.   [14] Th. 6.32.2.
[15] Th. 8.72–77; Amit (1965) 67.

The *thetes*, who provided most of the Athenian rowers, made up about half of the population of Athens.[16] They were probably proud of their work and their preeminent contribution to Athens' power. During the Peloponnesian War, farmers, normally of the hoplite class, may have rowed in the navy to supplement their incomes in the face of Peloponnesian invasions.[17] Finally, the liturgical class – to which Thucydides almost certainly belonged – often captained and outfitted ships as trierarchs. During the Peloponnesian War, they seemed to have taken pride in their performance of these duties. In his description of the preparations for the Sicilian expedition, Thucydides tells how the trierarchs provided extra pay for some crew members and spared no expense on making their ships both fast and impressive.[18]

The prestige of the navy came out of the involvement of these different classes as well as from the navy's centrality to Athenian power. We can see the status of the navy and the claims that even just rowing bestowed in the contemporary comedies of Aristophanes.[19] The chorus of the *Wasps* treats rowing and fighting on land in parallel. They were both ways that an Athenian might earn the right to jury pay.[20] Their mock-epic pride first boasts of Marathon, but then of the Athenian navy that acquired the empire: they value rowing well more than oratorical tricks.[21] In the *Acharnians*, the *thranatai*, the top row of oarsmen crucial to a trireme's efficiency, are even called the "saviors of the state."[22] Even pseudo-Xenophon, an enemy of both the people and the navy, conceded that the common people in Athens had some right to control the government because they rowed the ships upon which Athens' empire depended.[23]

---

[16] B. Strauss (1986) 70–86. I am only concerned with the approximate proportion of *thetes* and not Strauss' particular argument for a decline.

[17] Rosivach (1985).

[18] Th. 6.31.3: cf. Ar. *Ach.* 544–554, esp. 547. In the fourth century, rich Athenians involved in lawsuits would claim to have been particularly generous and careful in the performance of their trierarchies (Ober [1989] 216, 227, 231–233). Thucydides' evidence is perhaps more trustworthy since he is not pleading an actual legal case.

[19] Sargent (1927) 265; Ehrenberg (1951) 213–214.

[20] Ar. *Vesp.* 1118–1119; cf. Ar. *Eq.* 567, 781–785, *Ach.* 677.   [21] Ar. *Vesp.* 1093–1102.

[22] Ar. *Ach.* 162–163. See Casson (1994) 65–66 for the role of the *thranatai*.

[23] [Xen.], 1.2; cf. Arist. *Ath. Pol.* 33.2. An oligarchy could also be based on the equivalence of soldier and citizen: Xenophon's Theramenes favors governing in company of all "who have the means to be of service, whether with horses or with shields" (*HG* 2.3.48). See below pp. 185–192 for ideologies that associate rights only with certain branches of the military.

Athenian naval pride is paradoxically most prominent in the *Knights*, a play devoted to the cavalry of Athens. Poseidon, a patron of horses and thus the cavalry, is also invoked as a god of the sea, delighting in Athenian triremes.[24] Both competing demagogues, the Paphlagonian and the Sausage-Seller, bring gifts to Demos, "the People," to help the Athenian navy, which the goddess Athena watches over.[25] Earlier, the cavalrymen were praised for their participation on a naval expedition.[26] Naval concerns, references, and imagery crop up throughout the play; the whole audience – of Athenian citizens since the play was produced at the Lenaea – is expected to share in these jokes and jargon.[27] Such a world, in which the Athenians as a whole identify strongly with the navy, is far from what we shall see later in Xenophon: a speaker in Xenophon even slips into the mistake of assuming that the Athenian assembly is made up only of hoplites and cavalry; that indeed reveals a contempt for and neglect of naval service.[28]

Little in Aristophanes is a transparent representation of the attitude either of the poet or of Athenians in general; some individual references to the navy could no doubt be explained away. Nevertheless, one leaves Aristophanes with the overwhelming impression of the importance of the navy and the esteem in which its crews were held.

Two pieces of evidence suggest more specifically that the presence of slaves among the crews of the navy was awkward. The crews of the state ships Paralus and the Salaminia consisted entirely of free Athenian citizens.[29] Apparently these ships represented an ideal to which the rest of the navy did not live up: ships ought to be manned by free Athenians. The converse and more subversive proposition appears in the *Frogs*: Aristophanes argues that everybody who fights in the navy should be treated as "a relative and citizen with full rights."[30]

A high regard for the navy is what we see in Thucydides too. Only once does Thucydides refer to the "naval mob", a favorite bugbear

---

[24] Ar. *Eq.* 554–555.   [25] Ar. *Eq.* 1182, 1182–1186.   [26] Ar. *Eq.* 598–610.

[27] Ar. *Eq.* 541–544, 602–603, 830, 1063–1066, 1071–1074, 1300–1315, 1350–1354, 1366–1368; cf. Ar. *Au* 108, Ar. *Ach.* 94–97, 189–190, 647.

[28] *HG* 7.1.13.   [29] Th. 8.73.5.

[30] Ar. *Ran.* 701–702. By this time the Arginusae slaves had been given citizenship and Aristophanes is arguing for the reinstatement of the rights of the disenfranchised oligarchs of 411.

of fourth-century elitist writers.[31] Even this reference may not be derogatory, since Thucydides often uses the term translated "mob" in a neutral sense.[32] Nor is the "naval mob" doing anything untoward when so described.

This isolated reference is overwhelmed by the regard Thucydides shows for naval power. Beginning in the *Archaeology* and then throughout the history, Thucydides concentrates on the theme of the importance of the navy.[33] If anything, Thucydides overestimates the value of sea power.[34] Most interesting for our argument is Pericles' injunction that the Athenians should consider themselves islanders.[35] The primacy of the hoplites and cavalry are completely over-shadowed in this view of Athens as completely dependent on its navy. Thucydides' class sympathies were largely with the hoplites and cavalry: the "best men" who died during the war were hoplites.[36] Nevertheless, the navy was, in fact as in Thucydides' account, the basis of the Athenian power whose greatness Thucydides emphasizes.[37]

SLAVE AND CITIZEN

Non-citizens other than slaves also played a significant role in the Peloponnesian War. Metics of hoplite status served in garrisons and manned the walls of Athens itself.[38] Mercenaries provided Athens with special skills and weaponry. Most crucial of all were the foreign or metic rowers, who may have outnumbered citizens in the Athenian navy.[39] All these groups were exceptions to the connection between rights within a city and military service. None presented the ideological quandary of slave fighters. Slaves were not merely non-citizens. They were the outsiders within, in opposition to whom all citizens could feel united.[40]

---

[31] Th. 8.72.2; cf. 8.86.5. Amit (1965) 58–60.

[32] Thucydides uses the term ὄχλος twenty seven times. In many cases its force is probably or certainly not pejorative: Th. 1.80.3, 6.20.4, 6.57.4, 7.75.5, 8.25.4, 8.92.1. Thucydides, in contrast to pseudo-Xenophon, does not connect naval power with democracy or mob rule (Starr [1978] 344–347).

[33] E.g., Th. 1.15.1, 2.62.2, 6.17.7. See Kallet-Marx (1993) for a recent treatment.

[34] Cf. above pp. 90–101.   [35] Th. 1.143.5.   [36] Th. 3.98.4.   [37] Th. 2.65.12.

[38] Th. 2.13.6–7 with *HCT ad loc.*

[39] Indeed, the common contrast of free and slave strategically ranges the metics on the side of the citizens (Mactoux [1980] 74).

[40] See Patterson (1982) ch. 2 on this phenomenon in a variety of slave societies.

A wide variety of evidence shows that slaves were emphatically marked out as different, opposite, and inferior to citizens.

In the classical period vase painting emphasizes the division between slave and free. While women are distinguished by a light color in black-figure pottery, slaves are the little people. Vase painters had to make sure that nobody would mistake slaves and free men.[41] In vases and in reliefs on grave steles, slave women were distinguished by their size and dress.[42] In comedy slave characters were marked as distinct by the red hair on their masks as well as their costumes.[43]

In jury courts and public assembly the accusation of slavishness or slave ancestry was apparently a potent one.[44] Even citizens who were not slaveholders were expected to feel antipathy towards the descendant of slaves or a "slavish" man. Several orators affect to assume that everybody owns slaves.[45] Some members of their audience did not, but nevertheless must have felt that they were members of a group, the citizens, naturally distinct from and hostile to slaves.

Demosthenes twice argues that the greatest difference between slaves and the free is how they are punished: slaves are answerable with their bodies whereas the free are not.[46] Slaves indeed were subject to brutal corporal punishment, both publicly and at the hands of their masters. To treat a free person in this way was an outrage. Although some exceptions to the immunity of the free can be found, modern scholars generally accept Demosthenes' distinction.[47] The legal requirement that even slave witnesses give their testimony under torture may seem bizarre and cruel; it may have been merely a legal fiction.[48] Whether a common practice or not,

[41] Himmelmann (1971) 16, 19, 22–30.   [42] Himmelmann (1971) 32–33, 39–40, 43.

[43] Wiles (1991) 65, 157, 165–166, 189. These conventions, attested in later sources, probably originated in the Classical period.

[44] Ober (1989) 279–281. Ober is particularly concerned with the accusation of having participated in "slavish occupations"; many Athenians must have done work that the aristocracy considered "slavish." Nevertheless, the closest any of the orators come to defending "slavishness" itself is to claim that πολλὰ δουλικὰ καὶ ταπεινὰ πράγματα τοὺς ἐλευθέρους ἡ πενία βιάζεται ποιεῖν (Dem. 57.45).

[45] Lys. 5.5: οὐ γὰρ τούτοις μόνοις εἰσὶ θεράποντες, ἀλλὰ καὶ τοῖς ἄλλοις ἅπασιν. οἱ πρὸς τὴν τούτων τύχην ἀποβλέποντες οὐκέτι σκέψονται ὅ τι ἀγαθὸν εἰργασμένοι τοὺς δεσπότας ἐλεύθεροι γένοιντο (ἄν), ἀλλ᾽ ὅ τι ψεῦδος περὶ αὐτῶν μηνύσαντες.

[46] Dem. 22.55, 24.166–167.

[47] Finley (1980) 93–95; Hunter (1994) 154–184. See also below p. 168.

[48] Dubois (1991) 39–45. Gagarin (1996).

the idea itself shows the deliberate marking off of slaves from the
citizen population.[49]

The argument of Vidal-Naquet's article, "Slavery and the Rule of
Women in Tradition, Myth, and Utopia," provides an apt summing
up of the absolute dichotomy between chattel slaves and citizens.
Not even in the upside-down worlds of comic utopias or myth are
states envisaged in which slaves rule: "An Aristophanic utopia can
put women on top, just as Plato later can set them almost on the
same level as men. But chattel-slaves are simply not part of the city
at all."[50]

All this evidence concerns slaves directly. The use of the metaphor
of slavery for a number of stark and hierarchical dichotomies – such
as the relation of mind and body in philosophy – shows that slaves
were indeed a category apart in Athenian thinking.[51] Although the
contrast between freedom and slavery is not a central organizing
theme in Thucydides as it is in Herodotus, his common use of the
metaphor of slavery shows that the distinction between slave and
citizen was nevertheless important. In Thucydides unjust systems of
government could be likened to slavery: Brasidas promises not
enslave "the many to the few, or a minority to the whole people."[52]
More commonly states could be enslaved to other states: Sparta
declared that it was fighting to liberate Greece from Athens.[53]

In consequence of Thucydides' comparison of interstate with slave
and master relationships, loss in war could bring "slavery." In some
cases, this slavery might involve actual enslavement: Athens' treatment of Melos and Scione – where they enslaved the women and
children – added plausibility to Gylippus' and the Syracusan
generals' claim that if the Athenians had enslaved Syracuse they
would have inflicted "the worst indignities upon our wives and

---

[49] Garlan (1988) 42–43; Dubois (1991) 41; Gagarin (1996) 17. Dubois argues that the torture of
slave witnesses was also symptomatic of the notion of a buried truth that needed to be
extracted by violence.

[50] Vidal-Naquet (1986b) 218. Vidal-Naquet is also concerned to mark off chattel slaves from
Helot-like classes whom he considers a part, albeit subordinate, of the city.

[51] See Vlastos (1941) for Plato's use of the metaphor of slavery. For other dichotomies see
above pp. 46–47 and below pp. 158–160.

[52] Th. 4.86.4–5; cf. 6.40.2.

[53] Th. 2.8.4; *HCT* 3.646. The relations of city-states to each other are described using the
metaphor of slavery on 57 occasions in Thucydides, both in speeches and narrative. Athens
and, to a lesser extent, Persia, typically play the role of master in the metaphor. Predictably
enough, in many cases it is loss in war that leads to "slavery."

children."[54] Nevertheless, when Gylippus speaks of Athens' ambition to enslave Sicily, the Peloponnese, and the rest of Greece, it is metaphorical slavery that he is talking about.[55] The use of the metaphor of slavery to describe a variety of unequal relations suggests that the contrast between slave and free was a given in Thucydides' mental world – as in classical Athens in general. Significantly for our purpose, Thucydides associates metaphorical slavishness with cowardice and pacifism.[56]

Thucydides' association of slavery with loss in war and with a lack of manly courage – similar to Herodotus and what we will see in Xenophon – made slaves awkward participants in war. In Thucydides and in Greek mentality in general, we see two strongly opposed categories: citizen soldiers and cowardly slaves. Slaves who played a part in war and thus proved their courage upset this way of thinking about the world.

Mary Douglas' explanation of the Levitican dietary prohibitions shows the potential power of the need to keep categories straight and provides a productive parallel to our argument. The basic principle behind the Levitican rules seems to be that the categories of creation have to be kept distinct. Thus, to be clean an animal has to conform completely to its class.[57] Proper livestock consists of cloven-hoofed and cud-chewing animals. Domestic animals that do not chew the cud, such as pigs, or non-domestic ones that do, such as "rock badgers," are taboo. They violate the categories of creation.

The treatment of slaves in Greek warfare differs in several ways from Douglas' case. In one respect, our argument is easier; we do not need to explain as much by recourse to the inviolability of categories. In Thucydides we are faced merely with a reluctance to discuss a subject rather than an absolute prohibition of potentially nutritious foods. Escalation made the actual use of slaves in war inevitable. Greek categories made the acknowledgment of slave roles awkward. To this extent, we can say that fighting slaves tend not to be written just as pigs could not be eaten.

Douglas' explanation depends upon the wholeness and integrity of divine creation. We can find support for the inviolability of our opposed categories in the well-known Greek penchant for polar oppositions. Cartledge sums this up as follows: "the ideological habit

---

[54] Th. 7.68.2.   [55] Th. 7.66.2.   [56] Th. 2.63.3; cf. Th. 1.141.1, 4.34.1, 6.82.4, 7.71.3.
[57] Douglas (1966) 53, 55.

of polarization . . . .was a hallmark of their mentality and culture. Moreover, they pressed polarization to its (ideo)logical limits. Thus whereas Greeks were ideally seen as not-barbarians, barbarians were equally envisaged as being precisely what Greeks were not."[58] For example, Hartog and Redfield show how Herodotus' view of different cultures is largely structured by his search for opposites. Hartog discusses Herodotus' "excluded middle" that makes him collapse all cultural encounters to the one model of Greeks meeting their opposites: "the narrative proves unable to cope with more than two terms at a time."[59] Redfield notes Herodotus' proclivity for systematic oppositions. Most famously everything about Egypt is opposite to normal custom.[60] In Greek philosophy and medicine references to pairs of opposites are ubiquitous.[61] Early and even Platonic texts tend to treat these opposites as "mutually exclusive and exhaustive alternatives."[62] In medicine, opposites are cures for opposites.[63] That slaves must be opposite to citizens in every way should start to seem less surprising. Thucydides would certainly not be the first Greek whose account of the world was distorted by a false polarity.

Thucydides himself is known for his stark oppositions such as those between word and deed, between land and sea powers, between foresight and chance, between his truth and the opinions of the many. Even his writing style is marked by contrasts, often strained.[64] We have already seen Thucydides' commitment to the purity of the category of slave: his dichotomy between the Messenians in Naupactus and the Helots in Messenia kept him from acknowledging that the status of neither was unambiguous.[65] It should not seem strange that Thucydides plays down slaves who fight to maintain the integrity of the opposition between the slave and the citizen warrior.

The great virtue of such an explanation is that it does not posit the untenable view of Thucydides as deliberately working for the specific interests of a certain social class or for a political program. Certain factors, such as rebelling, deserting, or fighting slaves, tended to drop

---

[58] Cartledge (1993a) 11.   [59] Hartog (1988) 258–259.   [60] Redfield (1985) 103.
[61] Lloyd (1966) 7.   [62] Lloyd (1966) 7–8, 431–434.   [63] Lloyd (1966) 21.
[64] Rusten (1989) 12, 23–25. Dover (1965) xvii: the "underlying symmetrical and antithetical sequence of thought" can be concealed by Thucydides' taste for variation.
[65] See above pp. 68–69.

out of Thucydides' account of the Peloponnesian War because they did not fit the way he organized his world.

Nevertheless, such an explanation – an explanation at the level of Geertz's symbolic systems – leaves some questions unanswered. Why did these particular categories come into existence? How did they reflect Athenian society and how did they function within it?

At first glance it seems that the classification according to slave or citizen status simply reflects the realities of Athenian society.[66] Despite contentious debate about many aspects of ancient slavery, there is some agreement about its role at Athens. This consensus derives in a large part from the comparative work of M. I. Finley.[67] Finley showed that everywhere in the Mediterranean world, some form of dependent labor existed. What distinguished the slave society at Greek cities such as Athens was that such labor was provided by imported slaves rather than half-free peasants within a stratified social structure.[68] Rather than the complex hierarchies typical of the Mediterranean world, at Athens "statuses were bunched at the two ends, the slave and the free."[69]

The processes that produced this result were no doubt complex and are still obscure. One crucial step was taken when Solon ended the possibility of debt-bondage for citizens. Manville argues that the basic feature of the Solonic reforms was "the creation of boundaries."[70] Athenians citizens could not become slaves at Athens. Nor in general could slaves become Athenian citizens. Socially the boundary between slaves and citizens became almost impermeable.

In a connected development slaves began to be imported largely from the non-Greek world.[71] The foreign extraction of most slaves fed the feeling that they were completely and naturally different from and inferior to citizens. Most conspicuously, non-Greek slaves would not be able to speak Greek well. Xenophon has to specify that a hunter's net-keeper be able to speak Greek.[72] In drama, Phrygians and Scythian slaves speak Greek with ridiculous accents and do not

---

[66] See Lloyd (1966) 35–41 for a discussion of the basis of Greek polarities.

[67] Finley (1982a, c, e, f). His basic argument is accepted by scholars as dissimilar as E. M. Wood and de Ste. Croix, although Wood does argue that the rich derived some of their wealth from renting out land to the free poor (Ste. Croix [1981] 133; Wood [1988] 81–82).

[68] Finley (1982e) 166.   [69] Finley (1982f) 132.

[70] Manville (1990) 126–133. His interpretation of the reforms of Cleisthenes is similar (213).

[71] Garlan (1987) and Finley (1982d).   [72] *Cyn.* 2.3.

understand it well.[73] This was a sign of inferiority: in Aeschylus, Sophocles, Aristophanes, and Herodotus, we find sentiments or comparisons disdainful of non-Greek speech.[74] In his defense of slavery, Aristotle assumes the slavishness of "barbarians." It is only the enslavement of Greek prisoners of war that gives him pause: such slaves were often not natural slaves.[75] Differences in language, culture, and origin between imported slaves and Athenians tended to strengthen the contrast between slave and free.

Although the number of slaves at Athens is a controversial subject, slave ownership was certainly not restricted to the rich. Men of the hoplite class may have made up about half of the citizen population and cannot be described as an elite within the citizens.[76] To judge from a wide variety of evidence, including the ubiquitous slave servant on campaign, hoplites regularly owned slaves.[77] Some *thetes* even owned slaves.[78] The contrast between slave and free was experienced every day by slave-owning citizens.

A THREATENED IDEOLOGY

To some extent the polarity of slave and citizens was so important and sharp because the contrast between actual slaves and citizens was so important and sharp. But some readers may have noticed a certain excess in the way the Athenians emphasized the distinction. In vase paintings, in comic masks, in the law courts, the Athenians were not merely depicting the difference between slaves and citizens. They insist upon and mark out the opposition. As a variety of scholars agree, the contrast between slave and citizen tended to efface class distinctions and suppress social conflict among the citizens.[79] Even the poorest Athenian could take pride in his citizenship and in not being a slave. In this ideology – whose limits

---

[73] Ar. *Thesm.* 1082–1135. Eur. *Or.* 1369. Ehrenberg (1951) 131.

[74] Soph. *Trach.* 1060, *Ant.* 1001–1002, Aesch. *Ag.* 1050, H. 2.57.1, Ar. *Ran.* 679–682. In this paragraph I follow the arguments and citations of Rosivach (forthcoming).

[75] Arist. *Pol.* 1255a24–32.

[76] B. Strauss (1986) 173. According to Hansen (1991) 94 adult, male citizens made up only one-tenth of the people in Attica and only one-fifth of the adults. To denote half of these citizens as elite and the other half as mass is certainly a bit arbitrary.

[77] Ehrenberg (1951) 124; Garlan (1988) 61; Hansen (1991) 317; M. Jameson (1992) 143; R. Osborne (1995) 29. See Hunt (1994) n.62 on Wood (1988).

[78] Graham (1992) 266–267.

[79] Raaflaub (1983) 532; Vidal-Naquet (1986e) 163–164; Farrar (1988) 7; Wood (1988) 121; Todd

we will explore below – rich and poor citizens were not in opposition to each other, but rather all citizens were a unity in contrast with the slaves. In Mactoux's formulation the absolute distinction between slave and citizen provided an imaginary resolution of real social tensions among the citizens.[80]

Again, to a certain extent, slavery did minimize social conflict among the citizens. The creation of a legal barrier between citizens and slaves by Solon prevented the development of a "homogenous lower-class."[81] Poor citizens did not have the same economic interests as the rich, but neither were the rich and poor as polarized as in a society with debt bondage. By the time of the Peloponnesian War, all Athenian citizens enjoyed rights that went far beyond freedom from debt bondage. The rich could afford the legal equality of democracy since they derived their wealth largely from the labor of imported slaves.[82] The encroachment of the rich that led to calls for cancellation of debts and redistribution of land in many other Greek cities seems to have been avoided by democracy and slavery at Athens. The legal equality of the citizens and the independence of the poor that characterized classical Athens grew out of their economic independence, made possible by the importation of slaves.[83] Although they disagree on the contributory factors, Funke, Strauss and Ober all emphasize the relative harmony of the Athenian democracy.[84]

Nevertheless, the ideological insistence on the dichotomy of slave and citizen suggests anxiety both about the boundary between slave and free and about the unity of the citizens. Both problems are likely to have been particularly intense during and directly after the Peloponnesian War, the period in which Thucydides wrote.

First, wartime events and circumstances undermined in practice the boundary between citizen and outsider. Athenians could fall out of the category of citizen. The aftermath of the 411 coup involved the disenfranchisement of oligarchic sympathizers.[85] Even more dramatically, captured Athenians could be enslaved. Demosthenes refers to an individual who suffered this fate.[86] In the aftermath of the Sicilian disaster, many Athenians were enslaved.[87]

(1990) 164–165; Manville (1990) 126, 132–133, 217; Patterson (1991) 99; Ober (1989) 5, 27 n.63.

[80] Mactoux (1980) 215.   [81] Ober (1989) 62–63.

[82] Hopkins (1967) 170, Ste. Croix (1981) 141; Manville (1990) 133; cf. R. Osborne (1995) 38.

[83] Finley (1982a), (1982g).   [84] Funke (1980) 6; B. Strauss (1986) 5; Ober (1989) 17–19.

[85] See Arnott (1991).   [86] Dem. 57.18.   [87] Th. 7.85.3–4.

More visible and upsetting may have been the incorporation of non-Athenians into a body whose composition had previously been highly regulated: Pericles' law of 451–450 had required that both parents of an Athenian citizen be citizens.[88] From early in the Peloponnesian War, however, refugee Plataeans enjoyed almost full citizenship.[89] As we have seen, the Arginusae slaves obtained these same rights. Late in the war illegitimate children of Athenians were allowed to become citizens.[90] At the war's end Samians were offered Athenian citizenship.[91] Immediately after the war, citizenship was proffered to – but then withdrawn from – the metics and foreigners who fought against the Thirty.[92] The effect of all this can be seen in a decree that reinstated Pericles' citizenship law after the war: it contained the telling proviso that there were to be no inquiries into the descent of people born before 403.[93]

Second, if any period of Athenian history required an imaginary resolution of social conflicts, this war – marked in general by political and social strife, but especially the revolution of 411, its reversal, and the reign and fall of the Thirty – was it. This breakdown of political consensus is one of Thucydides' most constant preoccupations.[94] He admires the oligarchies at Sparta and Chios on the grounds that they maintained order and harmony among the citizens.[95] Thucydides may even go too far in his emphasis of the importance of civic harmony: he blames Athens' defeat on its internal problems. This conclusion is not borne out either by his own narrative or by other accounts of the end of the war.[96] Internal strife, such as that of 411, was certainly a severe threat to Athens. Thucydides, an exile, may well be forgiven, if antipathy to the disunity that his plight exemplified distorted his analysis of the war's conclusion.

Thucydides' own political views are hard to pin down; he clearly disapproved of extremists. He was critical of unfettered democracy:

---

[88] See Connor (1994) 35–37, 39, 41 for a critical appraisal of the exclusivity of Athenian citizenship.
[89] Dem. 59.104–106.   [90] M. Osborne (1981) 35.
[91] Meiggs and Lewis (1988) 283–287 (no. 94); _IG_ i³ 127.
[92] Krentz (1982) 110–113.
[93] Eumelus _FGrH_ 77F2; Dem. 57.30; Ath. 13.577b.   [94] Cf. Pope (1988) 288.
[95] Hornblower (1987) 162; _HCT_ 5.57–8 on Th. 8.24.3; cf. Th. 4.74.4.
[96] Thucydides states this opinion most explicitly in 2.65. The problems with Thucydides' emphasis have been noted by many scholars: Heath (1990) 259 cites Rusten, Gomme, Brunt, Westlake, Levy, and Dover as questioning the accuracy of Thucydides' judgment. Cf. _HCT_ 2.191–199 and Hornblower (1991) 340–348.

he approves of its moderation by a strong leader, a restriction of the franchise, and the elimination of pay for office.[97] His praise of Pericles is decidedly aristocratic;[98] his contempt for the fickle, vengeful stupidity of the masses is well known.[99] On the other hand, aristocrats such as Nicias and Alcibiades fare no better.[100] Thucydides' own presentation undermines Cleon's bitter attacks on democracy.[101] Thucydides approved of the government of the five thousand, in contrast to the hard-line oligarchy of the four hundred, as well as in preference to full democracy.[102] In the conclusion of Thucydides' account of civil war at Corcyra the distinctions between the democrats and the oligarchs are lost in his condemnation of both.[103]

Given his commitment to the slave/citizen distinction and to citizen unity, it was natural for Thucydides to want to maintain the purity of slave and citizen roles. The escalation of the Peloponnesian War ensured that slaves intruded upon the citizen realm of warfare. But, as the same intensification of the conflict drove Athens towards civil war and blurred the actual boundaries of citizen and slave, the citizen versus slave contrast most needed to serve its function of uniting the citizens. The war demanded unity among the citizens, but it also required the use of slaves. Thus it subverted the ideological basis of that unity. Thucydides pushes slaves to the margins of his history to resolve this contradiction.

EXTREMISTS

Our argument will be enriched by a consideration of its converse. Although the evidence is scanty, the centrifugal thinking of extremists tended to concentrate on boundaries and divisions within the citizens and to blur the categories of slave and citizen.

At the same time as mainstream democratic discourse divided people into slaves and citizens, in oligarchic or elite circles the

---

[97] M. Chambers (1957) 82 on Thucydides 2.65.8–10, 8.97. Since my modest point is no more specific than that Thucydides approves of something less than full democracy, the obscurities and difficulties of these passages are fortunately irrelevant.

[98] Edmunds and Martin (1977) 193.

[99] E.g., Rawlings (1981) 110; Edmunds (1993) 847; Roberts (1994) 55.

[100] Roberts (1994) 58.   [101] Roberts (1994) 57.

[102] Th. 8.97. De Romilly (1963) 102; Connor (1984) 221–230; Orwin (1994) 188.

[103] Th. 3.82.

primary opposition was between the elite and everybody else. If we look ahead to the fourth century, we see that Xenophon's contrast between the knowledge that makes some men aristocrats – *kaloi kagathoi*, literally "beautiful and good" – and slavish ignorance seems to imply the slavishness of all but the aristocracy.[104] Xenophon – as well as other elite Athenians – blurred the free/slave distinction by assimilating free people to slaves in terms of their occupations which are characterized as slavish.[105] In oratory too, tradesmen could be accused of slavishness.[106] Pseudo-Xenophon depicts Athenian support for the Spartans against the Messenians as a mistake; the Athenian *demos* should support the analogous lower class in other cities. Thus pseudo-Xenophon treats the Messenians, often referred to as slaves, as similar to the Athenian *demos*.[107] As Kurt Raaflaub points out, in an aristocratic society that "characterized the poor as low, base and bad," the distinction between slaves and commoners could no longer be considered decisive.[108] In fact, the very goal of oligarchy, the restriction of citizenship to those who held sufficient property, was a re-inscription of the division between citizens and outsiders that would put the poorer free in the same class as slaves.

Slavery did play a part in elite thought. Plato, in particular, focuses on the contrast of slave and master.[109] Whereas in Thucydides the metaphor of slavery is used to condemn unfair or unequal regimes, Plato considers the distinction between slave and master a model for the relationship of ruler and ruled. The very existence of rulers and ruled may have been antithetical to the Athenian democracy.[110] The comparison of political power with the absolute power of a master over slaves was even less democratic. Its apogee was the three hundred helpers of the Thirty armed with whips,

---

[104] *Mem.* 1.1.16.
[105] Slavishness of working for pay: *Mem.* 1.2.6, 1.5.6, *Ap.* 30. Distaste for tradesmen: *Mem.* 3.7.6; *Oec.* 4.3, 6.6–7; *Cyr.* 1.2.3. The occasional jokes to the effect that the rich in Athens are treated like slaves are aimed at portraying the democracy as a tyranny that enslaves its subjects (*Smp.* 4.32, 4.45). The injustice of the rich being in any way like slaves is emphasized whereas in the case of artisans, it is the fact that they are not actual slaves that seems wrong. See Wood (1988) 51.
[106] Ober (1989) 272–277 discusses these passages in relation to the problem of how such accusations would work before juries that probably included just such workers. See also Todd (1990).
[107] [Xen.] 3.10–11.   [108] Raaflaub (1983) 535. See also Todd (1990) 165–166.
[109] I here follow the arguments of Vlastos (1941).
[110] Ober (1989) 7–8, 293–295, but see Rhodes (1995).

symbols of a master's rule over slaves.[111] This elite use of slavery did not efface difference among the citizens. Rather the metaphor of slavery accentuated hierarchies among them.

On the other end of the political spectrum, there are hints of an affinity between radical democrats and slaves. If poor Athenians had few slaves, their community of interest with the slave-owning elite may have been a fragile illusion. Some Athenians, as the stereotype of poor whites in the southern United States suggests, may have needed to feel superior to slaves to make up for their own low status. Such a feeling could explain their commitment to the slave/citizen dichotomy. But just as desertion plagued the South in the Civil War, the "rich man's war and the poor man's fight," the consolation of "at least being free" may have worn thin with some poor Athenians as the war dragged on.[112] We've seen that *thetes* and slaves worked together on triremes and in construction. Although such contact does not ensure fellow feeling, it makes it plausible.

Unfortunately, our sources for the views of radical democratic leaders – not to mention actual poor Athenians – are scanty and suspect. Antidemocratic, elite sources frequently accuse extreme democrats of being in some sense allied with slaves: pseudo-Xenophon complains that you cannot tell slaves from the free at Athens; according to Plato the ultimate democracy will equate free and slave; Aristotle argues that it helps democracies for slaves not to be under control.[113] In Xenophon's *Hellenica*, Theramenes defends himself against the accusations of Critias: he condemns those democrats who are not satisfied until "even slaves and those who, because of their poverty, would sell out the city for a drachma take part in the democracy."[114] These examples clearly show the oligarchic tendency to link extreme democrats, the poor, and slaves. But do such statements merely reflect anti-democratic rhetoric? Or do they also indicate, with some exaggeration, the actual position of radical democrats?

The claim that some democrats wanted ex-slaves, at least, to take part in government may have had a grain of truth. Aristotle's *Politics* states that Cleisthenes enrolled foreigners and ex-slaves among the

---

[111] Arist. *Ath. Pol.* 35.1.   [112] See Robinson (1980) on the Civil War.

[113] [Xen.] 1.10; Pl. *Resp.* 8,563 b; Arist. *Pol.* 1313b35, 1319b28.

[114] *HG* 2.3.48 (M). The accusation that Critias stirred up slaves against their masters in Thessaly was either slander or indicates that extreme oligarchs had little interest in the citizen/slave dichotomy.

citizens.[115] In the 460s Cimon was in favor of helping Sparta against the Helots whereas the founder of the radical democracy, Ephialtes, may have wanted to let them overthrow Sparta.[116] Despite the differences between Helots and chattel slaves, conservative Athenian slave-owners cannot have been pleased at sponsoring revolts of people whom the Spartans called their slaves. Later also, during the Peloponnesian War, it was the more radical Cleon and Demosthenes who vigorously pursued just this policy.[117] The period of the most extreme and – in our elite sources – despicable democracy was the last years of the Peloponnesian War during which the slaves who fought at Arginusae were freed and given citizenship. The *Athenian Constitution* states that slaves were among the people to be rewarded with citizenship for fighting against the Thirty to restore the democracy.[118] More certain is the role that metics, many of whom were ex-slaves, played in overturning the Thirty.[119] To stray from Athens, both oligarchs and democrats at Corcyra promised freedom to the slaves; most of the slaves joined the democrats.[120]

So there are hints of another way of slicing up the world, one that did not involve a sharp dichotomy between slave and citizen, one that did not smooth over division among the citizens. There were oligarchs who would restrict citizenship. They would lump together the poor and slaves as part of the same *okhlos*, the same mob. Poor Athenians might have no ideological or economic commitment to slavery. They saw themselves as opposed primarily to the rich. The sharp dichotomy between slave and citizen was implicated in the increasingly difficult struggle to maintain civic unity in the face of extremist threats during a protracted and divisive war.

THUCYDIDES

Nicole Loraux's exploration of the Athenian funeral oration, the *epitaphios*, provides a parallel for our study of the treatment of slaves in Thucydides. Like Thucydides, funeral speeches concentrate on war and politics, ostensibly the domains of citizens alone. They "insist on the unity of the city, suppressing political dissensions . . . ,

---

[115] Arist. *Pol.* 1275b37–38; cf. Arist. *Ath. Pol.* 21.4. Manville (1990) 180, 191 n. 103 believes that ex-slaves were enfranchised, but not in "some deliberate parliamentary manner."
[116] Ste. Croix (1972) 179.   [117] Ste. Croix (1972) 90.   [118] Arist. *Ath. Pol.* 40.2.
[119] Krentz (1982) 84, 129.   [120] Th. 3.73.1.

expressing . . . the strictly Greek homology of the civic community and its army of citizens."[121] The orations tended to suppress the plurality of the polis. The *epitaphios* also resembles Thucydides' history in not mentioning slaves.[122] The slaves who served as hoplite attendants – or slave rowers – were not even buried in the Kerameikos; the gap between citizens and slaves was too large.[123]

This correspondence between the world of the funeral oration and Thucydides brings us to a crucial problem. Loraux traces the "history of the funeral oration" in Thucydides' history. She takes issue with scholars who contrast Thucydides' narrative and the account of Athens in the *epitaphios*. She points out that the funeral oration of Pericles is an organic part of Thucydides.[124] Nevertheless, even Loraux admits that the Pentecontaetia has little relation to the history of Athens presented in the funeral oration. By Book 3 the idealized Athens of the *epitaphios* is faring poorly. From the Melian dialogue on "all trace of a collusion between history and the eulogy gradually disappears from Thucydides' work."[125] To get to the nub of our problem, is not Thucydides admired largely for the ways in which his history is not at all a eulogy of Athens, for his harsh and unrelenting honesty, for his objective condemnations of both sides?

To begin with, I am not portraying Thucydides as a conscious purveyor of Athenian war propaganda, trying to maintain citizen unity against the enemy. Thucydides is clearly not an Athenian apologist. Too much in his history is discreditable to Athens.[126] Rather the dichotomy between slave and citizen was pervasive. This world view, with its strategic consequences for citizen unity, was the sea in which Thucydides swam rather than a choice he made to further Athens' war goals. It is to this sea rather than to any pro-Athenian agenda that I attribute Thucydides' suppression of slave involvement.

But even the claim that Thucydides was trapped within the

---

[121] Loraux (1986) 270. Funeral orations concentrate on the hoplites as the model for all Athenians. See Loraux (1986) 278 and below pp. 190–194.

[122] Loraux (1986) 286, 334.

[123] Loraux (1986) 36. As in the whole of Thucydides' history, women are also excluded from the funeral oration. Compare Loraux (1986) 284 and Cartledge (1993b).

[124] Loraux (1986) 288–293.   [125] Loraux (1986) 295.

[126] Badian (1993) argues that Thucydides presents accounts of the *Pentecontaetia* and of the war's beginning that exculpate Athenian aggression. Even if Badian's arguments are accepted, they show perhaps more partiality for Periclean imperialism than for the Athenians, whose foibles and arrogance Thucydides highlights in the latter narrative.

categories of his society may strike some readers as strange. Many readers most admire Thucydides for his bitter insight and unsparing inquiry: fighting, fleeing, or rebellious slaves might fit perfectly well in a history which included the repeated defections of Alcibiades and the traitorous oligarchs of 411. In fact, Thucydides describes in great detail the disintegration of other boundaries in his accounts of the plague and of the civil war in Corcyra.[127] In his description of the naval battle near Pylos, Thucydides seems to revel in the breaking of categories: the Spartans fight a naval battle from land and the Athenians a land battle from their ships. This ostensible reversal of categories is so forced that Gomme writes "I would be glad to believe that Thucydides did not write this."[128] Clearly we need carefully to define our claims about Thucydides.

First, Thucydides did not actively lie about slave participation. He does not say that slaves were not important to Athenian naval power. He does not say that there were no Neodamodeis before 421. Nor have I even shown that Thucydides absolutely excludes slaves from his text. I do not have to explain a complete suppression of slave roles. Thucydides merely chose his emphases in such a way that slaves and Helots become peripheral to the main concerns of his history. When he decided what to pause over, whom to follow, what to focus in on, which tactics or strategies deserved center-stage, and which should be left unmentioned, he tended to neglect slaves.[129]

Second, many recent scholars of Thucydides highlight the way that he structures his account. The picture of Thucydides as an impartial, objective historian has lost considerable ground.[130] Cornford claims that Thucydides conformed to a tragic pattern.[131] De Romilly shows how Thucydides' speeches and narrative function together to elaborate a consistent theory of Athenian imperialism.[132] Rawlings argues that Thucydides divides the Peloponnesian War into two ten-year wars: in some cases Thucydides distorts his narrative to provoke comparison between the two wars as well as

---

[127] Th. 2.53, 3.81.5 – 3.84; cf. Connor (1988) 207; Orwin (1994) 175, 178–182.
[128] *HCT* 3.452 on Th. 4.14.3. Cf. 4.12.3 where Thucydides' delight in paradoxical reversals is more justified.
[129] I do not want to imply by the word decision an explicit, completely conscious process.
[130] Crane (1996) 27. Rhodes' clear and cogent article, "In Defense of the Greek Historians," takes issue with some of the more extreme attacks on Thucydides' reliability (Rhodes [1994]).
[131] Cornford (1907) 244.   [132] De Romilly (1963)

with the Trojan War.[133] Hunter also focuses on the patterns that Thucydides imposes on events despite his pretense of objectivity.[134] Connor concentrates on the way Thucydides plays on readers' knowledge of the war's end.[135] For none of these scholars is Thucydides' narrative a mere reflection of the course of the Peloponnesian War. Thucydides has aims in addition to neutral narration.

Most important for our thesis are approaches to Thucydides' selection or omission of material. Thucydides' oscillation between comprehensiveness and selectivity is a salient aspect of his history.[136] It has often been noted that Thucydides focuses relentlessly on politics and war.[137] Arnaldo Momigliano points out that "even the plague – the only extrapolitical experience he could not avoid – is eventually examined for its political consequences."[138] The love interests, the women, the servants, the prophesies, and the household intrigues that Herodotus details play no role in Thucydides.[139] It is, moreover, a particularly limited politics in which Thucydides is interested. For example, in his account of the Four Hundred, he ignores political slogans invoking the ancestral laws of Athens.[140] He neglects appeals to religion or to racial kinship. He minimizes the role of personal influence and family connections.[141] For Thucydides politics is exclusively the autonomous decisions of the citizens in assembly. So too Thucydides focuses on war as what the citizens do rather than a sphere of activity involving various classes.

We are not, however, required to deny Thucydides objectivity entirely. Rather Thucydides is able to be so objective because he has limited his scope.[142] We can acknowledge Thucydides' penetrating insights in the realm of the citizen and the city but still inquire into the reasons for what he selects or omits.

A brief discussion of the two occasions where Thucydides explicitly mentions chattel slaves' activity in his war will reinforce our conclusions. In 431 Theban forces made a surprise night attack and burst into the town of Plataea. When the Plataeans counterattacked, the plight of the Thebans was aggravated by women and slaves who pelted them with stones and tiles from the roofs.[143] In the civil war

---

[133] Rawlings (1981).   [134] Hunter (1973) 151.   [135] Connor (1984) *passim*, e.g., 51.
[136] Hornblower (1987) 42.   [137] Hornblower (1987) 191.   [138] Momigliano (1990) 40.
[139] Hornblower (1987) 7, 14; Crane (1996) especially chapters 3,4,6.
[140] Hornblower (1987) 142.
[141] Crane (1996) 24–25 and *passim*. See also Hornblower (1987) 82.
[142] Crane (1996) 24–25.   [143] Th. 2.4.2.

at Corcyra, slaves joined the democratic faction. Again at Corcyra women too took part. They threw tiles from the rooftop and endured the uproar of battle "contrary to their natures."[144]

In both cases, Thucydides could easily have skipped the slaves and women. Just as he often gives extraneous details about the activities or suffering of soldiers, here he proffers extra information about slaves and women. These two incidents mark the limits of Thucydides' notice of slaves. At Plataea, the slaves only partake to the extent of throwing tiles from roofs in the dark and confusion of an inverted battle within a city in peacetime.[145] At Corcyra, the involvement of slaves is a sign of the social disintegration of civil war.[146] Unfree participation can be acknowledged in these two cases more easily than at Pylos, with Brasidas, or in the navies so central to Thucydides' war.

The connection of slaves and women is also telling. Thucydides' neglect of women is notorious.[147] Although women did not usually take part in actual fighting, even their role in politics – and the whole influence of family ties – is minimized. The case of women is similar to that of slaves. They were a significant contrary against which Athenian males could define themselves.[148] Like slaves, their inferior status also seems to have served the function of uniting the rich and poor among the citizens.[149] Again Thucydides concentrates on the citizens, even at the cost of neglecting important factors in the politics he aims to describe and understand.

Thucydides' treatment of Persia provides another parallel for his treatment of slaves. The use of Persian funds was decisive in determining the outcome of the war. Like the recruitment and incitement of slaves the recourse to the Persians was a product of the escalation of conflict. Like the involvement of slaves in war, alliance with the barbarians transgressed a boundary that served to unite, in this case, all Greeks. Perhaps in consequence there are strange omissions in Thucydides' treatment of Persia. Thucydides makes no

---

[144] Th. 3.73–74.

[145] Th. 2.2.3, 2.3.3–2.4. The Plataeans also claim that the attack was during a sacred month (Th. 3.56.2).

[146] Crane (1996) 91. Additionally, after most of the slaves join the democrats, they disappear from the narrative. One can only presume that they took part in the enormities perpetrated by the democratic faction.

[147] See Cartledge (1993b) and Crane (1996) for discussion and bibliography.

[148] Vidal-Naquet (1986b) 206.   [149] Pomeroy (1975) 57ff. Halperin (1990) 98–101.

mention of the peace of Kallias, which seems to have put a stop to fighting between the Athenian league and the Persians in the mid-fifth century.[150] The possibility of Persian involvement in the Peloponnesian War figures nowhere in the introductory sections such as the *Archaeology* or pre-war predictive speeches. More significant, only when an embassy from Persia to Sparta is captured by the Athenians does it become apparent that there had been many previous communications between Sparta and the king.[151]

Current anthropological theory holds that dirt is not just matter out of place, but tempting matter out of place: there is no need for taboos on putting broken glass into food. It is materials or practices with potential appeal that need to be sanctioned.[152] So too the use of slaves in warfare was an awkward subject not merely because it was so contrary to Greek ways of thinking, but because it was so tempting during the Peloponnesian War. Similarly the dichotomy between slaves and citizens did not influence Thucydides' narrative because these opposed categories were so strong and natural an outgrowth of Athenian society. Rather, the Peloponnesian War tended to subvert the absolute distinction between slave and citizen. Extremists, always present but more prominent then, threatened the citizen unity to which this boundary contributed. It was not the strength, but rather the weaknesses of Athenian social structure that required Thucydides to maintain the division between slave and citizen.

[150] See Lewis (1992c) 121–126 for a trenchant and convincing defense of the Peace of Kallias; Badian (1993) 1–72.
[151] Hornblower (1987) 38; Th. 4.50. It is, however, possible that if Thucydides had finished the histories, he would have given more attention throughout to the Persians, whose importance became so obvious only at the end of the war (Cartledge [1993] 51).
[152] Levy (1997).

CHAPTER 8

Xenophon: ideal rulers, ideal slaves

This day will show what each man is worth.
                              Xenophon's Cyrus before a battle.[1]

Xenophon differs from Thucydides in the period of history he described and lived through, in the content of his thought as well as in the varied genres in which it is expressed. Thucydides, a rich general during the supremacy of the Athenian navy, was particularly concerned with the relations between *thetes* and the elite among the citizens. Thucydides emphasized the importance of naval power as well as the theme of different types of leadership throughout his work. During the Peloponnesian War, Thucydides was exiled and relations between mass and elite deteriorated, leading to violence in the oligarchic coup of 411. It makes sense to analyze Thucydides primarily in terms of the maintenance of the citizen-slave dichotomy especially since he provides no direct evidence about slave stereotypes.

In contrast, Xenophon recounted the re-establishment of citizen unity after the Peloponnesian War with the deposition of the Thirty in 403. Xenophon was not in general interested in the *thetes* or the navy. Rather he considered the hoplites and above the only real citizens. He even composed speeches which address the Athenian assembly as if it consisted of land forces only.[2] As was common among Athenians of oligarchic tendency, Xenophon thought not in terms of leadership of the *thetes* but of an elite alliance with the hoplites.[3] Xenophon had no particular interest in establishing a

---

[1] *Cyr.* 3.3.37 (M).   [2] *HG. 7.1.13.*
[3] The oligarchic Xenophon and [Xenophon] divide the hoplites and above from the thetes whereas the democratic Lysias divides the haughty cavalry from the hoplites and thetes (Hansen [1991], 116 on [Xen.] 1.2, *HG* 2.3.48 and Lys. 14.7–14, 16.13). In a manner

rapport between elite and *thetes*; his ideology concerning the use of slaves in warfare was primarily driven by a desire to maintain a stereotype of cowardly slaves and a link between military prowess and rule.

In many ways Xenophon is a richer source for our investigation than Thucydides. After observing Thucydides' treatment of slaves, we depended on other contemporary sources to explain it in terms of ideology. Xenophon wrote essays of military, political, and household advice and theory in addition to his history of Greece. Xenophon's handling of slaves in this history, less strikingly dismissive than Thucydides', can be set in the context of his own explicit thoughts about slavery, warfare, and the right to power: a whole complex of ideas informs Xenophon's attitude towards slaves in the military.

In addition, Xenophon's thinking was more driven by the demands of practice and common morality than by a philosophical need for consistency or a search for eternal principles. For example, Xenophon would rather suggest or report a useful military tactic than remain consistent in his professions. But the qualities which make him a "shallow moralistic prattler" in terms of philosophy make it more likely that Xenophon's professions are rooted in his society and actual world view rather than in the demands of philosophical abstraction.[4] Accordingly, contradictions in Xenophon's thinking about the military often reflect strains within his society. Nevertheless, Xenophon is not utterly inconsistent. One can find coherent systems of thought in his works. These cover such areas as the hierarchy of arms, the prerogatives of soldiers, the importance of tactics or, on the other side, the fairness of battle. These three chapters will analyze these systems and especially the contradictions among them and between them and the realities of fourth-century warfare.

---

reminiscent of modern United State politicians laying claim to the "middle class," both the oligarchic and radical democratic groups tried to lay claim to the hoplites.

Xenophon is critical of the extreme oligarchy of the Thirty and presents its ouster as the salvation of Athens. Nevertheless, he presents many of his criticisms through the mouth of Theramenes, a somewhat more moderate oligarch. Xenophon is also careful to distinguish between the oligarchic yet well-intentioned followers of the Thirty and the bloodthirsty tyrants themselves (*HG.* 2.3.50, 2.4.22–23, 2.4.26).

[4] Chroust (1957) 8; Guthrie (1969) 335 sees "little sign of any capacity for profound philosophical thought."

Several tendencies in Xenophon's thought required the exclusion of slaves from warfare. His explicit theories stressed that rulers needed to maintain their predominance in the military sphere. Conversely, slaves had no place in the army. Furthermore, the basic dichotomies through which Xenophon saw the world linked slaves with the categories soft, feminine, and barbarian. These alignments did not recommend the use of slaves as soldiers. Finally, Xenophon, like masters in many slave societies, depicts slaves as cowardly, childish, and unreliable.

Xenophon's participation in and fascination with fourth century warfare often contravened his ideals. Xenophon's theories depended upon war being a fair test of a man's worth; fourth century warfare was becoming more and more a matter of stratagems and specialized skills. The connection between rule and military service grew tenuous as semi-civilized mercenaries and the Neodamodeis rose in prominence. Xenophon was not merely a witness, but a key player in these changes in fourth-century warfare.

Xenophon's position as an Athenian aristocrat and as an associate of the Spartans also complicated his commitment to a way of thinking derived from Athenian democratic practices. Xenophon was not wedded to the hoplite ideal of equal participation in the army. An aristocratic officer might be in the same relation to his soldiers as a master to his slaves. Accordingly, there might be a place in the military for slaves. The Spartan army was a heterogeneous organization with a variety of levels for soldiers coming from different strata in society: the ex-Helot Neodamodeis played a particularly important role during much of the period of Sparta's ascendancy.

My goal is to include all these different contexts for the reading of Xenophon. Thus I do not have to argue that Xenophon is really an Athenian, or truly a Spartan, or essentially a Socratic philosopher or, on the other hand, a mercenary general. Perhaps it is due to his lack of philosophical depth that Xenophon so often incorporated contrary tendencies in his thought. It is easier to trace influences in his work than to exclude them.

THE MILITARY BASIS OF RULE

Xenophon insists upon a moral justification for leadership. Leaders, whether of soldiers or of slaves, ought to be better than those they command. But Xenophon does not quite separate the idea of rule's moral justification from that of rule based on force. The very qualities of self-control, bravery, and endurance that Xenophon emphasizes as indicative of superiority are those he identifies as leading to success in war. So Xenophon's ideal leaders are also his ideal warriors. Furthermore, Xenophon, in several places, portrays battle as a test of the combatants' inner nature rather than depending upon specific skills, tactics, or even luck. If battle is a test of essential worth, the most successful warriors deserve to rule.

Xenophon's theory of leadership is well known.[5] To begin with, Xenophon is concerned with intelligent rule. This consists of close supervision of subordinates, appropriate rewards and punishments, deception for the sake of morale, and good planning.[6] But most important of all is Xenophon's contention that it is the superiority of leaders that justifies their rule and ensures the willing adherence of their followers. We will base much of our discussion on a particularly illustrative passage in the *Cyropaedia*. Xenophon's ideal ruler, Cyrus, addresses his troops on how they are to maintain their dominance despite being far fewer than those they rule. After assuring them that the gods are on their side because of the justness of their conquest, Cyrus goes on to what, he says, is next in importance:

Namely, we must claim the right to rule over our subjects only on the ground that we are their betters. Now the condition of heat and cold, food and drink, toil and rest, we must share even with our slaves. But though we share with them, we must above all try to show ourselves their betters in such matters; but the science and practice of war we need not share at all with those whom we wish to put in the position of workmen or tributaries to us, but we must maintain our superiority in these accomplishments, as we recognize in these the means to liberty and happiness that the gods have given to men. And just as we have taken their arms away from them, so surely must we never be without our own, for we know that the nearer to

---

[5] Many scholars have discussed Xenophon's general theory of leadership. Breitenbach (1950) is the classic work on the subject. Nickel (1979) 24, Lengauer (1979) 158, 167 and Dillery (1995) 32–33, 63, 74, 86, 94 emphasize Xenophon's militarism. In her investigation of Xenophon's beliefs, Gray (1989) perhaps underestimates his concern to narrate a true history. Tatum (1989) and Due (1989) are particularly useful for the *Cyropaedia*.

[6] Supervision: *Oec.* 20.16–17. Rewards and punishments: *An.* 1.9.15, *Cyr.* 8.1.39, *Oec.* 13.9–10. Deception: *HG.* 4.3.13, *Cyr.* 8.1.40. Planning: *An.* 3.1.37.

their arms men constantly are, the more completely at their command is their every wish.[7]

Cyrus does not want military service to be shared "with those whom we wish to put in the position of workmen or tributaries to us."[8] Slaves were a subset of "workmen." The contrast between the sharing of hardship "even with our slaves" and retention of arms would lose its point if slaves were not at least included among those "whom we wish to put in the position of workmen or tributaries to us." That the gods gave weapons as "the means to liberty and happiness" also suggests the contrast with slaves who ought not to have arms. Let us look closer at the reasons behind this exclusion of slaves from the army.

In our passage, the Persians must rule on the basis of their superiority: "we must claim the right to rule over our subjects only on the ground that we are their betters." This is a ubiquitous motif in Xenophon's writings from the *Hiero* and *Oeconomicus* to the *Hellenica* and *Anabasis*.[9] Leaders can display their superiority in two spheres. The first, less usual one, is that of knowledge. Xenophon's Socrates connects knowledge with rule on several occasions. For example, women rule in the area of spinning because of their superior knowledge.[10] The second sphere in which leaders should

---

[7] *Cyr.* 7.5.78–79: τοῦτο δ᾽ ἐστὶ τὸ βελτίονας ὄντας τῶν ἀρχομένων ἄρχειν ἀξιοῦν. θάλπους μὲν οὖν καὶ ψύχους καὶ σίτων καὶ ποτῶν καὶ πόνων καὶ ὕπνου ἀνάγκη καὶ τοῖς δούλοις μεταδιδόναι· μεταδιδόντας γε μέντοι πειρᾶσθαι δεῖ ἐν τούτοις πρῶτον βελτίονας αὐτῶν φαίνεσθαι. πολεμικῆς δ᾽ ἐπιστήμης καὶ μελέτης παντάπασιν οὐ μεταδοτέον τούτοις, οὕστινας ἐργάτας ἡμετέρους καὶ δασμοφόρους βουλόμεθα καταστήσασθαι, ἀλλ᾽ αὐτοὺς δεῖ τούτοις τοῖς ἀσκήμασι πλεονεκτεῖν, γιγνώσκοντας ὅτι ἐλευθερίας ταῦτα ὄργανα καὶ εὐδαιμονίας οἱ θεοὶ τοῖς ἀνθρώποις ἀπέδειξαν· καὶ ὥσπερ γε ἐκείνους τὰ ὅπλα ἀφῃρήμεθα, οὕτως ἡμᾶς αὐτοὺς δεῖ μήποτ᾽ ἐρήμους ὅπλων γίγνεσθαι, εὖ εἰδότας ὅτι τοῖς ἀεὶ ἐγγυτάτω τῶν ὅπλων οὖσι τούτοις καὶ οἰκειότατά ἐστιν ἃν βούλωνται.

[8] In another passage Cyrus' policy is again spelled out. Οὓς δ᾽ αὖ κατεσκεύαζεν εἰς τὸ δουλεύειν, τούτους οὔτε μελετᾶν τῶν ἐλευθερίων πόνων οὐδένα παρώρμα οὔθ᾽ ὅπλα ἐπέτρεπεν (*Cyr.* 8.1.43). There may be some blurring of the line between slaves and subjects in general in these passages, but even if ἐργάτας ἡμετέρους or Οὓς δ᾽ αὖ κατεσκεύαζεν εἰς τὸ δουλεύειν could be construed as excluding slaves, Xenophon's argument would apply *a fortiori* to slaves.

[9] Both the *Hiero* and *Oeconomicus* are concerned throughout and conclude with this point. See L. Strauss (1963) *passim* and L. Strauss (1970) 209. For the *Hellenica* see Breitenbach (1950) 47, 60ff., 82ff., 98 *et passim*. See also *An.* 3.1.37, *Cyr.* 8.1.37, 8.1.40. In the light of such passages I would reject Higgins' (1977) *passim* esp. 132 rosier picture of Xenophon as essentially an Athenian political philosopher. Nevertheless, the arguments of Henry (1967) 193–210 forbid a return to the simplistic view of a Laconophilic Xenophon.

[10] *Mem.* 3.9.10. See also *Mem.* 3.3.9 and *Eq. Mag.* 6.

demonstrate their superiority is in the endurance of physical hardship. In our passage Xenophon spells this out:

Now the condition of heat and cold, food and drink, toil and rest, we must share even with our slaves. But though we share with them, we must above all try to show ourselves their betters in such matters.

This same emphasis appears in other places in Xenophon's work. In his study of Xenophon's historical works, Breitenbach shows that the requirement that a good general be able to endure cold, heat, sun, and toil is a standard theme in Xenophon.[11] For example, Agesilaus, praised for his physical toughness, believes that "a ruler's superiority over ordinary men should be shown not by softness but by endurance."[12]

Xenophon not only theorizes about toughness justifying rule and inspiring followers. He makes a point of showing how he embodies his teachings himself. He goes to some length to show how, during the retreat of the Ten Thousand, he personally learned how the endurance of *ponos*, "hard work," can inspire one's men. He was riding his horse and urging the hoplites to hurry up a hill.[13] A certain Soteridas complained about Xenophon's riding and the weight of his own shield. Xenophon dismounted, seized the man's shield, but could not keep up with his heavy cavalry gear as well as Soteridas' shield. Soteridas was pelted by other soldiers and forced to take his shield back. At first the incident seems not to have any particular point: Xenophon's gesture was unsuccessful and he gets back on his horse. The observant reader, however, will recall Soteridas when, during his campaign with Seuthes, Xenophon gets off his horse when the Greek hoplites need to hurry. Seuthes questions him. Xenophon points out that it is not he personally, but the whole phalanx that is needed and that "the hoplites will run faster and more cheerfully if I also am on foot leading the way."[14] Naturally this leads to a successful outcome and the capture of booty and slaves.

Xenophon displays the toughness of a good general when he is first to get up and start chopping wood without his cloak on a snowy morning, a display of overcoming the cold.[15] Perhaps Xenophon's finest moment in the *Anabasis* is presented as a victory over sleep:

[11] Breitenbach (1950) 61. See also Luccioni (1948) 54–56 and Tatum (1989) 190.
[12] *Ages.* 5.2–3. Examples of his toughness are given in *Ages.* 5.3.
[13] *An.* 3.4.47–49.   [14] *An.* 7.3.45.   [15] Breitenbach (1950) 61 on *An.* 4.4.12.

when awakened by a dream he decides to call a meeting of the
captains in the middle of the night instead of lying at ease. Xenophon's superiority over sleep leads to his election as general and
helps to save the Ten Thousand.[16]

Xenophon closely links this superiority in endurance and self
control, which justifies rule, with ability in war.[17] Xenophon predicts
victory for the Ten Thousand since "we have bodies more capable
than theirs of bearing cold and heat and toil."[18] These are the same
virtues as the toughness in "heat and cold, food and drink, toil and
rest" which Cyrus believes justify rule. That the word *ponos*, the
endurance of which is often praised by Xenophon, can mean either
hardship or battle reinforces our point that the Greeks considered
physical toughness a key quality for a good soldier. Those who have
bodies better able to endure *ponos* will do better in the *ponos* of battle.
Sparta, where Xenophon sent his sons to be educated, was renowned both for the toughness of its citizens and for their military
prowess; Xenophon praises both.[19]

Since the virtues that justify rule are also those that make one
fight better, in a just society the class that rules will also be most
capable of fighting. We can see why Cyrus complains "and how
would it be otherwise than base in us to think that we have a right to
enjoy security protected by other men's spears, while we ourselves do
not take up the spear for our own defense."[20]

The inverse of the qualities of endurance that justify rule are the
weaknesses that brand the slave. Just as toughness makes for warriors
as well as rulers, the softness of slaves makes them unsuitable for
either role. The best evidence for the association of vices and slavery
come from passages in which Xenophon likens soft men to slaves.
The vices which render one slavish include the following: lechery,
pleasures – sometimes specified as pleasures of the body – gluttony,
sleep, love of drinking, drunkenness, laziness, lack of self-control,
softness of the spirit, and negligence.[21] These are the opposites of

---

[16] *An.* 3.1.13–14, 47.

[17] Due (1989) 226ff. links the "ἐγκράτεια/πόνος ideal" with military prowess as well as with
the moral right to rule. She does not make the further connection of military prowess and
the right to rule.

[18] *An.* 3.1.23.   [19] *Lac.* 2.3ff., 11.1ff., *et passim.*

[20] *Cyr.* 7.5.84. Lengauer (1979) 158, 167 diagnoses Xenophon's militarism.

[21] The vices are λαγνεία, ἡδοναί, (sometimes specified as τοῦ σώματος ἡδοναί), γαστήρ,
ὕπνος, φιλοποσία, οἰνοφλυγία, ἀργία, ἀκρασία, μαλακία ψυχῆς, ἀμέλεια. The following
passages explicitly invoke the metaphor of slavery: *Mem.* 1.5.5, 1.6.8, 4.5.3–5 ; *Oec.* 1.16–23.

the virtues of endurance, training and self mastery that distinguish the ruler.

A brief consideration of Xenophon's recommended activities will corroborate the connection between physical toughness, freedom, and warfare. The activities that Xenophon sees as toughening one up and thus improving one's character are portrayed as appropriate for the free and good for soldiers. Gymnastics was an activity for the free.[22] It was also linked to war. Xenophon gushes about his hero Agesilaus and his soldiers returning with garlands from the gymnasium.[23] Xenophon asserts that Spartan law required soldiers to practice gymnastics on campaign.[24]

Farming was another activity connected with freedom as well as with war. It trains the body to be able to do everything "that a free man should be able to do."[25] Farming provides food for a horse and riding practice for a cavalryman and it makes a foot soldier's body energetic.[26] Farming also teaches you how to manage men. This is useful for war: the same techniques used to get slaves to work on the farm are needed by a officer leading soldiers.[27] Hunting makes for the best soldiers.[28] It is certainly not an activity for slaves: Xenophon assumes that his reader will own a slave net-keeper to help him hunt.[29]

Gymnastics, farming, and hunting are ideal free activities in Xenophon's world. Each contributes to a person's soldierly qualities.[30] In contrast, the trades which are characterized as slavish are those that Xenophon believes ruin one's body and martial courage.[31]

Xenophon's hope that rulers be tougher than their subjects is a case of the typical Greek connection between the internal dynamics of a personality and external social relations. Xenophon tried to

---

In *Mem.* 2.6.1 a criterion for choosing a friend is that he rule his vices. In *Oec.* 10.10 Ischomachus tells his wife to not always sit around δουλικῶς. No vice is named, but Xenophon may have something like ἀργία in mind.

[22] Aeschin. 1.138.   [23] *HG* 3.4.18. See also Delorme (1960) 24; *Vect.* 4.51–52.

[24] *Lac.* 12.5.   [25] *Oec.* 5.1.   [26] *Oec.* 5.5, 11.17–18.   [27] *Oec.* 5.14–17.

[28] *Cyn.* 12.1–8, 13.11–12.

[29] *Cyn.* 2.3. Xenophon needs to specify that the net-keeper should be able to speak Greek.

[30] These activities were all free in the sense of being non-slave. However, hunting, gymnastics and the type and scale of farming envisioned in the *Oeconomicus* were more appropriate to an aristocrat than to the free in general. More *thetes* were tradesmen themselves than took a serious interest in hunting.

[31] *Oec.* 6.6–7; *Mem.* 4.2.22.

establish within himself and within individuals of his class the same hierarchy that he desired in society.[32] He was a strict general and a slave-owning male who found the correct basis for rule in military superiority. The hierarchy he tried to establish within himself was just as harsh. As the weak, cowardly, or untrained deserved death or enslavement, so the body needed to be subjugated with cold, heat, sun, and *ponos*. Excellence requires that the body serve the mind: "you must accustom your body to be the servant of your mind, and train it with toil and sweat."[33] In contrast, the vices that Xenophon characterizes as slavish often consist of a slavelike relationship to some pleasure. Since these pleasures are generally those of the body, this type of slavery is linked to an improper relationship of body and soul.[34]

This connection between control of society and of the body is often all but explicit in Xenophon.[35] In our passage Xenophon's Cyrus wants his men to master their bodies so that they will be able and justified in controlling their inferiors. In various passages, including those cited above, Xenophon is actively engaged in trying to change the way the elite use their bodies so that they may better use their slaves and inferiors: Xenophon's Socrates asks questions that show how disgraceful it was for slaves to be tougher than their masters.[36] Xenophon seems to commend the converse measure to preserve the social hierarchy: in the *Cyropaedia*, Cyrus not only barred slaves from free activities but took care of their physical

---

[32] Michel Foucault (1990) 63–83 reaches a similar conclusion about the sexuality of the Greek citizen male: those who were to rule others needed to rule themselves (83). A lack of self-restraint could lead to tyranny (81). My approach is more akin to Winkler (1990b), who links the self-restraint demanded of the citizen with the hoplite service by which he deserved his position in society. The ideal of self-restraint, like the ideal of the hoplite, could be used to distinguish the citizens in general from other inferior groups or to distinguish among the citizens. Halperin (1990) 95–99 shows how the Athenian sexual ideology suppressed differences among the citizens. In contrast Xenophon seems more interested in justifying the rule of an elite within the citizens.

[33] *Mem.* 2.1.28.

[34] The only exception I found was slavery to φιλοτιμῶν τινων μώρων καὶ δαπανηρῶν which, although some sort of luxury, is not a vice of the body (*Oec.* 1.22).

[35] The central and explicit metaphor of Plato's *Republic* is the equivalence of justice in the city and the soul (e.g. 441d). In Plato's conception, the appetite ought to be in the position of slave to the rational part of the soul (444b). The extent to which Plato and Xenophon reflect the influence of Socrates as well as the social and political import of Plato's analogy are beyond the scope of this thesis. For slavery in Plato see Schlaifer (1936); Morrow (1939); Vlastos (1941); Vogt (1975) 32–36; Patterson (1991) 172–180.

[36] *Mem.* 3.13.3, 3.13.6.

needs: slaves were allowed to take food with them on the hunt whereas the free men were not. The purpose of this was so that the slaves "always continue without complaint in their slavery."[37] Xenophon would like to burden slaves with the softness he attributes to them just as he urges elites to acquire the qualities that ought to justify their position.[38]

Douglas argues for an approach to the relationship between attitudes toward the body and social structures opposite to that of psychoanalysis: "Just as it is true that everything symbolizes the body, so it is equally true (and all the more so for that reason) that the body symbolizes everything else."[39] In our case, we may speculate that Xenophon wants to rule his body because such control symbolizes the desired, but insecure, rule over inferiors in society. In the fourth century Xenophon was attempting to defend a system in disrepair. When Xenophon insists again and again on how military virtues justify rule, one suspects that he "doth protest too much." As the connection of military service with rule was breaking down in Greek society, Xenophon turned away from the luxurious aspects of the aristocratic ethic and towards the Spartan (in both senses) ideals of a warrior elite.[40]

WAR AS TEST

For practical reasons Xenophon considers war to be of paramount importance. The course of wars can determine whether one is happy, rich, and a slave owner or a slave or dead.[41] Xenophon promotes physical training and unity on the grounds that, in the event of war, it will lead to glory and the opportunity to take away the possessions of the weaker.[42] It is hard to judge exactly when the

---

[37] *Cyr.* 8.1.43–44. Due (1989) 213 n. 21 convincingly argues for the acceptance of the end of paragraph 44. Regardless of its genuineness Cyrus' purpose was, in fact, ὅπως ἀναμφιλόγως ἀεὶ ἀνδράποδα διατελοῖεν. A similar story is told of Agesilaus: the king refused fancy foods from the Thasians and ordered that the food be distributed to the Helots with the army (Ath. 14.657c). Another Spartan custom provides a parallel. Although the Spartans censured public drunkenness, they sometimes forced the Helots to get drunk in order to humiliate them (Fisher [1989] 43).

[38] Cf. Winkler (1990b) 54.   [39] Douglas (1966) 122.

[40] See Kurke (1992) 98ff. on the negative fifth-century view of ἀβροσύνη. Cf. Halperin (1990) 99.

[41] *Mem.* 3.12.1–5.

[42] Taking from weaker: *An.* 5.6.32, *Eq. Mag.* 8.7–8; Glory: *Mem.* 3.12.4, *Eq. Mag.* 8.7–8 *et passim*.

appreciation of victory, or anticipated victory, no longer explains Xenophon's enthusiasm. Certainly, he praises effusively the military preparations of Agesilaus in Ephesus. Among other compliments Xenophon says that Agesilaus made "the entire city, where he was staying, a sight worth seeing."[43] Foot soldiers or cavalry riding in good order is "a noble sight to friends" and victorious soldiers have an aura that makes them seem taller and worth looking at.[44] Xenophon's *Hiero* complains bitterly and at length that a tyrant is deprived of the amazing delights and glory of victory in battle.[45]

Beside the practical advantages of victory, war was so important and the subject of such raptures because it was the arena in which the Greek male could display the most important virtues.[46] Xenophon, in particular, sometimes idealized war as testing the character rather than the skill, luck, or numbers of the antagonists. Cyrus in the *Cyropaedia* tells his men that it is a matter of common knowledge that "battles are decided more by men's souls than by the strength of their bodies." At another point Cyrus asks his officers to remind the troops that the day of battle will reveal what each soldier is worth.[47] Xenophon includes the superiority of the Greeks' souls as well as the toughness of their bodies among the reasons that they should expect to defeat the Persians.[48] In terms of Xenophon's theory of leadership, war provides an ideal test of the military virtues that ought to determine one's success in the world.

In the *Cyropaedia*, Cyrus insists that souls and thus military prowess could be improved not by a pre-battle speech, but only if laws were in existence that ensured a life of honor and freedom for the brave and one of humiliation for the cowards.[49] Xenophon approves of Lycurgus for establishing heavier penalties for the "base and cowardly" than for the crimes of enslavement, fraud and robbery.[50] Most interesting for our argument, Cyrus the Younger especially honored and rewarded those who had done well in war: "Thus, the

---

[43] *HG* 3.4.17. Pritchett's claim (*GSW* 5.312) that the Greeks were "too close to spear thrusts" to romanticize war is untenable for Xenophon in the light of passages such as *HG* 3.4.16–19, *Hier.* 2.14–17 and *Oec.* 8.6.

[44] *Oec.* 8.6 cf. Sappho 16 1–4. *HG* 4.5.6, *Cyr.* 4.4.3.　　[45] *Hier.* 2.14–17.

[46] Havelock (1972) 51ff.; cf. N. Wood (1964); Garlan (1975) 60.　　[47] *Cyr.* 3.3.19, 3.3.37.

[48] *An.* 3.1.23. Xenophon recommends physical training for war because there are advantages to a fit body, but also because training confirms the mastery of soul over body that distinguishes the free and thus the warrior.

[49] *Cyr.* 3.3.51–52.

[50] *Lac.* 10.6 (M): τῶν κακῶν καὶ ἀνάνδρων; cf. *Lac.* 9.3–6.

brave were seen to be most prosperous, while cowards were deemed fit to be their slaves."[51] Since, in Xenophon's conception, war provides just such a discrimination between rulers and slaves, the internal regulations of these kings are admirable: they prepare their people for the external test of war whose criteria are exactly the same.

In theory, if not always in practice, slavery was the result of loss in war; slaves have already failed the test of their manly qualities. Even in cock-fighting terminology, we can see this attitude: the defeated bird was called the "slave. "[52] In the *Anabasis* Xenophon describes many slaving operations in which he took part with no indication of any qualms.[53] Xenophon's most notorious expression of this attitude comes in the *Cyropaedia* when Cyrus declares that "it is a law established for all time among all men that when a city is taken in war, the persons and the property of the inhabitants thereof belong to the captors."[54] This view of the origin of slavery dominates Greek thought even though it is unclear whether most slaves were actually captured in war.[55]

The hypothetical origin of slavery in war has important consequences in terms of slaves' suitability as soldiers. The loss of freedom in war could be ascribed to cowardice. Xenophon set a high value on fighting to the death. For example Xenophon considered that the only members of the Spartan brigade destroyed by Iphicrates' peltasts who were really saved were those who were wounded early and evacuated rather than those who escaped by running away and swimming.[56] Even Plato, less militaristic than Xenophon, considers surrendering to the enemy a servile and base action.[57] Thus slaves were typed as cowards who had lost their liberty through surrender in war.

---

[51] *An.* 1.9.15. The textual problem here does not effect the argument.

[52] Ar. *Au* 70 with scholia in White (1914) 28 and Sommerstein (1987) 205.

[53] *An.* 6.3.3, 6.6.38, 7.3.35, 7.6.26, 7.8.16, 7.8.19. Outside of war, to enslave a citizen was a heinous crime. It could even be a capital offense (Westermann [1955] 6; see also *Smp.* 4.36, *Lac.* 10.6, *Mem.* 2.2.2, 4.2.14–16; cf. *An.* 7.2.6, 7.3.3).

[54] *Cyr.* 7.5.73. Ducrey notes that the belief that capture in war justified slavery was a general feature of the Greek world view (Ducrey [1968] 284).

[55] Garlan (1987); *contra* Pritchett *GSW* 1.82; cf. M. Jameson (1977) 140 n.93 for further arguments and a survey of the bibliography. Wiedemann makes the interesting suggestion that the ancient lack of interest in the slave trade was due to uneasy consciences about slaves who were acquired outside of warfare (Wiedemann [1987] 23). This is the complement to our argument that warfare was the theoretically correct source of slaves.

[56] *HG* 4.5.14.   [57] Pl. *Ap.* 38e–39a.

To go back to the *Cyropaedia*, two arguments for monopolizing "the science and practice of war" are implied in our passage.

First there is the practical advantage that "the nearer to their arms men constantly are, the more completely at their command is their every wish." Arms are not only good for use against another state but also to maintain superiority over one's workmen and slaves.[58] Xenophon asserts that Lycurgus set down exemplary laws for the Spartans and even set out regulations for the safety of their army camps. These included, as we have seen, the mandate that the Spartans "keep slaves from the weapons."[59]

This concern for the practical, internal advantages of possession of weapons was more general than just the barring of slaves. Aristotle believes that the type of arms favored by a city may determine which side will win in case of *stasis*. He envisions each side in a civil war using the same weapons as they use in the city's army.[60] Anderson generalizes that the willingness of the rich to serve in the army and pay for their equipment was due to their fear that "if poorer citizens were hired to fight, they might overthrow the state."[61] Xenophon gives an example of this: the Arcadians stopped paying their elite brigade, the Epariti. The poor could no longer serve and the rich then joined the troop so that "instead of being under the control of the Epariti, they should control this army themselves."[62] This practical argument for not letting any inferior groups fight for a city is predicated upon the idea that the respective classes are likely to become enemies. This was a common Greek conception of the relation between slave and free.[63] This whole line of reasoning was antithetical to the use of slaves as soldiers.

The second implication of the *Cyropaedia* passage is that the advantageous policy, the restriction of military participation, is also the moral one. In our passage this is hinted at in that Xenophon describes weapons as gifts from the gods. In other passages, Xenophon implies that serving the state in the military gives one a moral

---

[58] When Cyrus takes the arms from Babylonians and orders that all the occupants of a house in which arms were found should be killed, the Babylonians are on the threshold between being foreign enemies and domestic subjects (*Cyr.* 7.5.33). In our passage the phrase ἐργάτας ἡμετέρους καὶ δασμοφόρους is on this same border.

[59] *Lac.* 12.4 (M).   [60] Arist. *Pol.* 1321a5–28.   [61] Anderson (1970) 5.

[62] *HG* 7.4.34 (A). Underhill (1900) 298 points out that there is disagreement between Xenophon and Diodorus about this whole incident. Xenophon's perception of the motives of the rich is the point here.

[63] Dover (1993) 48.

right to participate in politics. Xenophon contrasts the evil politicians who hold back their money and are utterly unfit for war with hunters who offer their bodies and wealth in good condition for war.[64] Perhaps a specific example of these bad politicians is Peisander whose right to leadership in Athens is mocked because of his cowardice.[65] A man has the right to contribute nothing while his female relatives are making clothes, because he is the watchdog and protector of the house.[66] In the *Anabasis*, Xenophon urged the army leaders to show their superiority to the common men in a crisis on the grounds that they had received more pay and respect in times of peace.[67] Military service justifies one's position in society. Therefore one's position in society might demand – or exclude in the case of slaves – participation in war.

Although each of these two arguments for linking military service with political participation may seem natural on its own, there is an inharmonious redundancy about their combination. In the moral argument those who fight for a country gain legitimacy in that they confer a benefit upon other classes. The practical view sees the soldiers as ready to kill these same other classes. Some scholars view early classical wars as rituals conducted for internal purposes rather than directed at real external threats.[68] Xenophon's emphasis on military participation justifying rule may be a reactionary appeal to this arrangement. Such an interpretation makes sense of the discordance between the practical and moral advantages of restricting military service. The practical advantages of possessing arms which may be used against threats within is in harmony with the internal ideological power of being the city's protectors.

That Xenophon's theory of rule excluded slaves from war does not mean that this was its sole motivation. Fourth-century aristocrats were not afraid that they would lose their power to slave warriors. Xenophon's theory of rule was primarily aimed at establishing a military basis for elite or hoplite rule. It was perhaps an unintended outcome of the theory's consistency that it so clearly excluded slaves.

---

[64] *Cyn.* 13.6.11–12. In both this and the previous passage the other main way one could help the state is by contributing money. Thus both the rich and the fighting class have the right to participate in politics.

[65] *Smp.* 2.14; cf. the remarks of Phocion reported in Plut. *Phocion* 9, 10.

[66] *Mem.* 2.7.12–14.   [67] *An.* 3.1.37.

[68] Garlan (1975) 31; Connor (1988) 17, 27. Thus it was not until later that the idea of military service as an obligation to be avoided appeared (Garlan [1975] 89).

As we shall see in the next chapter, some aristocratic views of the army did not mandate the exclusion of slaves.

BINARIES

The aim of Xenophon's militarism may have been the reassertion of elite rule, but slave participation in war was also anathema to ways of thinking that had a far wider currency in Greek society. Slaves were often linked with other groups such as women, barbarians and children against which all free citizens could define themselves.[69] A quick rehearsal of the way that the free/slave distinction interacted with those of Greek/non-Greek, man/woman and adult/child will show how deeply rooted in the Greek mentality was the exclusion of the slaves from warfare. The warrior, in contrast to the slave, needed to be on the top side of each of these pairs.[70]

Several of Xenophon's ideas about slavery appear in his representation of barbarians.[71] Xenophon fashions the incident in which he unmasks the Lydian Apollonides, a mercenary captain, to show how the true, cowardly nature of this barbarian ex-slave is revealed during this crucial test: Xenophon ends his speech against Apollonides by saying that he is a disgrace to the whole of Greece, since he, though Greek, is such a coward. Lo and behold, a soldier immediately points out that he is not really a Greek but a Lydian, probably an ex-slave.[72]

Xenophon also corroborates our conclusions from Herodotus about the slavishness of the Persians. The Persians seemed natural slaves due to military inefficiency. In the *Anabasis* not only Xenophon, but Cyrus the Younger himself insists on the superiority of the Greeks troops.[73] So naturally the Ten Thousand were particularly

[69] Wiedemann (1987) 25; Golden (1985) 101; cf. Halperin (1990) 103.

[70] Cf. Garlan (1975) 90. Aristotle, who did not believe in a single science of rule as Xenophon did, differentiated between the type of rule exercised over slaves, children, and wives (Treggiari [1991] 187). Whether they were conceived of as identical or different, these binaries were basic to the Greek world view. See Cartledge (1993a).

[71] I do not accept the claim of Hirsch (1985) that Xenophon was essentially an admirer of the Persians, but his book is a sufficient antidote to the opposite view. Xenophon's attitude was complex and probably inconsistent.

[72] *An.* 3.1.30–31. This passage shows Xenophon's association of barbarians, slaves, and cowardice regardless of Apollonides' actual status and origin, which can admittedly never be known for sure.

[73] *An.* 1.7.3, 3.1.23.

upset when they fled from barbarians despite being present in large numbers: this was the first time this had happened.[74]

The Persians were already metaphorically slaves of their king.[75] They also were inferior to the Greeks in terms of physical toughness. As we have seen, the Greeks' bodies were superior in terms of enduring "cold, heat, and hardship."[76] The Greeks have exactly the qualities vis à vis the Persians that justify rule. That barbarians seemed ideal slaves to Xenophon was due to their perceived military weakness, their position as subjects of an absolute monarch, and their physical softness.

That slaves can be referred to as *bought barbarians* makes the link between non-Greek status and slave status clear.[77] In several places Xenophon notes expressions of the view that Greeks should not be enslaved but only barbarians.[78] Rarely practice, this was an ideal in line with Xenophon's thinking. In the *Ways and Means* Xenophon suggests that metics should not be required to serve as hoplites in Athens: Athenians should not be "in the same company as Lydians, Phrygians, Syrians, and barbarians of all sorts."[79] This is consonant with his belief that the barbarians are slavish as well as with the fact that barbarian metics at Athens might well be ex-slaves.[80]

Xenophon likens an object or person to a woman, as to a slave, in order to emphasize military weakness. Cavalry horses and men that are carelessly trained will be just like women struggling with men.[81] Fighting with white and soft barbarians will be just like fighting with women.[82] Spartan soldiers wore red capes. Red was easy to keep clean, did not show blood and had magical and royal connotations; it was also not worn by women in Xenophon's time.[83] So Xenophon

---

[74] *An. 5.4.18.*   [75] *An.* 2.5.38, 3.4.25; *HG* 4.1.36, 6.1.12. See Chapter 3.

[76] *An. 3.1.23.*   [77] Garlan (1987) 38.

[78] *HG* 1.6.14–15, 2.2.20. Jackson (1970) 48 sees this as a tendency in Greek thinking about the treatment of prisoners of war. See also Hopkins (1967) 175.

[79] *Vect.* 2.3.

[80] Hansen believes that Xenophon's statement that many metics are barbarians from Lydia, Phrygia, Syria, and other places refers to freedmen metics since these are the places from which Athens recruited her slaves (Hansen [1991] 119).

[81] *Eq. Mag.* 8.2; cf. Pl. *Leg.* 1, 639b; Hall (1993) 110–112. See also Winkler (1990b) 47 fn., 50–51. Just as the sharp distinction between slave and citizen soldier was an ideal not adhered to in practice, so too the complete seclusion of women was an unattainable ideal – if even desired – for most Greeks of average wealth and typical house size. See Just (1989) 105–125; D. Cohen (1989); M. Jameson (1990) 99–100, 104, n.15, 16.

[82] *HG* 3.4.19; *Ages.* 1.28. See Isoc. *Philip* 90 for a similar expression.

[83] Ollier (1934) 54.

adds the claim that Lycurgus chose red, because it was least like women's clothing.[84] Warriors should be unlike women in the same way that they should be unlike slaves.

Slaves were linked with boys in a variety of ways. The most obvious is the linguistic equivalence common in many languages: *pais* like the Latin "puer" or the English "boy," can indicate either a boy or a slave. Significantly for our purposes slaves and boys are also alike in their absence from politics and war. A slave is permanently barred from war: he never ceases being a "boy." Free-born boys became adults with their entrance into the political and military life of a city.

The exclusion of slaves from warfare was connected to how Xenophon, and Greek free males in general, interpreted their world in terms of age, sex, and nationality. Slave participation in war was anathema since slaves were seen as inverses of the free, male, adult Greek, the ideal soldier.[85]

XENOPHON, SAMBO, AND NAT

This picture of slaves seems to have deep roots in a specifically Greek world view. But, although the details and particular slant of this image are specifically Greek, a similar slave stereotype appears in every major slave society. The image of slaves is related not only to Greek culture, but also derives from the nature of slavery. On the one hand, the practice of slavery encouraged certain patterns of behavior on the part of the slave. On the other hand, masters had a

---

[84] *Lac.* 11.3.

[85] B. Williams (1993) 114 has recently claimed that while most Greeks felt they needed to have slaves (the argument from above), they did not think it was necessary for some particular person to be a slave (the argument from below). To be enslaved in war was merely bad luck, so slaves were not felt to be inferior (105). Aristotle was exceptional in insisting on the argument from below as well as the argument from above (115). Although Williams' argument is conceptually very interesting, it does not present an accurate picture of Greek culture for two reasons. First, there is abundant evidence – some of which is recounted above – that slaves were considered inferior barbarians who did, in fact, deserve to be slaves. The idea that slaves are just like the free, only unlucky, is as rare as Aristotle's fully developed idea of natural slavery. Second, capture in war is not just bad luck. The strain in Greek culture that regards war as the ultimate test of a man's worth is strong from Homer, through tragedy – note that only women can be unlucky captives – to Herodotus, the Funeral Oration, and Xenophon. See Pomeroy (1994) 67 for an argument similar to that of Williams. See now Garnsey (1996).

need to despise the people they oppressed. The more that slaves seemed not to be content with, or not to deserve their condition, the more intensely masters clung to the stereotype of a childish, cowardly Sambo. Since Greeks viewed the slave as the inverse of the citizen warrior, it was particularly unsettling for slaves to display the qualities of a warrior.

Patterson, who has studied a wide spectrum of different systems of slavery, concludes that the Sambo stereotype is "an ideological imperative of all systems of slavery, from the most primitive to the most advanced."[86] Sambo is childish, lazy, usually cowardly, thievish, and sneaky. We have seen that Xenophon depicts slaves as cowardly and lazy. In Attic oratory too, slaves are "naturally cowardly."[87] Several other aspects of the Sambo stereotype can be found in slaves in Athenian comedy: slaves typically try to steal food;[88] slaves are lazy.[89] One main function of slaves in Aristophanes is to evoke laughter by being hurt, threatened, or frightened.[90] The few good and trustworthy slaves in Aristophanes are outnumbered by "the vast crowd of their lazy, insolent, randy, cowardly, thieving and dishonest companions."[91] Their lack of martial qualities is manifest when even a woman, Lysistrata, can ask her baffled enemies in indignation "Did you think you were attacking slaves?"[92]

This stereotype derives in part from the realities of slavery. Bradley, for example, links many of the aspects of the Sambo stereotype to slaves' efforts to "soften the rigors of everyday life in bondage and to frustrate the will of the owner." Slaves often have no interest in the productivity of their masters' enterprises.[93] Why should they not be lazy? They are being kept in captivity by force. Why should they not steal?[94] For slaves to be scared of masters who could beat them at will should occasion no surprise. A show of deference would smooth a slave's lot; open resistance could bring on

---

[86] Patterson (1982) 96. Genovese (1971) 49 and Davis (1966) 59–60 concur. Cartledge (1985) uses the term "Sambos" for Greek slaves, but his concern is with actual rebelliousness rather than stereotypes of slave personality.

[87] Ober (1989) 271.

[88] Ehrenberg (1951) 131. A priestess was accused by Demosthenes and executed. Among her crimes was that she taught slaves dishonest practices, τοὺς δούλους ἐξαπατᾶν διδασκούσης (Plut. *Dem.* 14).

[89] Dover (1993) 49.   [90] Dover (1993) 43.   [91] Vogt (1975) 8.

[92] Ar. *Lys.* 463–465.   [93] Genovese (1972) 309.

[94] Lichtenstein (1989). Bradley (1990) 148.

severe punishment. Although the behavior of relatively powerless slaves provided some basis for the Sambo stereotype, this image also reflected slave-owners' ideological needs. Masters seized upon "the worst or most easily patronized traits" and expanded them into a theory of slave personality.[95]

This stereotype, however, was not entirely the product of masters' power, but also of their insecurity. Even when Sambo appears to be the primary slave stereotype, there is ample documentation of intense paranoia among slave holders. In the American South perpetual insecurity could coexist with professed belief in the loyalty and childishness of slaves.[96] The less famous inverse of Sambo was Nat, a cruel, vengeful brute who might rise up in rebellion at any time: false alarms of slave revolts could send masters fleeing into the woods.[97]

Xenophon too displays the strange amalgam of paranoia and contempt that characterizes so many slave-owning classes throughout history. That running away seems to be the most typical slave action in Xenophon, regardless of the actual reasons for flight, shows slaves as undignified cowards.[98] Xenophon explicitly links slavery with cowardice in the *Cyropaedia*. Cyrus argues that a quick follow-up to his previous victory will so upset the enemy that they will be like slaves caught trying to run away: "some of them will beg for mercy, others will try to escape, others still will not even have presence of mind to do either."[99]

Although Xenophon found nothing more ridiculous than a runaway slave, he also assumed that masters were in danger of their lives from their slaves: "Citizens guard one another without pay from their slaves and from evildoers, so that none of the citizens may die a violent death."[100] A tyrant could earn popularity if he used his bodyguard to prevent slaves from murdering citizens, seemingly a common occurrence.[101] Thus *mutatis mutandis*, Blassingame's question about the slave South seems equally appropriate to Greece: "If whites really believed that a majority of slaves were Sambos, how

---

[95] Patterson (1971) 217.   [96] Genovese (1972) 615.

[97] Blassingame (1979) 230; Stampp (1956) 137.

[98] See pp. 106–107.   [99] *Cyr.* 4.2.21.   [100] *Hier.* 4.3 (A).

[101] *Hier.* 10.4 (M).See also Plato, *Resp.* 578d–579b for a similar sentiment. Dover finds a whole strand of Greek thought that portrays slaves as naturally hostile to their owners and to the citizen body in general (Dover [1974] 114; [1993] 48).

could they also believe that these pathetically loyal and docile blacks would rise up and cut their throats?"[102]

This dramatically dichotomous view of slaves may derive in part from contrasts in the behaviors of different slaves at different times. But such exaggerated and contrasting stereotypes of slaves are, on the whole, more likely to reflect the psychological needs of masters than social realities. Blassingame has argued that, with Nat in the wings, "the creation of Sambo was almost mandatory for the Southerner's emotional security," and that "the more fear Whites had of Nat, the more firmly they tried to believe in Sambo in order to escape paranoia."[103] We may hypothesize that Xenophon too defended the picture of slaves as cowardly, lazy, soft, and womanish more intensely in proportion to its fragility. The citizen-slave binary in Thucydides was threatened by oligarchic and radical thinking that could tear the citizenry apart. So too the image of the unwarlike slave was more precarious than our original treatment of Xenophon would suggest.

Neither distrust of slaves nor the belief that they are lazy cowards would tend to recommend their use in war. The actual threat of armed slaves could be minimized: slaves could be used in the navy where entrusting them with oars made them no more of a threat; the families and villages of Helots were hostages for their good behavior; slaves would fight hard for the promise of freedom or other rewards. Nevertheless, however safe their use was in practice, slave soldiers threatened the notion of slaves as the inverse of the citizen warrior. Not merely were the categories and justice of the Greeks' social arrangements in the balance. At stake in the maintenance of the slave stereotype was any confidence that threat of punishment could deter your own slave from killing you.

By way of conclusion let us consider a particularly effusive passage. Xenophon describes how, in preparation for a campaign in Asia Minor, Agesilaus was encouraging all sorts of military preparations. Xenophon describes these exercises with loving care and evident approval. Xenophon also relates that, for the sake of his troops' morale, Agesilaus gave an order that the "barbarians" who had been taken prisoner should be put up for sale naked. Since Persians differed from the Greeks in considering nakedness in itself shameful, such exposure was a considerable extra humiliation added

---

[102] Blassingame (1979) 230.   [103] Blassingame (1979) 230, 233.

to the horrors of being captured and enslaved.[104] But Xenophon enthusiastically describes the effect of this spectacle:

The soldiers, seeing that these men were white-skinned because they never were without their clothing, and soft and unused to toil because they always rode in carriages, came to the conclusion that the war would be in no way different from having to fight with women.[105]

These slaves had surrendered rather than showing the valor that characterizes the free. Their slavery is completely appropriate since they are physically soft and white. These new slaves were barbarians and were likened to women. In contrast, the soldiers who watched this spectacle had been training, practicing virtue, and the arts of war and could thus anticipate easy victories. In Xenophon's world this is a picture of things just as they ought to be. Lest we take this "pretty picture" for the reality of warfare in Xenophon's time, recall that Agesilaus' army included only thirty Spartiates but three thousand Neodamodeis recruited from the people the Spartans called their slaves.[106]

---

[104] H. 1.10.3. One assumes that, in general, slaves for sale had to undergo physical inspection. Perhaps, slaves had only to disrobe at the request of specific buyers or buyers just looked under their clothes.

[105] *HG* 3.4.19; cf. Plut. *Ages.* 9. The raiding parties could hardly have captured only Persians of such high status that they rode around in carriages. Xenophon is stereotyping all Persians as soft in order to make his point.

[106] Cartledge (1987) 210 and Parke (1933) 43 using data in *HG*.

CHAPTER 9

Xenophon: warfare and revolution

For what is more useful in war than men?
Xenophon suggesting that mine slaves could be used as rowers and
soldiers in case of war.[1]

＊

Xenophon's social and political position determined his opposition
to the use of slaves in war; his war experience led him to very
different conclusions. Xenophon was to suggest in the *Ways and
Means* that slaves should be recruited for the Athenian navy and
army in the event of invasion. When this suggestion is juxtaposed
with our passages from the *Cyropaedia* and *Hellenica*, it seems an
aberration to be dismissed or discounted. Most scholars have done
just that. An account, however, of Xenophon's experiences with
slaves in war reveals the precedents of this otherwise dissonant
passage. Not only Xenophon's knowledge of slave and Helot soldiers
but his whole experience and participation in fourth-century warfare
were at odds with the ideal of military exclusivity, whose roots we
have been probing.

XENOPHON THE SOLDIER

Our exploration of Xenophon's actions and experience will pick up
his activities after the Peloponnesian War, which we have treated in
connection with Thucydides, its main historian. Xenophon's *Anabasis*
describes numerous emergency situations faced by the Ten Thousand during their retreat out of Asia in 401–400. We might expect
customary Greek practices to break down among this group of
mercenaries stranded in the middle of the Persian empire. In fact,
Xenophon does describe tactical innovations including the creation
of a slinger and a cavalry corps: Rhodians agreed to serve as slingers

---

[1] *Vect.* 4.42: τί γὰρ δὴ εἰς πόλεμον κτῆμα χρησιμώτερον ἀνθρώπων;

in exchange for some unspecified exemptions; some other soldiers were promoted to form a cavalry corps.[2] More significant than these shifts in status was the freeing of slaves. At a difficult point in their journey the Greeks got rid of much of their baggage train. They also freed all of their recently captured slaves. The army hoped to speed up their march, reduce the number of men required for guard duty, and to cut down on the number of people to feed. The scrutiny of the generals enforced this measure, which involved a considerable loss for the soldiers.[3]

Most startling of all, Xenophon himself, so convinced that his class should monopolize the conduct of war, seems to have persuaded the Ten Thousand to free and arm some slaves. Xenophon suggested getting rid of superfluous baggage. In contrast to the aim of his earlier recommendation that the Greeks burn their wagons and tents, Xenophon's goal here was not the mobility of the army. Rather he wanted as many men as possible under arms and the fewest number carrying baggage.[4] To accomplish this slaves who had previously been carrying baggage must have become fighters. This surprising inference, however, requires some expansion and justification.

In support of his proposal Xenophon began with the conventional claim that the Ten Thousand should not worry about their belongings, since the possessions of the loser belong to the winner anyway. Xenophon did not finish – as he does elsewhere – by pointing out that the Greeks would recoup their loss of baggage with booty from the Persians if they won.[5] Instead he concluded "if we win, we should consider the enemy our baggage carriers."[6] Xenophon's point may have been merely that the Persians were carrying baggage for the Greeks, if only the Greeks defeated them and took it. His formulation, however, may also imply that the Greeks would be able to enslave the defeated Persians. Then the Greeks could replace the baggage carriers who had been promoted to soldiers. Accordingly

---

[2] *An.* 3.3.15–20.

[3] *An.* 4.1.12–14. The soldiers obeyed except in cases where a slave was the object of a soldier's affection and was smuggled through.

[4] *An.* 3.2.28.

[5] Xenophon ends his final speech of that same evening with the simple topos (*An.* 3.2.39): those motivated by desire for wealth should fight hard τῶν γὰρ νικώντων ἐστὶ καὶ τὰ ἑαυτῶν σῴζειν καὶ τὰ τῶν ἡττωμένων λαμβάνειν.

[6] *An.* 3.2.28 (M): ἢν δὲ κρατῶμεν, καὶ τοὺς πολεμίους δεῖ σκευοφόρους ὑμετέρους νομίζειν.

the Greeks "should consider the Persians their baggage carriers," that is, their future slaves.

The Greeks referred to the men who carried an army's supplies as "followers," "baggage carriers," or "attendants."[7] Such men could serve the army as a whole or – especially in the case of attendants – they might be single servants accompanying individual hoplites. When Xenophon emphasizes the leanness of the Ten Thousand after his reforms, he reveals that even hoplite attendants had been promoted. For the benefit of readers used to armies in which each hoplite had an servant, Xenophon points out that as soldiers were wounded many people were taken out of action. The wounded men themselves were lost, but so were the soldiers carrying the wounded and those who took the arms of these carriers.[8] If there had been an attendant for each hoplite, it would not have been necessary to take additional soldiers out of the ranks. For example, during the Spartan debacle at Lechaeum, the attendants by themselves evacuated wounded men.[9] This reduction of the Ten Thousand's logistical support was not unprecedented: in their retreat from Syracuse Athenian hoplites did without their attendants. They no longer trusted these slaves since so many were deserting.[10] The Ten Thousand probably promoted their baggage carriers in a more systematic and moderate way; the Ten Thousand's policy resulted from public deliberation rather than desperate, individual expedience. The standard scholarly view is that most, if not all, "attendants" were slaves.[11] This seems also to be true of "followers" and "baggage carriers."[12] Indeed, slaves are attested accompanying the Ten Thousand before the reduction of baggage: after treacherously killing the Greek generals the Persians rode around the plain killing all other Greeks they met, whether slave or free.[13]

---

[7] The Greek words are ἀκόλουθοι, σκευοφόροι, and ὑπηρέται. The Greeks did not always clearly distinguish between these groups (*UAK* 1.58–62).

[8] *An.* 3.4.32. The wounded man is presumably carried in his armor – on his shield? – or else Xenophon has forgotten to mention the men needed to carry the wounded man's armor.

[9] *HG* 4.5.14.

[10] Th. 7.75.5. This passage is one of the clearest indications that the attendants in Athenian armies were slaves.

[11] Sargent (1927) 204–206; *GSW* 1.49–51; *UAK* 1.59, 1.64. M. Jameson (1992) 141 n.41 gives further bibliography and explains the one apparent exception to this rule in Isae. 5.11.

[12] *UAK* 1.59.

[13] *An.* 2.5.32. Since these slaves were Greek, they must have been intrinsic to the army rather than recently captured.

Naturally, the Greeks did not arm all of the slaves in their army. The Ten Thousand needed slaves for essential support services. There is ample evidence of a baggage train and slaves among the army later in the march.[14] In fact, Xenophon relates an incident near the end of the Anabasis that indicates the presence of free men in the baggage train even after the arming of some "baggage carriers."[15] Does this imply that the army only promoted free baggage carriers and had not even used all of these? The details of Xenophon's narrative rather indicate that it was exceptional and shameful for a free man to serve in the baggage train. First, some background. Various men had accused Xenophon of hitting them during the campaign.[16] Xenophon had in effect treated them as slaves, subject to corporal punishment, instead of as free men.[17] In his cross-examination of his main accuser, Xenophon went down the military hierarchy and discovered that the man was neither a hoplite nor a peltast but rather "had been assigned by his tentmates to drive a mule although he was a free man."[18] Xenophon was implying that this man was doing a servile job. Accordingly, he probably deserved to be treated as a slave, to be hit. Xenophon's accuser turned out to be the man whom Xenophon had caught trying to bury an ill, but still living, comrade.[19] So the characterization according to his job stuck: Xenophon was acquitted. This vignette does show that some free people served as "baggage carriers," but also reveals the common expectation that a slave would be doing the job.[20]

---

[14] Xenophon anticipates the continued existence of the baggage train and large crowd of camp followers in the very speech in which he proposes reducing the baggage (*An.* 3.2.36). For the slaves and the baggage train see e.g., *An.* 3.3.6, 4.2.20–21, 4.3.15, 4.3.19, 4.3.30, 4.5.4, 6.1.12, 6.5.3, 7.3.20. The army's supply of slaves probably varied as they captured, sold, and released slaves e.g., *An.* 4.1.13, 6.6.38.

[15] *An.* 5.8.5.   [16] *An.* 5.8.12, 5.8.1–2.   [17] Morrow (1939) 190 n.2, 195.

[18] *An.* 5.8.5 (M): ἡμίονον ἐλαύνειν ταχθεὶς ὑπὸ τῶν συσκήνων ἐλεύθερος ὤν. The participle ὤν must be considered concessive rather than causal, since being free cannot possibly explain his position in the baggage train rather than among the hoplites and peltasts. It is interesting that the man was assigned by his tent mates to his job. The decision of who should fight and who drive the mule was made on a low level.

[19] This presumably took place during the difficulties described in *An.* 4.5. With respect to other soldiers whom he had struck, Xenophon portrayed himself as a father or doctor: either might cause pain for a person's own good (*An.* 5.8.19).

[20] Cf. *An.* 3.1.30. Wood (1988) 48ff. believes that in aristocratic discourse many jobs could be typed as slavish even though free people did them. In one sense, this is the case here. The mule driver was free and yet Xenophon was trying to characterize his job as slavish. However, the conclusion that σκευοφόροι were not usually slaves does not follow. That slaves predominated among σκευοφόροι could be the reason that the insult works.

In contrast, Xenophon mentions an ex-slave peltast.[21] This unnamed man, originally from Macronia in northern Asia Minor, had been a slave in Athens. The Ten Thousand were on the verge of attacking the Macronians across a stream in difficult terrain, when the peltast realized that this was his homeland. He spoke with the Macronians and arranged a truce for the Ten Thousand to travel peacefully through their land. In the turbulence of the Peloponnesian War period any number of paths may have led this Macronian to peltast service with the Ten Thousand. He might have started out as an attendant for one of the Athenians on the expedition. If he had run away to Decelea, he might have become a slave attendant of a Peloponnesian member of Cyrus' army. In either case he could have joined the peltasts as a result of Xenophon's reorganization. Perhaps, he had been freed after Arginusae or had run away from Athens and ended up rootless, homeless, and happy to join a mercenary army. Simple individual manumission at Athens is also possible but is less probable than these mass events: Arginusae and Decelea may have resulted in the freeing or emigration of tens of thousands of Athenian slaves.

Earlier in the retreat we hear of an Apollonides, another ex-slave member of the Ten Thousand. His history, if known, would also testify to the turmoil of the age. He was an officer among the Ten Thousand, who spoke in the Boeotian dialect. He disagreed with Xenophon but was mocked and driven away when another officer revealed that he had his ears pierced in Lydian fashion.[22] Although an object of Xenophon's contempt for his cowardly advice, one can only wonder how a Lydian slave in Boeotia managed to become, not a mere mercenary, but an officer. It cannot have been through cowardice.

After his escape from the middle of the Persian empire, Xenophon and some remnants of the Ten Thousand joined a Spartan-led army in Asia Minor. In the winter of 396/395 its leader, Agesilaus, raised cavalry for his impending campaigns against the Persians. He allowed

---

Furthermore Xenophon's apparent inclusion of peltasts among the reputable ranks of the army is distinctly unaristocratic.

[21] *An.* 4.8.4.

[22] *An.* 3.1.26, 3.1.31. Roy (1967) 300 draws the conclusion that he was an ex-slave. How else would a Lydian learn the Boeotian dialect and pose as a Greek? Unfortunately, the false accusation of barbarian or slave ancestry was common enough in Attic oratory to preclude complete confidence in this story. See Ober (1989) 279–280.

each rich man, who would normally have had to serve in person, to provide a horse and a good rider. This policy was antithetical to any link between status in society and in the military. Still Xenophon wryly notes that the cavalry was raised with the energy one would expect "when men were eagerly looking for substitutes to die in their stead."[23] He also notes Agesilaus' just pride when this cavalry later beat the Thessalians, famous for their horsemen.[24]

Who ended up serving in lieu of the wealthy? Some poorer free men might have been happy for a chance at glory and booty. But where would they have learned to ride? Only the rich could afford to keep horses and their reluctance was the very reason for Agesilaus' policy. Perhaps, the reluctant well-to-do recruited the same outland people who were later to serve in the prestigious mercenary cavalries of the mid-fourth century. But were such men available individually? Agesilaus, furthermore, might have preferred Greek speakers in his army.

Although some riders may have come from these sources, slaves may have been best suited for the job. Slaves' willingness to serve would not be an issue. They would have had no choice and might even have preferred military discipline to personal service. Men who owned horses often had slave grooms. These grooms were not only familiar with the daily care of horses, but often knew how to ride.[25] If a noble had to give up his horse for Agesilaus' cavalry, why not his slave groom also? The riders had to be *dokimoi*, "approved," but this only implies that their riding skills were to be tested. Agesilaus wanted to get the best cavalry from whatever source and had made no provision nor had any motive to exclude slaves.[26]

THE NEODAMODEIS

From the end of the Peloponnesian War to beyond the period of Messene's foundation, Sparta continued its policy of using Helots in

---

[23] *HG* 3.4.15; cf. *Ages.* 1.24.   [24] *HG* 4.3.9; cf. *Ages.* 2.5.

[25] In the *Oeconomicus* Ischomachus hands his horse over to his groom to take from the farm into town (*Oec.* 11.18). Anderson (1961) 95, 137 cites two other pieces of evidence for slaves knowing how to ride: The trick of making a body of cavalry look stronger by giving the grooms real or fake lances and interspersing them with the cavalry depends upon the grooms being mounted, though perhaps only on pack animals (*Eq. Mag.* 5.6); Vegetius 1.56.11–13 urges masters not to let their grooms recklessly race their horses since the grooms have little concern about possible damage to their masters' horses.

[26] Cf. *Cyr.* 2.2.26.

its military. Xenophon describes how Gorgopas rounded up men to counter an Athenian attack in 388: he ordered the free men from the ships' crews to join him.[27] Perhaps Gorgopas wanted free men because they alone were trusted to fight well on land and not to desert. In any case the presence of slaves or Helots among the Peloponnesian crews is patent. A speech in the *Hellenica* assumes Helot rowers in 369.[28]

The navy was not the only place where Sparta employed Helots. During Epaminondas' invasion of the Peloponnese in the winter of 370/369, Agesilaus recruited several thousand Helots to defend Sparta by promising them their freedom.[29] This was a unique emergency measure, but the use of Neodamodeis seems to have been a regular Spartan practice. As I noted in the introduction, in the 390s the Spartans often had more Neodamodeis in the field than there were Spartan citizens in total.[30] The Neodamodeis were used when an expedition needed to be organized quickly, when it involved great distances, such as Agesilaus' in Asia Minor, or a long time away from Sparta, such as garrison duty.[31] In all these roles Neodamodeis not only replaced citizen hoplites but may have been superior to them. Unlike most Peloponnesian soldiers, the Neodamodeis seem to have been professionals, who did not need to go home to take care of their farms.[32]

Sparta's use of Neodamodeis spanned five decades, from before

---

[27] *HG* 5.1.11.   [28] *HG* 7.1.12.

[29] *HG* 6.5.28–29. Diod. 15.65 has only one thousand helots enrolled and only after Epaminondas retreated to Arcadia. Welwei and Underhill prefer Xenophon's six thousand (*UAK* 1.155; Underhill (1900) 262). Garlan attempts to reconcile the figures by supposing that Diodorus' figure is the number of Helots freed whereas Xenophon's is the number enlisted. The difference is then to be ascribed to desertions (Garlan [1972] 43). Neither figure is consistent with *HG* 7.2.2 where Xenophon claims that all of the Helots revolted, but this statement is an exaggeration serving to show the loyalty of the Phleiasians to best advantage (*UAK* 1.155).

[30] Hamilton (1991) 78; Talbert (1989) 26 estimates that in the 390s there were perhaps 3000 Neodamodeis in the field at a time.

[31] Urgency: *HG* 5.2.23–24 – no Spartiates at all accompanied this expedition which was also distant and lengthy. Garrisons: *HG* 1.3.15, 6.5.24. Asia Minor: *HG* 3.1.4, 3.4.2–3. Ducat (1990) 163.

[32] The Spartiates were also professional soldiers, but they tended to stay close to home because of fears of a Helot revolution. The *perioeci* who fought as hoplites were probably farmers and thus could not be sent on long expeditions without provoking discontent. The Neodamodeis may have eventually been settled on the land (Th. 5.34.1), but were able to serve for many years away from home before being settled anywhere.

421 to at least 370.[33] Although this long-lived policy provides an incontrovertible argument for their utility, several passages raise doubts about the loyalty of these freed Helots. Most significant, Xenophon has Cinadon include the Neodamodeis among the discontented upon whose support he counted.[34] Xenophon also attributes special precautions to the Spartans' fear of potential rebels on campaign.[35]

Three other passages are ambiguous. Agesilaus hid the results of Spartan defeat at Cnidus in 394 to keep the support of his men, because "if they saw anything unpleasant, they were under no compulsion to share in it."[36] Agesilaus' insecurity, however, was more appropriate to the mercenaries recruited from the remains of the Ten Thousand and the volunteers from Asia Minor; the Neodamodeis were perforce to share the fortunes of their Spartan patrons.

In the *Agesilaus* Xenophon praises the quality of this army: the greatness of Agesilaus at Coronea in 394 did not consist in defeating a superior army but in making his own army so good.[37] This is a clever reversal of a typical encomiastic technique, but Xenophon may be responding to those who held Agesilaus' motley army in low esteem.

In 374 Polydamas requested Spartan help against Jason of Thessaly. Xenophon has Polydamas declare that an army consisting of Neodamodeis with a private citizen at its head will not be sufficient.[38] This complaint – further evidence for continued regular use of Neodamodeis – may be a slur about the quality of the Neodamodeis either reported or shared in by Xenophon. But this is not a necessary inference. Polydamas wanted a full Spartan and allied army. Such a force would outnumber even the largest contingents of Neodamodeis. Polydamas also wanted a Spartan king as its leader to commit Sparta more fully to his cause.

Sparta played a precarious game with all of the men that bolstered her army whether they were allies with their own ambitions, Neodamodeis, *perioeci* or the numerous, obscure grades of partially disenfranchised Spartans. Nevertheless, non-Spartiates formed a

---

[33] Th. 5.34.1; *HG* 6.5.24.   [34] *HG* 3.3.6.
[35] *Lac.* 12.4; *UAK* 1.110.   [36] *HG* 4.3.13.
[37] *Ages.* 2.7–8. This army contained the remains of the 3000 Helots who had served with Agesilaus.
[38] *HG* 6.1.14.

crucial element of Spartan strength. Even in the early fifth century, when Sparta may have been able to field five thousand hoplites at the battle of Plataea, her preeminence depended upon an equal number of *perioeci* hoplites, a greater number of light-armed Helots and a vastly larger army of subordinate allies. It was a matter for pride rather than condemnation that so few Spartans ruled such a great empire.[39]

Several modern scholars consider the Spartan use of Helots a dangerous practice indicative of Spartan weakness, later revealed by Sparta's rapid decline after Leuctra. Cartledge, for example, characterizes the use of Helots as a desperate expedient, which threatened the equivalence of citizen and soldier upon which Sparta was based.[40] Sparta's military hierarchy, however, made it possible to incorporate men from different levels of society without disruption to the rule of the Spartiates: even the inferior status of the Neodamodeis, no threat to Spartiate supremacy, was desirable enough to provide Sparta with a large reserve of full-time soldiers. Despite Xenophon's hints of distrust, no reports have come down of mass desertion or rebellion by Neodamodeis during the long period of Spartan preeminence.[41] Finally we should note that the Neodamodeis were an important element of Spartan might, not in her decline, but during a period of at least fifty years including the heyday of her empire.

Lest we overemphasize the precarious basis of Spartan power, let us recall that the hegemony of Thebes' citizen army lasted all of ten years. Twentieth-century experience seems to indicate the superiority of citizen armies motivated by having some share in society. At other times poverty or the desire for personal freedom were just as cogent spurs. Weaknesses were indeed inherent in the Spartiates' power due to their small – and perhaps diminishing – numbers and to the hatred with which they were regarded among the different subservient grades of society. But we need not exaggerate the picture of fragility and inevitable decline. Rather than seeing Sparta's decline as a fall from the ideal of citizen soldiers, which at no time characterized Sparta, we should attribute it to military defeat and a

---

[39] *Lac.* 1.

[40] Cartledge (1987) 40. See also Finley (1982b) 40.

[41] *UAK* 1.157. As might be expected some of the Helots recruited in 369, as well as some *perioeci*, deserted (Plut. *Ages.* 32). The desertion of Helots seems rather mild at a time when Messenia had just been liberated and full Spartiates were plotting revolution.

precarious system of alliances.[42] During its primacy Sparta had
recruited outsiders into its armies and hired mercenaries; it was a
symptom of her decadence that, after Leuctra, Spartans were hired
as mercenaries by other states.

Xenophon was not merely a distant observer of the Spartan use of
Helots. He was a high officer for five years in a Spartan army, which
contained up to three thousand Neodamodeis. For the last two of
these years he served under the Spartan king Agesilaus. Xenophon's
treatment of this army is highly laudatory. There is no hint that
Agesilaus had to deal with soldiers of inferior quality.[43] In his
enthusiasm Xenophon may even have distorted Agesilaus' mediocre
and inconclusive accomplishments in Asia Minor.[44]

Later Sparta gave Xenophon an estate in Scillus. Scillus probably
belonged to territory that Elis claimed as its own, but whose
autonomy Sparta guaranteed.[45] The Scilluntians would have been
happy to oblige the Spartans, their liberators. The settlement of
Sparta's friends and allies at Scillus would commit the Spartans
more fully to the maintenance of the Scilluntians' independence. In
a similar action during the Peloponnesian War, Sparta had settled
Neodamodeis and the Brasidian Helots at near-by Lepreum, which
had also been asserting its autonomy from Elis with Spartan help.[46]
Could the Spartans have settled Agesilaus' Neodamodeis, who had
served so well in Asia Minor and at Coronea, near to Xenophon at
Scillus or, as before, at Lepreum? If so, Xenophon's personal contact
with the Neodamodeis could have continued beyond the five years
that they fought together.[47] Xenophon was personally implicated in
Sparta's use of Helots in war through his service in Asia Minor, his

[42] Hamilton (1991) 256; Cawkwell (1983). The lack of evidence from actual Spartans – as
opposed to their Athenian admirers and apologists – makes it hard to determine their
military ideology. It is clear that the Spartans did insist that all citizens should be soldiers.
Perhaps, like other Greek cities, Sparta also held to the converse ideal: all soldiers should be
citizens. In this case, the contrast between Spartan practice and ideal was so early and stark
that it can have little power as a historical explanation for Sparta's decline.

[43] Xenophon and the remains of the Ten Thousand were as liable to that accusation as
anybody to judge from Isocrates' negative portrayal of them (Isoc. *Paneg.* 4.146).

[44] Cawkwell (1966) 17.

[45] Krentz (1989) 2 on *HG* 3.2.21–31; cf. *HG* 6.5.2, 6.5.12.

[46] Th. 5.31.1–5, 5.49ff., 5.62.1. Thucydides gives Sparta's motive in settling the Brasidians at
Lepreum as enmity with Elis (Th. 5.34.1). See Malkin (1994) 83–89.

[47] This may be the explanation for Diogenes Laertius' report that, after Scillus was retaken by
the Eleans, Xenophon sent his sons and wife to Lepreum (Diog. Laert. 2.53). Admittedly it
may just have been the nearest friendly town.

friendship with Agesilaus, and perhaps the very location of his estate. Nevertheless, he routinely refers to Helots as *douloi* and condemns the use of *douloi* in wars.

SLAVE SOLDIERS IN THE *WAYS AND MEANS*

Practices such as recruiting slaves or Helots for the army were contrary to Greek ideology; they occurred nevertheless. When the sources talk about such unsavory – to ancient slave-owning eyes – methods, the information has already slipped through the screen of an ancient ideology which would rather not see it. We should not make the mistake of adding a second screen and discounting attested practices on the grounds that they were not consonant with ancient ideology. This dissonance between practice and ideology needs to be explored, not eliminated by disregard of known practices.

For example, Xenophon bluntly recommends in the *Ways and Means* that slaves be armed and serve in the army and navy in the event of an invasion of Attica:

For what is more serviceable for war than men? We should have enough of them to supply crews to man many ships of the state; and many men available for service in the ranks as infantry could press the enemy hard, if they were treated with consideration.[48]

Xenophon was here responding to fears of slave desertion as the result of an invasion since, after Decelea, this was an obvious objection to his plan of buying large quantities of slaves for the silver mines.[49]

Garlan makes several points in an attempt to soften the impact of Xenophon's suggestion.[50] He argues that the use of public slaves would have been less radical than commandeering private slaves, but his only parallel is from 85 BC. Nevertheless, Garlan's observation that Xenophon envisaged the use of slaves only for defensive wars is valid.

Garlan also points out that Xenophon first discusses the enrollment of slaves in the navy, this suggestion being unqualified and unjustified. Then Xenophon proposes the more subversive army recruitment with the qualifying clause "if they were treated with consideration." Garlan explains that the navy was of lower status

---

[48] *Vect. 4.42* (A).   [49] *Vect. 4.41. Pace* Gauthier (1976) 177.
[50] Garlan (1972) 49. Gauthier (1976) 176 endorses Garlan's views.

and consequently slave use was less outrageous. But Xenophon does not speak of hoplites but rather of foot soldiers.[51] Light-armed infantry was as definitely lower class as the navy.[52] In neither case need there have been the large status gap involved in arming slaves as hoplites. I believe that the use of public mine slaves in the navy was an extension of usual Athenian practice and would have caused little surprise. The use of slaves as combatants in any branch of the army was rare at Athens so Xenophon adds the condition of good treatment of the slaves.[53]

Despite his own attempts at weakening its import, Garlan still considers Xenophon's suggestion to be evidence of great intellectual audacity. He claims that Xenophon is the only ancient author to discuss the use of slaves in war "in cold blood."[54] But Xenophon was not so inept as to counter a potential objection to his mining plan by blithely suggesting a shocking and unprecedented expedient. To suggest the recruitment of slaves did not require imagination, only memory. During the Peloponnesian war, the Athenian fleet upon which the city's hopes – and perhaps even Xenophon's own life or freedom – depended was partially manned by slaves. The complete mobilization of slaves played a part in Xenophon's praise of the Arginusae generals. Xenophon may have personally suggested military reforms during the *Anabasis* that involved the arming of slave attendants. After this adventure Xenophon joined the army of his hero, Agesilaus, which contained three thousand Neodamodeis. Twenty-five years later, Agesilaus' desperate defense of Sparta depended upon thousands of Helots, who were promised their freedom in return for fighting.

So no intellectual audacity is needed to explain Xenophon's recommendation in 355 of arming mine slaves in the event of an invasion. Xenophon was advocating a series of practical reforms. However much he might insist in the *Cyropaedia* that slaves had to be barred from arms, Xenophon realized the practical advantages of arming slaves in certain circumstances.

A contrast remains between the reticence of Greek historiography

---

[51] Gauthier (1976) 176.

[52] Arist. *Pol.* 1321a14–15: "the light-armed and the naval forces are entirely of the common people."

[53] Gauthier (1976) 177 points out that whereas θεραπεύειν is often pejorative in Xenophon, this is not always the case.

[54] Garlan (1972) 49.

– including to a lesser extent Xenophon's own histories – and the bluntness of the *Ways and Means*. Part of the explanation may lie in generic considerations. As we have seen most conspicuously in Thucydides, history was the genre of citizen activity and ideology. In contrast, pamphlets of advice, especially military advice, seem not to shirk – and sometimes even delight in – the immoral and ideologically dubious as long as it is advantageous. An occasional disregard of propriety may have served to assure the reader that the author was sufficiently hard-headed and unsentimental. Such moral lapses also represented the author as serving the reader's interest exclusively. Aeneas Tacticus provides striking examples of the anti-ideological delight of such pamphlets.[55] Such sources have already provided us with several cases of slave involvement omitted by the historians. In fact, it is another book of practical advice for soldiers that provides a later, but close, parallel to Xenophon's statements about arming slaves. This is the late third-century BC work of Philon of Byzantium which advises a besieger to proclaim freedom for deserting slaves. Among other things such an announcement will prevent the arming of the slaves who will no longer be trustworthy.[56] Was this another startling and unusual announcement or were both the announcement and the arming of slaves well-known tactics? I hope my investigations will induce the reader to tend towards the latter possibility. In fact, if anything in Xenophon is startling, it is the survival of an ideology so out of touch with military reality. The *Cyropaedia* should surprise us, not the *Ways and Means*.[57]

THE FOUNDATION OF MESSENE

The archaic hoplite battle restricted war to a limited time, space and class in order to reaffirm the social structure; the incitement of slave revolts threatened a permanent state of hostility extending into the household and involved the lowest rank of a society in its overthrow. Herodotus skips the Messenian revolt of 490. Thucydides avoids dwelling upon this tactic in the Pylos campaign and skips it entirely in the case of Syracuse. Xenophon too avoids extended discussion of

---

[55] E.g. Aeneas Tacticus 17.1, 18.4–19.1.

[56] Philon of Byzantium 5.4.14–15.

[57] Cf. Aristotle's insistence that δεῖ δὲ τὴν πολιτείαν εἶναι μὲν ἐκ τῶν τὰ ὅπλα ἐχόντων μόνον at a time when mercenaries were described merely as στρατιῶται and it was the citizen soldiers who required a distinguishing epithet (Arist. *Pol.* 1297b1–2; Parke [1933], 21).

the Athenian loss of Pylos. More startling, he fails even to mention one of the decisive actions of the fourth century, the establishment of Messene by Epaminondas.

To turn first to Pylos – Coryphasium to the Spartans – Peter Krentz calls Xenophon's description of its recapture a "remarkably brief statement of Sparta's recovery of the site of Demosthenes' famous victory in 425."[58] Diodorus relates that in 409 the Spartans attacked the Messenian garrison of Pylos. After an Athenian relief mission failed, the Messenians surrendered under a safe conduct which allowed them to leave the country.[59] In contrast Xenophon's account consists of a single sentence in the Greek: "At this time the Lacedaemonians granted terms to the Helots who had revolted and fled from Malea to Coryphasium, allowing them to evacuate Coryphasium under a safe conduct."[60]

The brevity of Xenophon's account of the capture is notable. More interesting is the mention of rebellious Helots coming from Malea and Xenophon's implication that such Helots made up the entire garrison of Pylos. We know from Thucydides that Pylos was a base for raids and a haven for deserting or rebellious Helots. Xenophon clearly knows in addition of a specific revolt in Malea, whence some sizable part of the Pylos garrison.[61] The date and all circumstances of this event are unknown, but Xenophon blandly refers to

---

[58] Krentz (1989) 117.

[59] Diod. 13.64.5–7. Anytus, the future accuser of Socrates, headed this expedition and was put on trial for his performance. Perhaps Xenophon is reticent for some reason connected with Anytus or his trial.

[60] *HG* 1.2.18 (A): The Messenians who, a generation earlier, capitulated at Ithome had also been given a safe conduct (Th. 1.103.1). In the light of our discussions of Thucydides' usage, it should come as no surprise that Xenophon uses the expression "Helots" where Diodorus uses the honorable "Messenians."

[61] There are two possibilities for the location of Malea. The well-known peninsula of Malea was an area subject to Athenian raids and even a coastal fort from 414 to 412 (Th. 6.105.2, 7.26.2, 8.4). Perhaps, when the Athenians abandoned their fort, they relocated to Pylos any rebellious Helots who had joined them. Xenophon's wording, however, suggests a direct defection of the Helots from Malea to Pylos: τῷ δ' αὐτῷ χρόνῳ καὶ Λακεδαιμόνιοι τοὺς εἰς τὸ Κορυφάσιον τῶν Εἰλώτων ἀφεστῶτας ἐκ Μαλέας ὑποσπόνδους ἀφῆκαν. A "long march" from the peninsula of Malea would not be impossible but would involve crossing the whole of Laconia as well as Messenia. Bölte prefers the Malea near the border of Arcadia, Laconia, and Messenia (*RE*, s.v. "Malea" (4): vol. XIV.1 col. 868). This Malea – sometimes called Malaia – was part of the territory of Aegys, conquered by Sparta in the early eighth century and retained until 368 (Cartledge [1979] 99–100, 300; Frazer [1965] 305 on Paus. 8.27.4). Thus the area of Malea probably contained Helots and was closer to Pylos than the peninsula of Malea.

the garrison of Pylos, probably more than five hundred men, as if they all came from Malea.[62]

In this case Xenophon is merely tantalizing and brief. He is infamous for outright omissions. The formation of the Athenian naval alliance, most of the life of Pelopidas, Epaminondas at Leuctra, and the founding of Megalopolis do not find their way into the *Hellenica*. Many gaps can be at least vaguely correlated with his disapproval: "it can with some confidence be asserted that to say nothing was his principal means of censure."[63] It is tempting to suppose that Xenophon is in this case so reticent out of a distaste for the tactic of inciting slave revolts, manifest in the fortification of Pylos. Additionally, the Helots at Pylos, although defeated, were allowed to leave under a safe conduct. The escape of rebellious Helots might have been a particularly touchy subject among Xenophon's Spartan friends in the Peloponnese.[64]

This explanation must remain speculative. Xenophon omits entirely the equally important Megarian recapture of Nisaea and seems to include one year too few in his account of the Ionian War.[65] Xenophon seems to leave out important events or historical factors for reasons such as lack of information, carelessness, or indifference.[66] Often the reasons for Xenophon's omissions are obscure. Nevertheless, our next case, the founding of Messene, is one of the most glaring of Xenophon's omissions. He did not just forget to mention it.

The establishment of the city of Messene by Thebes in 370/369 was a more robust version of the Athenian fortification of Pylos. The

---

[62] Demosthenes was able to defend Pylos in 425 against a large-scale attack with somewhere between five hundred and a thousand men (Th. 4.5.2, 4.8.3, 4.9.1). The Spartans took Pylos after a siege rather than by storm so the garrison is likely to have been at least on the same order of magnitude as Demosthenes'; it could have been much larger. The last reference to the composition of the garrison of Pylos was in 419/418 when the Athenians reestablished Messenians as a garrison (Th. 5.56.3). During the Peace of Nicias, Messenians, Helots, and other deserters had been removed from Pylos and settled at Cranii in deference to the Spartans (Th. 5.35.7).

[63] Cawkwell (1966) 35–36, 43.

[64] Note that when the Spartans let the Helots go from Ithome they cited an oracle as a justification for their leniency in order to make the exceptional nature of their "generosity" clear.

[65] Underhill (1900) 12. See Krentz (1989) 11ff. on the Ionian War.

[66] His battle descriptions are regularly full of unmotivated gaps and often betray his lack of interest in obtaining information from more than one source: Ehrhardt (1970); Littman (1968).

dominance of the Theban army allowed them to raise the whole of Messenia in revolt and found a city to solidify their achievement. More than any other blow, the founding of Messene ensured Sparta's plummet from dominance to mediocrity.

Xenophon devotes what amounts to fourteen pages in the Oxford Classical Text to events from the return of the Spartan army after Leuctra to the withdrawal of the Theban army from the Peloponnese. He makes no mention of the building of Messene.[67] Affection for Sparta, hatred of Thebes, or Xenophon's typical lack of thoroughness all help to explain this lacuna. The habitual neglect of Helot revolt by Greek historians suggests another possible factor: a sense of unease about Sparta's problematic "slaves."

In addition to Messene's absence in the narrative – by itself suggestive of disapproval – we can detect another oblique expression of Xenophon's distaste. At the very point in the winter of 370 where Xenophon ought to have reported the founding of Messene by Thebes, he relates a debate at Athens on the issue of aiding Sparta.[68] Xenophon ascribes one particularly strange argument to the Spartan envoys. They contrast Athenian support for the Spartans during the Ithome revolt with their current inactivity. But Spartan suspicion of the Athenians under Cimon on the prior occasion led to the First Peloponnesian War. In fact, the Athenians subsequently helped the Helots who surrendered at Ithome and later even tried to start another revolt from their base at Pylos.

Requests for help, like prayers to the gods, often contained references to services received as precedents for the aid requested. Perhaps, the Spartans did in fact refer to Ithome despite the unhappy result of Cimon's mission and Athens' subsequent policies. Xenophon also mentions Athens' succor of Sparta to throw Thebes' unspeakable policies into the harshest possible light. The citizens of Greek states should defend each other against slave uprisings. They should not let their enmity reach the point of fostering such rebellions.

---

[67] *HG* 6.5.1–6.5.52. Fewer than 4 of these pages cover the debate at Athens; the rest are narrative. Xenophon later omits the foundation of Megalopolis in the summer of 369 as a capital for the Arcadians. Both cities may have been established with the same goal: the freedom of Messenia. Megalopolis is close to the best approach to the Messenian plain from Laconia (Ste. Croix [1972] 151; Cartledge [1987] 386).

[68] *HG* 6.5.33. Delebecque (1957) 459 n.31 locates the omission of the foundation of Messene between *HG* 6.5.32 and 6.5.33.

Xenophon's judgment on the Messenians is similar to that of Thucydides'. On the one hand, just as Thucydides speaks of the Spartans' slaves, *oiketai*, Xenophon refers to Helots as *douloi*: when describing the initial revolt of Messenia, Xenophon praises Agesilaus for defending Sparta "when the *douloi* . . . were in revolt."[69]

On the other hand, Thucydides' references to the free Messenians from Naupactus are unobjectionable. So too Xenophon, once Messene was securely free, sometimes describes it in the same terms as he would any other Greek city. He uses the expression, "the Thebans and all who had revolted from the Lacedaemonians," to describe the whole alliance against Sparta.[70] Thus he includes the "rebellious slaves" of Messene with former Peloponnesian League members, recognized Greek cities, which had defected from Sparta. On another occasion, Xenophon gives no special emphasis to an incident when the Messenians acquire some Spartan prisoners.[71]

Granted, Xenophon did not especially like Messene. He links the Theban foundation of Messene with Persian interference: Agesilaus wanted to fight Persia because of the King's demand that Messene remain independent.[72] Thus Xenophon appeals to pan-Hellenic sentiment against the Messenians and especially against the Thebans, always vulnerable to accusations of Medism.[73] No love was lost between Xenophon and the Messenians, but he did not insist that it was a city of slaves.

Like Thucydides, Xenophon tries to keep his categories straight: there are Helot slaves and then there are Messenians. He avoids the transition between the two, the establishment of Messene, entirely. Furthermore, from Xenophon's narrative it would be hard to guess that the status of the Messenians, both before and after Messene, was contested. He conceals these controversies, so subversive of a strict division between slave and free.

In other quarters this dichotomy was blurred and the debate was not so muted. It is hard to imagine that the conversion of Sparta's

---

[69] Th. 8.40.2; *Ages.* 2.24; cf. *Lac.* 12.4.   [70] *HG* 7.1.22.

[71] *HG* 7.4.27. In contrast, Isocrates declares that the equality of the Messenians to their former masters would be unendurable to the Spartans (*Archidamus* 96).

[72] *Ages.* 2.29; cf. *HG* 7.1.36.

[73] Xenophon smears Thebes in this way in other places (Cawkwell [1966] 37). Isocrates also contrasts Thebes' abandonment of the Greek subjects of Persia with its solicitude for the Messenians (*Archidamus* 27.)

douloi into a *polis* did not unsettle Greek thinking about slaves. In fact, Plato begins his discussion of slavery in the *Laws* with the observation that the question of the Helots was the most puzzling and controversial in Greece.[74] On the other side of the issue, a passage of Alcidamas dealing with Messenia contains one of the statements most critical of slavery to survive from antiquity: "god made all men free; nature has made nobody a slave."[75] A story recorded in Pausanias also suggests fellow feeling between the Messenians and Greek slaves at least. When the Messenians conquered Zankle they refused to enslave the inhabitants as Anaxilas ordered. Their commanders, Gorgos and Mantiklos, "beseeched Anaxilas not to force them to do to Greeks the same wicked things their own brothers had done to them."[76]

Slavery in Greece, of course, did not disappear. Debate over the status of slaves, however upsetting, remained marginal. Even the foundation of Messene could be defended without reference to the question of slavery in general. Most advocates of Messene did not emphasize the rights of slaves, but rather the unjust oppression of Greeks with a noble and long genealogy. Dinarchus includes the restoration of Messene after four hundred years among the noble deeds of the Thebans.[77] The reference to four hundred years shows that he was thinking in terms of Messenian mythology rather than the sponsorship of a slave revolt. The fourth-century elaboration – some scholars say creation – of early Messenian history displays this same approach.

Thebes, for its part, was the staunch ally of the nascent city. In his account of 368 – Xenophon's first admission of Messene's new status – Xenophon states that Thebes refused to agree that Messene be subject to Sparta.[78] The independence of Messene was Thebes' first priority at Pelopidas' conference with the King in 367.[79] Regardless of Thebes' motives, probably complex, for its actions, the foundation of Messenia was publicly defended on moral grounds. On the base of Epaminondas' statue in Thebes, an inscription summed up his greatest accomplishments:

---

[74] Pl. *Leg.* 6,776c.
[75] Alcidamas, scholia to Arist. *Rh.* 1373b18 (M): "ἐλευθέρους ἀφῆκε πάντας θεός, οὐδένα δοῦλον ἡ φύσις πεποίηκεν".
[76] Paus. 4.23.9.   [77] Dinarchus *Against Demosthenes* 73.
[78] *HG* 7.1.27; cf. *HG* 7.4.9.   [79] *HG* 7.1.36; cf. Plut. *Pel.* 30–31.

By my strategies was Sparta deprived of her glory,
And holy Messene received back her children at last.
By the arms of Thebes Megalopolis was circled with walls,
And all Greece was independent and free.[80]

Thebes was proud of its role as liberator, but the statement that "Messene received back her children at last" refers to Messenian mythology rather than to a controversy about slavery. The Thebans were not about to free their own slaves, or to insist on calling their allies ex-slaves.

Isocrates wrote the *Archidamus* in 366 as a rhetorical exercise, but also as a defense of Sparta's claim to Messenia. While Xenophon is silent or elliptic, Isocrates is insistent and emphatic. He tries to distinguish between the true Messenians and the Helots, whom he refers to elsewhere as slaves:

Even if they had restored people who were truly Messenians, they would have acted unjustly. Nevertheless, they would have harmed us in a more reputable way. But, in fact, it is our Helots that they have settled on our borders.[81]

Although Isocrates goes to some lengths to deny the rights of the Messenians, he would rather deny altogether the contemporary existence of Messenians: the ex-Helots in possession of Messenia are just slaves.

Why does Xenophon tread so warily, rather than consistently condemning the Messenians as slaves in revolt as Isocrates does? Some of his reticence may be due to the ideal of historical fairness in contrast to Isocrates' rhetoric. As the years passed, Messene remained a city with an army. Even the alliance of Sparta and Athens could do nothing to alter that. To insist that the Messenians were slaves, a commonplace before 370, was more likely to subvert the dichotomy between slaves and free than to rouse indignation against Messene. Even the Spartans, the intransigent adversaries of Messene, might have tired of hearing that their opponents were mere slaves.

The debate was perhaps too bitter for necessarily futile discussion. Xenophon's philosophy was better suited to defending the status quo than to questioning the judgment of war. Or perhaps we should give Xenophon credit for sticking to his guns. Just as rule is justified by

---

[80] Paus. 9.15.6.
[81] Isoc. *Archidamus* 28.1. In *Archidamus* 88, Isocrates refers to the Messenians as οἰκέται.

success in battle, so might insurrection be justified by its accomplishment. Xenophon reacted to the upheavals in which the Spartans lost their slaves and he his home with resignation and disillusionment rather than the hare-brained schemes of Isocrates.[82] So Xenophon censures by omission, covers up, condemns obliquely, classes the Messenians first with slaves and then with free cities.

[82] During the second half of 371 Xenophon lost his estate at Scillus in the aftermath of Leuctra (Delebecque [1957] 304).

CHAPTER 10

Xenophon: the decline of hoplite ideology

I don't know what effect these men will have on the enemy, but, by God, they frighten me.

The Duke of Wellington[1]

So far, we have portrayed slave participation in war as a practice which contravened Greek ideology in a particularly awkward way. This is, indeed, the big picture. Nevertheless, there are some aspects of classical thought and practice that a simple opposition between ideology and practice cannot explain. Some ideologies of military service did not insist upon the exclusion of slaves. Even the exclusionary ways of thinking that we have traced so far could not continue unaffected by the intrusion of the base-born onto the battlefield. The prestige of warfare suffered as it became a matter of technical skills and no longer the province of the citizen or the noble. Contempt for the unfree may occasionally have been shaken by their participation in war.

MILITARY HIERARCHIES

The prohibition of slaves was neither an abstract nor a universal law. The ostensible exclusion of slaves from warfare was a result rather of specific political interests and the attitudes of particular social classes. Contrary ways of thinking could spring from other interests and classes. Already our consideration of Thucydides has revealed that extreme groups, both democratic and oligarchic, were not primarily committed to the citizen/slave dichotomy. A strain of Xenophon's thought divergent from the hoplite ethos did not insist on the exclusion of slaves from war. Hoplite ideology tended to see

[1] In MacNeill (1995) 131.

every farmer in every state as an equally armed and equally important member of the phalanx. But in Xenophon's world there was a wide difference between the different branches of the military, and between the aristocrats whose job was to command and the common soldiers whose was to obey. Inequality within the army allowed for differences in the status of those who could take part.[2]

There had been a hierarchy of military service at Athens at least since the creation of the cavalry in the archaic period.[3] In the archaic and early classical period, however, the hoplite was central both to the state and to battle.[4] Both the cavalry on top and the light-armed below were relegated to marginal roles in combat. Their insignificance may reflect their lack of political clout: the aristocracy had lost their former monopoly of power; the *thetes* had not yet even threatened to supplant the class of hoplite farmers as the ostensible backbone of the state.

During the fifth century the military centrality of the hoplite first began to fade. The importance of the Athenian navy to her defeat of Persia and subsequent empire was indisputable. In the late-fifth and early-fourth century the victories of Demosthenes and Iphicrates showed the potential of peltasts. Xenophon himself helped mold the inflexible, primarily hoplite army of the Ten Thousand into a mixed force with slingers, cavalry, and elite divisions with special duties. This growing diversity within the military – most of all the growth of naval power – provided more flexibility as to who could carry arms and what rights this would entail.

We can discern two reactions to the increased complexity of the military. On the one hand, the hoplite model of military service as the exclusive prerogative of citizens – and conversely as conferring rights – could expand to include the new services. This line of thought lies behind, for example, pseudo-Xenophon's admission that the *demos* deserves its power since it provides rowers for the navy. For slaves to fight was blatantly contrary to this view: slave use could be recommended only by necessity. On the other hand, an aristocrat

---

[2] The notion of military hierarchy corresponds to Garlan's theory of status congruity: the Greeks tried to avoid too great a gap between the status of a position and of the person who filled it (Garlan [1972] 47–48; [1988] 175). Welwei interprets the participation of slaves in warfare in terms of necessity over-riding an ideology which would exclude them, what I describe as the hoplite ideal of purity (*UAK* 1.179–180).

[3] Bugh (1988) 4.

[4] Hanson (1989) 89, 223; Hanson (1991a) 6; Cartledge (1977) 24; Garlan (1975) 132.

might deny that light-armed soldiers or rowers deserve any rights: who cares what low-life rows in the navy? To turn to Xenophon in particular, his theory of the right-to-rule exemplifies the hoplite ideal of personal participation. An aristocratic notion of a military hierarchy also features prominently in Xenophon's world view. In some cases, this line of thought assigns slaves a place in the military.

Cyrus in the *Cyropaedia* forced ill-disposed or unarmed subjects to practice with the sling, which he considered the most slavish weapon.[5] Xenophon also describes slingers – as well as peltasts and archers – as using "servile weapons." We possess no evidence that slingers were actually slaves, but Xenophon's explanation of their slavishness is pertinent to our inquiry: slingers are useful to assist other troops; they are of no account on their own. In contrast the heavy-armed play the role of masters in this system.[6]

This theory did not represent the actual mutual dependence of different types of infantry. Although hoplites were the best troops for decisive battles on the plains, Xenophon had ample experience of the vulnerability of hoplites on their own. In the *Anabasis*, he himself suggested the creation of a slinger corps: the Ten Thousand were not self-sufficient even with peltasts and archers.[7] Xenophon, nevertheless, portrays the relation between these different arms of the military as analogous to the relation between masters and slaves. Xenophon here depicts the military as a structure in parallel to a stratified society. There are places for masters and slaves and not just for equal and equally armed farmers. Slaves could be tools and proxies for their masters in the military sphere just as they could in private life.[8]

---

[5] *Cyr.* 7.4.15. Xenophon was not alone in this characterization of slingers. Demosthenes makes fun of Charidemus for having served as a slinger in the same way he might have mocked him for servile ancestry (Dem. 23.148). The low status of slingers may have made it necessary to reward those willing to serve in this capacity during the Ten Thousand's retreat from Persia (*An.* 3.3.18). Pritchett believes that the cheapness of his equipment may have contributed to the low status of the slinger (*GSW* 5.53).

[6] *Cyr.* 2.1.18: τοῖς ὑπηρετικοῖς ὅπλοις. See *Cyr.* 1.5.5 for the composition of the Persian army. When Cyrus offers to give heavy arms to all his soldiers, the slingers are skipped and the soldiers addressed as archers and peltasts only. Either Xenophon is portraying Cyrus' oratorical technique in glossing over the low status of some of the men whom he is addressing or he is whitewashing Cyrus of the charge of promoting such lowly fighters as slingers to heavy armor.

[7] *An.* 3.3.15.

[8] Cf. Arist. *Pol.* 1253b33. Probably both Xenophon and Aristotle are reflecting a common way of thinking about slaves.

Xenophon has little interest in the navy. In his voluminous works with their constant military interest the navy is conspicuous largely by its absence. Neither farming, nor hunting, nor the endurance of *ponos* is recommended on the grounds that it will make one a good rower and thus able to help the state in war. On two occasions Xenophon even implies that rowing in the navy is typically the work of the unfree.[9] The concept of a hierarchy of services explains Xenophon's indifference as to who rowed in the navy.

This idea of hierarchy could even influence the treatment of the hoplite phalanx itself. Rather than the ethos of hoplite egalitarianism expanding to encompass the whole military – as we saw in Aristophanes' view of the Athenian navy – elitist distinctions could infiltrate the ostensibly equal hoplites. The difference in risk depending upon whether one fought in the front or rear rank was a potential source of hierarchy within the phalanx. Classical monuments to those who died fighting as *promachoi*, "front-fighters," seem to have no referent: nobody fought, in the heroic style, in front of the line. Perhaps the use of *promachoi* was a way of solemnizing the higher risks of fighting in the front rank.[10]

Xenophon brings this often submerged distinction within the hoplite phalanx to the fore. Sometimes this prominence is because Xenophon is describing the Spartan army. Here, as we have seen, the usual vague injunction to put the best men at the front and rear had become an official principle: every front-rank man was an officer.

The Helots fought in the Spartan army at Plataea according to this distinction between the front rank and the rest of the phalanx. *Perioeci* too fought in the same formation with the Spartans; they did not usually fight in the front rank.[11] At Leuctra, the proportion of full Spartiates in the four *morai* involved may have been as low as nine percent.[12] Not only was the front rank a position of superiority in the Spartan army, but there was an elite corps called the

---

[9] *HG* 6.1.11, 7.1.13; cf. Arist. *Pol.* 1327b7–13.

[10] Anderson (1984) 152. On the other hand, *GSW* 4.88–89 believes that the term was a non-specific laudatory term: it could be used of all of the dead who fought at a certain battle. The term is not used by tactical writers when they describe the first rank. Even if the prefix was applied loosely, the honorific use of the term implies that fighting "in front" had a higher status and thus that the phalanx was not a completely egalitarian formation.

[11] Cawkwell (1983) 387; Toynbee (1969) 366, 369; *UAK* 1.140. See p. 37.

[12] Lazenby (1985) 58.

"horsemen" among the hoplites.[13] The Spartiates as a whole may have claimed superior prerogatives on the grounds that they were the only professional, true soldiers.[14] The Sciritae also had a special role. They held the position of honor on the left flank, but were also responsible for unpleasant jobs such as sentry duty.[15] Even the ideology of equality, never mind its practice, included only the small proportion of the Spartan army that consisted of Spartiates. In such a system the use of lower classes, even Helots, would not contaminate a pure formation of citizens, the hoplite ideal.

Although there was nothing approaching a modern officer class in most other cities, the rising professionalism of the armies led to a separation between the figure of politician and general at Athens.[16] The Spartans and the Ten Thousand, both professional armies, had articulated systems of command.[17] Xenophon seems to approve of such stratification within the army: that each front-rank man was an officer was an important factor in the high morale of Cyrus' army, which also had a complex hierarchy of officers.[18] The distinction between soldier and officer explains Xenophon's recommendation of farming on the grounds that it teaches how to lead men. The farmer who needs to inspire his slaves is like the man "who is leading men against the enemy."[19] In the *Cyropaedia* too, Xenophon explicitly compares the command of slaves and of soldiers.[20] In contrast to the ideal of hoplite generals fighting in the first rank, in the *Anabasis* we find Xenophon as an officer on horseback urging the hoplites on.[21] Xenophon did not always conceive of military service as an egalitarian experience. From the point of view of an officer the common soldiers might even be in a position analogous to slaves. This outlook was completely at odds with the exclusive and egalitarian hoplite ethos.

---

[13] Hodkinson (1983) 249. [14] Plut. *Ages.* 26. [15] *Cyr.* 4.2.1; *Lac.* 12.3–4; Th. 5.67.1.
[16] Anderson (1970) 40; Lengauer (1979) *passim.*
[17] Ten Thousand: Roy (1967) 317; Nussbaum (1959) 27. Sparta: Th. 5.66.3–4. The cavalry formation Xenophon recommends would also have file and half-file leaders (*Eq. Mag.* 4.9). He also advises stationing officers chosen for their courage and ambition in the front ranks (*Eq. Mag.* 2.2, 2.6). By modern standards stratification within the army was minimal. Even as a general Xenophon was involved in close combat and praises Agesilaus, who although a king, fought in the front ranks and had the scars to prove it (*Ages.* 6.1–2).
[18] *Cyr.* 2.1.22–24, 3.3.57. [19] *Oec.* 5.15–16. [20] *Cyr.* 5.3.49, 8.1.4.
[21] *An.* 3.4.46, 7.3.45.

HOPLITE PURITY

In contrast to a complex hierarchy with the cavalry at its top is the conviction that the hoplite is the only real and important soldier. Among the hoplites everybody from the generals down ought to take the same risks in interchangeable positions in the formation, just as everybody ought to be fighting for similar farms.[22] Our thesis that the notion of an aristocratic hierarchy would allow slaves to serve in certain branches of the military finds corroboration in its opposite. The hoplites were a particular locus for citizen exclusivity. More than any other service, hoplites needed to be citizens.

In the fourth century, mercenaries encroached more in the other divisions of the military than among the hoplites. Many, if not most, mercenaries were peltasts, especially from Thrace.[23] Cretan archers and Rhodian slingers also enjoyed high repute. Mercenaries made up a large proportion of the crews in the Athenian navy. Xenophon even reports that everywhere mercenary cavalry had a high reputation.[24] In the *Cyropaedia* slings, bows and javelins are called mercenary arms in contrast to the heavy weapons of a state's own people.[25] Both above and below the level of hoplites there seems to have been less resistance to the use of mercenaries.

When Xenophon presents Cephisodotus' argument before the Athenians against the terms of an alliance with Sparta the connection between hoplite service and citizenship is again patent. That the Athenians will command on sea and Sparta on land will led to the result that "they become leaders of your own selves, while you become leaders merely of their slaves and their men of least account."[26] Not all the citizens whom Cephisodotus was addressing would fight on land. In fact, many were likely to row in the navy. Nevertheless, his slip was an easy one to make: citizens, even in the fourth century, ought to be hoplites and perhaps liked to be addressed as if they were. So Xenophon here assumes the ideal of

---

[22] Hanson (1989) 37, 107ff. The general was even supposed to fight in the first line; cf. Wheeler (1991).

[23] Best (1969) 134. Parke (1933) 44 n.6 notes that Isocrates occasionally uses the term "peltasts" to indicate mercenaries in general.

[24] *Eq. Mag.* 9.3–4.   [25] Anderson (1970) 132 on *Cyr.* 2.1.18.

[26] *HG* 7.1.13. Cf. Vidal-Naquet (1986d) 88 on Th. 4.101.2.

the hoplite state that appears again and again in the work of moderate oligarchs.[27]

The ideal service for citizens was not the navy, but neither was it the cavalry. Lysias claimed that a certain knight, Mantitheus, volunteered for the hoplites and subsidized the provisioning of two other hoplites.[28] The motivation for this action – and for Lysias to mention it – was twofold at least. Since hoplite status was closely linked to citizenship, this knight was showing himself to be an exemplary citizen by his efforts for the phalanx. At the same time he was deferring to the egalitarian, hoplite ethos by demoting himself to the lower status hoplites rather than staying in the suspiciously elite – and perhaps safer – cavalry.

The special link between the hoplite phalanx and citizenship is again patent in Xenophon's suggestions for the reform of the Athenian military. He proposes that metics be allowed in the cavalry but excluded from the hoplites.[29] Many scholars have found this passage troublesome, because it goes against the theory of status congruity. Low-status metics were even further from the elite cavalry, into which they were to be incorporated, than from the hoplite phalanx, from which Xenophon would bar them. Part of the explanation may be that the status of hoplite was most closely linked to citizenship. The purity and self-reliance, which Xenophon includes among the reasons for this reform, were especially desirable in this branch of the military. Significantly, Xenophon characterizes the metics as barbarians from Lydia, Phrygia, and Syria.[30] Such metics would probably consist largely of ex-slaves; these areas supplied a large portion of Athenian slaves.

Significantly Xenophon shows no concern about the large number of metics that served with the navy. About the question of metics in the navy Gauthier concludes that "Pour un homme de son milieu et de sa formation, le seul soldat est l'hoplite."[31] This seems like a strange opinion to ascribe to the cavalryman who instituted a slinger corps among the Ten Thousand, but at least part of Xeno-

---

[27] Th. 8.97.2; Arist. *Ath. Pol.* 33.1; *HG* 1.3.48; Arist. *Pol.* 1297b1–2, 1279a38–b5, 1291a33–34, 1297b1–2.

[28] B. Strauss (1986) 122 on Lys. 16.14.

[29] *Vect.* 2.2–6. In his *Cavalry Commander*, Xenophon recommends allowing metics to serve in the cavalry as well as the hiring of mercenaries (*Eq. Mag.* 9.3–6). Scholarly discussion and bibliography are summarized in Gauthier (1976) 65–66. See also Whitehead (1977) 128.

[30] *Vect.* 2.3–4.   [31] Gauthier (1976) 62.

phon's thinking was dominated by the centrality of the hoplites, their link to citizenship, and a special concern for their purity.[32]

Our treatment of Xenophon first presented a picture of a pellucid stream. As we piled up reasons for Xenophon's explicit prohibition of arming slaves, this exclusion may have seemed obvious and almost natural. The dissonance we observed between Xenophon's theories and the military practices of his age began to undermine the apparent solidity of the prohibition against slaves. Through the clear water of Xenophon's thought we began to see the rocks, litter, and bottom-feeders of fourth-century warfare and society.

The revelation of the entirely different, aristocratic conception of the relation of army and society has truly muddied the water. The ideal of equal military participation seems less a reflection of Greek society than one particular distortion of it. An army of aristocratic officers and slave-like men was as natural a conception as the hoplite model.

The strength of the hoplite, egalitarian ideal in war reflects the predominant, democratic conception of politics as a realm of personal participation rather than of representation or rule.[33] What distinguished these exclusively free realms, war and politics, from other "free activities" was the inadmissibility of representation. First, warfare. A slave could not fight for his master in the same way he might farm for him. Slaves could carry their masters' equipment as in times of peace; in the actual fighting, slaves could not act as the tools to which they were likened in the civilian sphere. To turn to politics, while Sicilian tyrants could win chariot races from hundreds of miles away, political representation was undemocratic. Even the temporary delegation of the assembly's power was suspect and limited.[34]

---

[32] Isocrates, speaking around 356 (*On the Peace* 48), showed a similar concern for the purity of the hoplites when he complained that "in those days we were hoplites and slaves and foreigners rowed, now hoplites are foreign and we row." This evidence is not as conclusive as Xenophon's since only the lower-class rowing is considered acceptable for slaves and foreigners rather than the services both above and below the hoplites. The citizen's dominance was fading all around. There is no evidence of a purification of the hoplites, but by the time of Demosthenes, mercenaries made up most of the cavalry who were even commanded by a mercenary (Bugh [1988], 160).

[33] This model is democratic in that all citizens have an equal role, not in terms of the extent of citizenship, which varied. It could, perhaps, just as easily be termed oligarchic. See Hanson (1995) 203–214.

[34] Arist. *Pol.* 1317a40–1318a2.

A commonly noted tension in Athenian democracy is that between political equality and economic distinctions.[35] The requirement of personal participation in war was a way that political equality was maintained while the admission of complete use of slaves in the private sphere was an aspect of the economic superiority that the elite at Athens never lost. Slaves or metics were excluded from the phalanx; they could be killed for trying to participate in the assembly.[36] Outside of war and politics, on the other hand, hierarchy allowed for slave participation. Hunting was a free, if not aristocratic activity. Nevertheless, as we have seen, the net-keeper was a slave.[37] Farming teaches everything "that a free man should be able to do," but for slaves to work on farms presented no problem.[38]

The distinction between an hierarchical, representational economic sphere and the ideal of purely personal participation in politics and war seems almost natural until we consider alternatives such as military hierarchy or powerful magistrates. Perhaps the hoplite participatory ideology had its roots in the Archaic period, when both the hoplite battle and citizenship were being established.[39] The growing power of the *mesoi*, middling hoplite farmers, may have been fundamentally a matter of agricultural economics.[40] The emerging hoplite class also stood to gain by the requirement that everybody fight in person, with a single attendant, and with similar weapons. In contrast, an aristocrat would have gained symbolic capital if his slaves or dependents fought in the army. Many of these attendants would be armed and play a role in battle equal to an independent citizen, who might well not maintain that position for long.[41] Although the *Iliad* focuses on personal competition

---

[35] E.g., Ober (1989) 293.   [36] Hansen (1991) 62 *et passim*.

[37] *Cyn.* 1.3, 6.5, 6.10, 6.18, 9.6.   [38] *Oec.* 5.1.

[39] Hanson (1995) 221–244 provides a balanced discussion with full bibliography. For a recent contrary view see Van Wees (1994). My argument does not require a particular temporal order of economic growth, military dominance, and political power, but points at a strong link between the military and political roles of hoplites. The question of whether hoplites dominated society because they fought the wars or whether war was limited to the hoplite battle because of the power of hoplites is probably unanswerable. The dynamic behind hoplite power was probably the result of military, economic, and political factors reinforcing each other.

[40] Hanson (1995) 25–126.

[41] In Etruria, hoplite warfare did not threaten the aristocratic social structure. At Rome, the Fabii are reported to have gone to war accompanied by their clients. Aristocrats could indeed have armed their retainers as hoplites (Snodgrass [1965] 119–120; Greenhalgh [1973] 150).

among aristocrats, Nestor's statement that "he [Agamemnon] is mightier since he rules over more men," would have boded ill for the farmers who were to become hoplites and equal citizens.[42]

The original issue was not whether the lowly retainers, or the barbarian slaves that superseded them, would acquire status and power for themselves by fighting. The question was rather whether the aristocracy could have shut out what was to become the hoplite class, if warfare had continued to be waged by aristocrats with their followers or slaves.[43]

Something like this may have occurred in Thessaly. Even in the classical period, Thessalian nobles were sometimes escorted in battle by large numbers of the Helot-like *penestai*, also on horseback.[44] Rather than fielding large numbers of heavy infantry, the army in Thessaly continued to consist of an aristocracy, backed by low-status retainers if need be. Reflecting this Thessalian society continued to be dominated by a small elite of large landowners, whose domination was only challenged by growing cities in the classical period.[45] In most of Greece, however, the nobles were "kicked upstairs" to the irrelevant cavalry. The hoplites scheduled wars in a break in their farming schedule and according to conventions that tended to perpetuate their own political weight.[46]

Both the egalitarian aspect of hoplite warfare and the requirement that only citizens fight may derive from this struggle. The power of the hoplite class depended upon restricting the military contribution of the aristocracy to personal service rather than allowing them to gain symbolic capital by fighting with large numbers of retainers. Conversely, to fight in similar positions in the phalanx, with one non-fighting slave attendant each, crystallized the hoplites' growing sense of themselves as the bulwark, and thus center, of the city.

IGNOBLE BATTLES

In theory slave participation could have lowered the prestige of war or raised the esteem in which slaves were held. Xenophon takes neither tack, but we can see the possibility of each in his work. The

---

[42] Hom. *Il.* 1.281.

[43] Greenhalgh (1973) 151–153 posits that early hoplite battles were such contests between armies of nobles with their retainers and believes that Alcaeus fr. 357 may refer to such a situation. See also Hanson (1995) 238.

[44] Dem. 13.23, 23.199.   [45] Westlake (1969b) 29–37.   [46] Ober (1994) 14.

prestige of war was lowered with the increasingly technical nature of fourth-century war, a trend in which Xenophon played his part. The status of slaves might in fact rise as a result of their military service. On the level of ideology, an emphasis on military prowess as the basis of social status can be subversive. The results of war may not turn out to correspond to preexisting hierarchies based on wealth or birth.

The status both of aristocratic officers and of equal hoplites derived from the high value that the Greeks gave to military prowess. We have already seen that war revealed a person's fitness to rule or to be ruled. Hoplite battles in particular were considered tests of the participants' worth. In the *Cyropaedia*, Pheraulas, a commoner favored by Cyrus, insists that using hoplite arms is as natural as for a bull to use his horns: hoplite warfare was an activity which "demands courage more than skill."[47] The prowess of a hoplite came from his inner quality and from the activities that characterized the free.

The fourth century, however, saw the development of tactics, technical advances, and the growing participation of manifestly ignoble persons in warfare. The innovations that made up this escalation had the potential to undermine both the high value of warfare and the link with citizenship from which much of its prestige derived. For example, the use of long range catapults was a fourth-century development. When Archidamus, the Spartan king, was shown such a machine, he reportedly stated that "manly prowess is dead." His discomfort reflects the extent to which such technical advances undermined the nobility of war.[48]

Xenophon did not merely record such novelties. He embraced them. Xenophon even claims that armies win the most and greatest victories by deception.[49] We are far from the "test of souls" that could justify the rule of a military class. In his historical works Xenophon portrays ability to concoct ambushes, contrive innovations, and make surprise attacks as part of the good general's repertoire.[50] Xenophon justifies such an approach to a war with a witty comparison attributed to the father of Cyrus the Great: Cyrus does not try to kill lions in fair, face-to-face fights; war is like

---

[47] Garlan (1975) 163 on *Cyr.* 2.3.11. In the pure hoplite clashes of the archaic and earlier classical period, this was probably the case (Hanson [1989] 227).

[48] Gabriel and Metz (1991) 38; Ober (1991) 191–192 on Plut. *Mor.* 219a.

[49] *Eq. Mag.* 5.11.   [50] Breitenbach (1950) 81, 96, 97.

hunting; Cyrus must be clever and a thief to win at war.[51] The common Greek analogy between war and an athletic contest, an *agon*, whose outcome is only valid if the rules are followed, is turned on its head here.

The new ways of fighting not only involved the unfairness of tactics and stratagems, but required specialized training. Peltasts required more specialized skills than hoplites. Many peltasts, such as those of Iphicrates, were highly trained, professional soldiers.[52] In the late fifth century war began to be seen as a matter of specific skills: the first experts in fighting in armor are attested.[53] In addition to the need to acquire specialize skills, war became a year round activity. Wars no longer took place during a short period in the summer when Greek farmers could afford to leave their farms.[54]

These pressures tended to break the link between citizens and soldiers. Fourth-century sources report elite and professional units in several cities. The *ephebes* at Athens gave up other occupations during their period of service but were not permanently divided from the civilians. The *epilektoi*, however, were a permanent group of elite troops at Athens.[55] Thebes maintained the Sacred Band as full-time soldiers. Elite units also appear in Arcadia and at Elis.[56] Military training was central to Xenophon's world even in the *Hellenica*.[57] In the *Cyropaedia* Xenophon stresses that the army of Cyrus had the advantage of being a professional one. Their morale was high since the men knew that they were maintained for no end other than to fight. The warring kings even agreed that the farmers should not suffer in the war, which would be entirely between the soldiers.[58] Nothing could be further removed from an army of hoplite farmers than the notion that the farmers should have no place at all in war.

Many cities responded to the greater demands of military service

---

[51] *Cyr.* 1.6.27–28.

[52] *GSW* 2.124; Parke (1933) 77; Anderson (1970) 121. The Dema wall with its sally ports was designed for well-trained, if not professional, defenders (Munn [1993] 48).

[53] Garlan (1975) 169; Lengauer (1979) 108. Pl. *La.* 178a, 179e, 182, *Euthydemus* 271d, 273c, *Leg.* 813d-e, 833e. Garlan (1995) 77–78 believes training may have been important earlier, but paints the same general picture.

[54] Ober (1994) 11.   [55] Plut. *Phocion* 13.2–3; Munn (1993) 189 on Aeschin. 2.169.

[56] *HG* 7.4.13, 7.4.34.   [57] Breitenbach (1950) 76.

[58] *Cyr.* 2.1.14, 2.1.21, 4.3.12, 5.4.24–27; cf. Ar. *Pol.* 1267b30–35. See also Hanson (1995) 351. Due (1989) 211 contrasts the *Cyropaedia* and the *Republic* in that the *Cyropaedia* does not separate military and political functions. The passages cited show that this is not the case.

by hiring mercenaries.[59] Their use, like the freeing of slaves for military purposes, was originally associated with tyranny.[60] Like the use of slaves in war, mercenaries represented a breakdown in the equivalence of soldiers and citizens. Elite or professional forces were at least from the city that they defended; mercenaries typically came from the impoverished fringes of the Greek world.[61] Xenophon, nevertheless, goes out of his way to present at great length a speech in the *Hellenica* about the advantages of mercenaries. He also recommended that the Athenians hire mercenary cavalry.[62]

It was hard for war to maintain its glamour when citizens and aristocrats were no longer the only ones who fought. How could an activity in which violent, thieving, semi-civilized mercenaries excelled be a test of true worth?[63] The prestige of the military, and thus the reason to restrict participation in it, derived from the model of the hoplite battle between citizen armies. As war became a matter of specialized skills, its luster faded.

Some Athenian evidence supports the thesis of a decline in prestige. Isocrates' *On the Peace* strongly condemns war.[64] The popular Athenian leader Eubulus was later condemned for doing nothing but ensuring a good economy. Such an accomplishment was a far cry from the successful wars that mark out the great statesman.[65] Demosthenes too denounces and exhorts the pacific and apathetic Athens of the mid-fourth century. Scholars, however, now suspect that much of Demosthenes' portrayal is exaggerated. For example, he distinguishes between his own active patriotism and the lethargy of Eubulus. The real difference may have been between

---

[59] Parke (1933); Best (1969). Xenophon mentions that the later stages of the Corinthian war were fought mainly by mercenaries with the opposing cities no longer sending out large armies but merely garrisons (*HG* 4.4.14).

[60] *Hier.*10.

[61] Arcadia, a prime recruiting ground for mercenaries, was geographically central, but was marginal in terms of its cultural development and its relative lack of city-states (Paus. 8.27.1).

[62] *HG* 6.1.5–6; *Eq. Mag.* 9.3. It is no surprise that Xenophon praised the quality of the Ten Thousand, honed by their continual service (*An.* 5.6.15).

[63] Ober (1985a) 47 on Pl. *Leg.* 1, 630b and Isoc. *On the Peace* 8.44. Isocrates and Demosthenes speak of the threat to citizens posed by large groups of wandering mercenaries (McKechnie [1989] 85). Best (1969) 133 points out that Thracian peltasts were known as robbers and were probably very poor; Xenophon describes some peltasts plundering after a victory, ὥσπερ εἰκός (*HG* 3.4.24; *Ages.* 1.32.).

[64] Isoc. *On the Peace* 5, 12, 19, 22 and *passim*.

[65] Plut. *Mor.* 812 f. I follow the arguments of Cawkwell (1963) esp. 53, 65–66 in this paragraph.

two strategies for combating Philip. In fact, Demosthenes' policy may have been foolish; Eubulus may have been energetically preparing Athens for war.

The decline of Athenian power needs also to be considered. Trouncing a recalcitrant fifth-century subject with a navy paid for by the empire was not the same as paying out of your own pocket and then fighting a defensive war against a Macedonian army, professional, experienced, and large. The obsessive Athenian pipe dream of recapturing Amphipolis was even less likely to attract the enthusiasm of intelligent statesmen.[66] We may be getting an exaggerated picture of a peace-loving Athens, where in fact Athens was merely weak. Conversely, an awareness of the horrors and tragedy of war is clear already in Homer, who was, nevertheless, hardly a pacifist: he emphasizes military prowess as the basis of personal worth. The thesis that war lost much of its prestige in the fourth century looks hard to prove.

A more modest goal can be salvaged. Both Plato and Aristotle argue, not against war in general terms, but against a militaristic basis of social structure. The political thinking that they address is the same as Xenophon's. Its failure is precisely that war is no longer a good test of worth.

Plato's *Laws* was probably written in the decade before Plato's death around 348.[67] In the first book, the interlocutors, one Cretan and one Spartan, both praise their countries' constitutions on the grounds that they are aimed primarily at military efficiency. Clinias, the Cretan, claims that all of his country's institutions and laws aim at successful warfare.[68] The Spartan Megillus believes that his state's social regulations are also designed to make good warriors. Like Xenophon, he includes among these customs the harsh training of the body that produces good soldiers.[69]

Plato demolishes his interlocutors with a variety of arguments. Most interesting for our purposes are two that fundamentally undermine Greek militarism – such as we have seen in Xenophon – and seem to come directly out of the experience of fourth-century warfare. Plato first brings up the poem of Tyrtaeus who would "neither mention nor take account of a man . . . if he did not excel at war."[70] Tyrtaeus' position is like that of Xenophon. Both believe

---

[66] Cawkwell (1963) 51.   [67] Stalley (1983) 3.   [68] Pl. *Leg.* 1, 626a-b, 628e.
[69] Pl. *Leg.* 1, 633b-c.   [70] Pl. *Leg.* 1, 629a-b.

that military effectiveness should be the primary criterion of a person's worth and place in society.

Plato, no ex-mercenary like Xenophon, points out that the qualities needed within a society are not the same as those that distinguish a man in warfare against an external enemy: many mercenaries fight well and to the death; almost all of them are "heedless, unjust, violent, and stupid."[71]

Warriors would not make the best ruling class. Plato's criticism does not come out of a society where hoplite citizens or aristocratic cavalry dominated warfare as well as their cities.[72] Rather Plato sees the goal of military efficiency as being in conflict with that of civic harmony. The detachment of prowess from civic responsibility forces Plato to seek another basis of rule; participation in warfare can no longer serve this function.[73]

Plato's argument here is presented as a criticism of Doric militarism.[74] He was also opposing himself to more prevalent ways of thinking. Plato would surely have taken issue with pseudo-Xenophon's admission that the people of Athens deserved their democracy since they manned the navy and with Aristophanes' argument that everybody who fights in the Athenian navy deserves citizenship. More surprising, in the *Laws*, Plato would not even agree with Xenophon's ideal of a militarily efficient elite.[75]

When Megillus is pressed to defend the Spartan practice of abstaining from drink, he appeals to the notion of war as a test of a society's worth. There may be warlike nations that are hard-drinking, he concedes, but "we rout them when we have weapons in our hands." Plato will have nothing of this romanticized view of war as the final touchstone of virtue: the result of war is hardly a

---

[71] Pl. *Leg.* 1, 630b.   [72] Pl. *Leg.* 1, 628b.

[73] Silverthorne (1973) argues that Plato's insistence on military order in society in *Leg.* 12, 942a5–943a3 is a rhetorical stand appropriate to a preamble and out-of-line with the predominant anti-militaristic strain of the dialogue; *contra* Powell (1994) 273–274. Powell's arguments (284–302), however, for non-rational persuasion in the Laws leave room for Silverthorne's reading.

[74] On Plato, Sparta and militarism, see Morrow (1960) 40–63 and esp. 49–51. More recently, Powell argues that Spartans or Athenian Laconophiles were a significant intended audience of the Laws (Powell [1994] 308–312).

[75] Vidal-Naquet (1986d) 95–97 contrasts the position of war in the *Laws* and in the *Republic*, where the need for experts in warfare dictates the existence of the guardian class – contrast e.g., Pl. *Resp.* 2, 374a-e and Pl. *Leg.* 4, 706a-707d. Vidal-Naquet argues that the first three books of the *Laws*, anticipated by the *Laches*, present an extended critique of militarism; see the similar views of Barker (1959) 108, 122, 160, 202.

dependable criterion of a government's virtue; for example, a more populous city may defeat a smaller one, regardless of the constitutional virtues of the latter.[76]

Such a rejection of military achievement as the sure sign of political superiority seems utterly trivial and obvious, until we recall how common was the connection between a city's or person's worth and their success at war. Herodotus considered their military success to be proof of the superiority of Athenian freedom to tyranny and of Greece's superiority over the slavish Persians.[77] In the Funeral Oration, Pericles' concludes his praise of Athens by pointing to the memorials of Athens' victories in every land. In his second speech Pericles is more blunt: Athens owes its high reputation to its devotion to warfare and consequent power.[78] We have seen Xenophon's repeated insistence that war is the final measure of activities and states as well as individuals.

Plato's criticism of this view has a bite to it in the aftermath of Leuctra and the foundation of Messene. Sparta was no longer the militaristic hegemon of the Greek world. Sparta's internal regulations no longer glowed with the aura of patent success. For Plato war was an activity at which the "heedless, unjust, violent, and stupid" excel and in which the Spartans cannot even subdue their *douloi* – as Plato calls the Helots.[79] Military prowess and success can no longer serve as the foundation of a political philosophy as they did for Xenophon.

In Xenophon's world, war was not only a key determinate of ideal rule, it also largely determined who deserved to be slaves. In his famous discussion of natural slavery, Aristotle entertains, but then rejects this way of thinking.[80] Aristotle considers the law by which prisoners of war are considered slaves. As we have seen, Xenophon is perfectly happy with this custom, since military prowess and courage are particularly apt markers of a person's nature, whether slave or master. In fact, acceptance of this practice seems widespread.[81] Aristotle concedes Xenophon's argument in part:

---

[76] Pl. *Leg.* 1, 638 a-b.   [77] H. 5.77–78, 5.91.   [78] Th. 2.41.4, 2.64.3.

[79] Pl. *Leg.* 6, 776 c-d.

[80] Barker (1959) 184–185, 188 notes other similarities between Plato's *Laws* and Aristotle's *Politics*; see especially Arist. *Pol.* 1271b1–11. Most recent philosophical scholarship on Aristotle's theory of natural slavery tends to have little interest in the rationales, rejected by Aristotle, for the enslavement of prisoners of war: e.g., Nichols (1983), Garver (1994), Dobbs (1994).

[81] Cambiano (1987) 24–25; cf. Rihll (1993) 79.

When it obtains the wherewithal, excellence is particularly capable of wielding force, and the ability to overpower always comes from a superiority of some good, so that it seems that force is not devoid of excellence.[82]

Havelock describes this as the "crude doctrine that might is right." He believes that Aristotle introduces it here merely to confuse the issue.[83] The context of the treatment of prisoners of war makes this position less of a straw man and Aristotle's concern with it more comprehensible. Two distinctions are necessary. First, war is often considered a sphere outside of conventional civic morality.[84] Greeks – such as Xenophon – who would never accept the enslavement of other, weaker citizens could quite easily countenance this treatment of captives.[85] Second, we have seen that for Xenophon military success derives from positive virtues such as courage, self-control, endurance, and intelligence. In this way of thinking, might is due to right. Might does not determine right as in Havelock's formulation.

Nevertheless, although Aristotle admits that "the ability to overpower always comes from a superiority of some good," he does not buy the whole package: people who are not natural slaves, even men of the highest nobility, can be enslaved in unjust wars; nobody would say that such men are real slaves just because they happened to be captured and sold.[86] As in Plato, the accidental aspect of war is opposed to its function as a true test of the worth, in this case of slaves.[87]

It is hard to resist putting these arguments in the context of the increase in military technique and the severing of the actual links between warrior and citizen. At the risk of assigning a grandiose importance to a modest topic, I would even suggest that the changes in warfare, including the use of unfree soldiers, contributed to the development of political philosophy. The decline of the hoplite battle from early in the fifth century and the use of mercenaries, Neodamodeis, and slave navies in the late-fifth and fourth century, left a hole in the ideologies that had previously justified elite, hoplite, or even

---

[82] Arist. *Pol.* 1255a13–16.   [83] Havelock (1957) 349–350.

[84] Walzer [1992] 3–20 on Thucydides' Melian dialogue. Aristotle finds it necessary repeatedly and explicitly to insist that morality applies to foreign as well as domestic affairs (Arist. *Pol.* 1324b23–1325a14, 1333b13–1334a10).

[85] See above pp. 153–155.   [86] Arist. *Pol.* 1255a24–28.

[87] Brunt (1993) 353 presents a similar interpretation of Aristotle and also refers to the rejection of warfare as a test in Plato's *Laws*.

citizen rule. Social structure had lost one of its most solid foundations in military participation. One of the functions of fourth-
century political philosophy may have been to fill this gap.

It would be nice to think of these two great thinkers simply as
early critics of a brutish militarism. Indeed, after his criticisms of
Megillus and Clinias, Plato proposes an education in philosophy as a
better goal than military victory.[88] But, despite this benign beginning, Plato ends up proposing another elitist, totalitarian state.[89] It is
Aristotle's concept of natural slavery that makes up the deficits in the
judgment of war. He immediately follows his criticism of the
militaristic argument with an ethnocentric distinction between
Greek nobles and barbarians: "they do not mean to say that those
men are slaves when captured, but that barbarians are."[90]

THE STATUS OF SOLDIERS

The contamination of slave, as well as mercenary, participation may
have diminished the role of war in Greek thinking. We need now to
consider whether these participants gained any prestige from the
activity whose éclat they were contaminating.

In practice, slaves or Helots could advance by serving in the army
or navy. The Neodamodeis and the slaves freed to fight at Marathon
and Arginusae escaped from bondage. When military participation
was not restricted, yet still retained its ideological and practical
importance, it could become an avenue of social mobility. In fact,
the higher the prestige of the military, the easier it was for fighting to
erase social distinctions.

In fact, K. J. Dover tentatively suggests that the slaves who saved
Athens at Arginusae and became free citizens form the backdrop to
the character Xanthias in Aristophanes' *Frogs*. Xanthias' dominant
personality may mark a break with previous comic slaves. Although
the general attitude of masters toward their slaves probably did not
change very much, "the implications of a contrast between a foolish
master who cannot row and a bold slave who could have won his

---

[88] Pl. *Leg.* 1, 641 c.

[89] The classic and generally correct statement of this argument is Popper (1966); see Stalley
(1983) 179–185 for discussion and Gill (1995) 54 for bibliography. Morrow (1939) shows that
Plato's recommendations in the *Laws* concerning the control of slaves were even harsher
than contemporary Athenian practice and law.

[90] Arist. *Pol.* 1255a28–29 (A). Cf. *HG* 1.6.14–15, 2.2.20; Jackson (1970) 48; Hopkins (1967) 175.

freedom by rowing cannot have escaped Aristophanes or his audience."[91]

We have already seen that martial prowess was central to the world of the *Cyropaedia*. Xenophon also constructs an episode in which the Persian commons are promoted to the status of heavy-armed soldiers. Cyrus later even instructs his officers to get the best soldiers from whatever source they can.[92] Luccioni believes that this policy was the invention of a new principle for a new situation, but the new situation, the Persian inferiority in numbers, is probably Xenophon's creation.[93] Xenophon could have had the Persians overcome this problem in a variety of ways. He chose not only to depict the advance of the commons, but also to justify it, especially in several debates on whether all should share equally in the rewards of victory.[94] These discussions expose the subversive aspect of the notion that war is the ultimate test of a person's worth.

Cyrus makes the unexceptionable and conventional declaration that the day of battle will show the worth of each man.[95] Typically, the restriction of military service served to ensure that only the right classes would prove their worth. But here, when the lower classes fight, the importance of military prowess can undermine the social hierarchy rather than confirm it.

The low-born Pheraulas is more extreme. Arguing to convince his fellow commoners that the rewards of victory should be distributed according to merit, he points out that the poor are stronger because of their hard physical labor. He concludes with the bold statement that the nobles "have been trapped in a democratic contest."[96] Xenophon seems to be reveling in problematic aspects of the Greek ideology about war. When participation is not restricted, war ends

---

[91] Dover (1993) 50.

[92] *Cyr.* 1.5.5, 2.2.26. In an aside on the subject of the type of weaponry appropriate for mercenaries, Anderson (1970) 132 makes the same comparison as I make here: in the same way that Sparta hired mercenaries as peltasts, but armed Helots when hoplites were needed, so Cyrus invites the commoners to take up heavy arms and refers to light arms as mercenary weapons (*Cyr.* 2.1.18). Due (1989) 183 also talks about the meritocracy of Cyrus' empire but does not discuss the significance of the commoners' new arms; cf. Tatum (1989) 204ff. Tuplin (1994) 143 with n.24, who is generally skeptical of comparisons between Sparta and the *Cyropaedia*, considers this parallel to be one of the most convincing.

[93] Luccioni (1948) 226; see also Gera (1993) 165.   [94] *Cyr.* 2.2.20, 2.3.2ff.

[95] *Cyr.* 3.3.36.

[96] *Cyr.* 2.3.15 (M): εἰλημένοι εἰσὶν ἐν δημοτικῇ ἀγωνίᾳ; cf. Socrates' denunciation of masters who are softer than their slaves (*Mem.* 3.13.3, 3.13.6).

up not maintaining the status quo but changing it. Pheraulas begins life as a poor farmer, but his military prowess wins him wealth and status.[97]

The degree of similarity between the Persians in the *Cyropaedia* and the Spartans is a matter of controversy.[98] In any case, Xenophon's depiction of the promotion of the commons resembles the way that Sparta overcame its numerical inferiority and came to rule Greece.[99] No other state had the deliberate policy of incorporating inferior classes into the phalanx.[100] In emergencies the poor might be armed, but Xenophon not only describes Cyrus' policy but praises it – and not only in terms of necessity. Xenophon could either be creating out of whole cloth a policy for his ideal king or be depicting the Spartan practices with which he was so familiar.

But why would Xenophon incorporate Spartan practices in general and specifically this one into his portrait of an ancient Persian king? The answer is likely to be complex. Practices that Xenophon considered exemplary would increase the merit of Xenophon's Cyrus. Xenophon attributes to Cyrus many leadership practices that he approves of in his other works. But the recruitment of lower-class people into the phalanx was not a practice of which Xenophon or his audience can be expected to have approved. It may be that an actual practice, a Spartan practice, is being raised in status by being associated with a great monarch. Xenophon goes into great detail about the rationale for Cyrus' action and also explains the motivations of the commons that end up making Cyrus' army so successful. This emphasis supports the thesis that the recruitment was not an action that would naturally add luster to Cyrus: Cyrus' policy needed justification. Although we are deep in speculative territory now, I believe that Xenophon was, in part, defending the policies of Sparta and Agesilaus that had always been

---

[97] *Cyr.* 2.3.7, 8.3.2, 8.3.35.

[98] See Tuplin (1994) and Georges (1994) 207–246 for recent discussions with bibliography. I hope to argue elsewhere that recent scholarship underestimates the resemblance between the Spartans and the Persians of the *Cyropaedia*.

[99] The argument of Tuplin (1994) 138 that Persia, unlike Sparta, suffered from no lack of manpower was probably true in fact; this only makes the parallel of Xenophon's Persia with Sparta more striking. See Anderson (1970) 132 and Georges (1994) 230 on the similarity of Cyrus' policies and Sparta's use of inferior grades in the army.

[100] Later the *ephebia* at Athens incorporated youth of all classes and concluded their training by giving them hoplite arms (Hansen [1991] 108–109).

ideologically dubious and with which, as we have seen, he may have been personally linked.

Xenophon is flirting here with the idea of social mobility based on military prowess. Nevertheless, we should note some caveats. Pheraulas, who does rise to the top of the Persian aristocracy, was not a typical commoner, but was rather "a noble at heart."[101] Furthermore, hierarchy within the Persian army enables the incorporation of most of the commons at subordinate levels. The new soldiers are treated as a separate group under the command of officers from the nobility. These officers laugh good-naturedly at their soldiers: "they are so easily won by kindness that we can make many of them our firm friends with even a little piece of meat; and they are so obedient that they obey even before the orders are given."[102] The army is no array of equals in which commoner and aristocrat are homogenized. Even the equality of armament was temporary. After Cyrus' success, the elite became cavalrymen.[103] Most significantly, Xenophon never equates the commoners with slaves. For slaves to advance through their military service was not, in fact, impossible, but it was almost unthinkable.

---

[101] *Cyr.* 2.3.7 (A): τὴν ψυχὴν οὐκ ἀγεννεῖ ἀνδρὶ ἐοικώς.

[102] *Cyr.* 2.2.1–10. The soldiers are εὐθεράπευτοι and πιθανοί.

[103] *Cyr.* 4.3.1–23. At *Cyr.* 4.3.23 Xenophon reveals that it was men of the καλῶν κἀγαθῶν who eventually became the cavalry.

CHAPTER 11

Conclusion: Volones, Mamluks, and Confederates

If slaves will make good soldiers, our whole theory of slavery is
wrong – but they won't make soldiers.
Howell Cobb, Confederate General, 1865.

The arguments of this book lead to two general conclusions. The
first is that a specific historical confluence led to the widespread use
of slaves in classical Greek warfare. The second is that the ideological prohibitions against the use of slaves were also the products of a
specific situation and particular social interests. There is nothing
inherently contradictory about the use of slaves in warfare. A brief
excursus into comparative history will serve to highlight these
conclusions. Greece was not the only place where slaves were used in
warfare. In addition to the other conceptions of the military we have
seen in classical Greece, the relation of the army to society has been
conceived of in a myriad of ways in different historical circumstances. Many of these views did not require the exclusion of slaves
from the military.

LIVY AND THE *VOLONES*

The history of fighting slaves at Rome is a long and complex one
encompassing massive slave revolts, the use of slaves in the civil wars
that ended the Republic, and the imperial ruling making it a capital
offense for a slave to enlist in the army.[1] The relation of military
service and social status at Rome was also complicated and varied
over time. To a large extent Rome resembles Greece in the high
value put on war, an original link between social status and position
in the military, contempt for slaves, and their exclusion from

---

[1] *UAK* vol. III and Rouland (1977) offer comprehensive treatments of slaves in the Roman
military. Bradley (1989) covers the slave revolts.

warfare. But Livy's treatment of slaves in the Second Punic War provides an illuminating contrast to mainstream Greek ideology. One may grant that Livy's treatment is far from the whole story of Roman thought. Nor is this episode even typical of the general pattern of the representation of slaves in Livy. Nevertheless, it does show that the different society of the Romans made possible an entirely different way of looking at the relation of army and society.

The Romans recruited slaves as a matter of military necessity in the period after their disastrous loss at Cannae: "They bought 8,000 healthy, young slaves at public expense and armed them, after asking each individually whether he wanted to serve."[2] Since the senate paid the masters of slaves who *volunteered* for army service, the slave soldiers were known as the Volones.

Whereas slave participation in the defining Athenian victory at Marathon is not even mentioned in Herodotus, Livy celebrates the Volones. They are made part of his grand depiction of how all of Roman society drew together in the struggle against Carthage: "such virtuous habits and such a love of country uniformly penetrated all classes of society."[3] The recruitment of slaves is one of a number of extreme measures by which the Romans signaled their resolve and hoped to strengthen their cause.[4] Livy carefully follows the fortunes of the Volones: they crop up in his narrative again and again.[5] He even brings the example of the Volones into speeches on extraneous subjects.[6] Not only is slave participation in a great war acknowledged, but – in striking contrast to Xenophon's omission of the liberation of the slaves who fought at Arginusae – Livy follows the whole process by which they obtain their freedom with great interest.[7]

The motif of the social mobility provided by war is underlined by

---

[2] Livy 22.57.11–12.

[3] Livy 23.49.3; cf. Livy 22.1.18, 26.35.2, 27.50.5. The ex-masters of the Volones refused compensation until the end of the war (Livy 24.18.12). When the Volones attained their freedom, they prayed for Tiberius Gracchus and the Roman people (Livy 24.16.10).

[4] Livy 22.11.8 (freedmen recruited for navy), 22.57.6 (human sacrifice), 23.14.3 (criminals recruited), 23.32.14–15 (scorched earth policies), 24.11.7–8 (the rich supply sailors for the navy – from their slaves?).

[5] Livy 23.32, 23.35–37, 24.10.3, 24.14–18, 25.1.5, 25.17.7, 25.20.4, 25.22.4, 27.38.8–9, 28.10.11, 28.46.13, 29.5.9, 29.13.4.

[6] Livy 25.6.19, 26.2.9; see also Livy 24.15.7–8.

[7] Livy 24.14–17. Livy even includes such details as Gracchus' request to the senate and the senate's reply on the subject of emancipation.

the contrary case of the Roman soldiers who had surrendered to Hannibal at Cannae. They were not ransomed, even though this is represented as being cheaper than the purchase and arming of the Volones.[8] Livy details how, despite their repeated pleas, the survivors of Cannae were treated with deliberate contempt for the rest of the war: they were not permitted to winter in a town, nor to return to Italy as long as any Carthaginians were there.[9]

This contrast comes out of a way of thinking in which war is the most important determinant of status. As in Xenophon's story of Cyrus' arming the Persian commons, if war became important enough, it could become an avenue for social mobility. Both this world view and the hoplite ideal of restricted military participation assume a congruence between army service and social status. In Livy, however, social status varied according to military service rather than military service being determined by social status. Their general instructs the officers of the Volones not to despise their low-born soldiers:

He wanted the old veterans to allow themselves to be ranked equal with the recruits, the free-citizens with the slave-volunteers, and for all to consider that anyone to whom the Roman people had entrusted its arms and standards was well-born and noble enough.[10]

In practice too, the army was one of the most important avenues of upward social mobility – though not usually for slaves – throughout Roman history.

It was not only the place of the army in Roman life that made the contrast between the Volones and Cannae veterans possible, but also the more open nature of Roman society. Rome was highly unusual in that ex-slaves regularly obtained citizen status.[11] Orlando Patterson argues that Rome was so willing to assimilate foreigners and slaves, because the citizen body was already highly stratified.[12] In classical Athens an enfranchised slave would have acquired a citizen status that was largely unitary. Accordingly it was rare for ex-slaves to become citizens. At Rome, however, enfranchised slaves were

---

[8] Livy 22.57.12.

[9] Livy, 22.59.12, 22.60–61, 23.31.1–2, 25.5.11, 25.7.3–4, 27.7.11, 29.24.11–12. The survivors were stationed in Sicily. In one place the survivors of Cannae are depicted as asking for the same treatment as the Volones. They want to be able to regain their status by battle service (Livy 25.6.21). The terms of service of the Cannae survivors were also assigned to other cowardly soldiers (Livy 24.18.9, 26.1.10).

[10] Livy 23.35.8.   [11] Patterson (1982) 30, 211.   [12] Patterson (1991) 218.

often bound as clients of their ex-masters.[13] As voters they were enrolled in the four urban tribes and usually the lower centuries. No matter how rich they still could not obtain the status of *equites* without special dispensation. They could not marry a person from the senatorial order. So while the Athenian system was largely designed to eliminate all such explicit distinctions between citizens, at Rome legal stratification and an elitist ideology enabled the state to include outsiders at lower levels without undermining existing privilege. Thus the advance of the Volones could be celebrated rather than regarded as a contamination of the citizens.

ISLAMIC SLAVE SOLDIERS

In contrast to our examination of one case in a single writer of the Augustan period, there is no danger of Islamic slave soldiers being a marginal case.[14] Islamic states from Spain to India to sub-Saharan Africa systematically used slave soldiers.[15] Military slavery is first attested around AD 820 and was still being used at the end of the nineteenth century.[16] The tradition of slave soldiers may even be an essential context for understanding the rule of Idi Amin.[17] Although military slaves never made up the entirety of a state's army, they were generally the elite troops.[18] So, in an area larger than Europe, for more than a millennium, the use of slaves for soldiers was – if not the standard – a standard way of raising armies.

In the case of the Egyptian Mamluks, on which I will concentrate, slaves were acquired from the European-Asiatic steppe. These non-Muslims were enslaved as youths, converted to Islam, and trained in military skills for a period of years before becoming professional, life-long soldiers devoted to the service of the sultan.[19] Ordinary

---

[13] In Greece the ex-slave was often bound to the master by economic ties, but his client status was not institutionalized (Patterson [1982] 253).

[14] My familiarity with the modern bibliography on Islamic slave soldiers is far from comprehensive. I also lack the familiarity with Middle Eastern history and original sources that would allow me much independence of outlook. But, by canvassing a variety of opinions, I do hope to have avoided blind adherence to any one interpretation.

[15] Pipes (1986) 167.   [16] Pipes (1981) 159; D. H. Johnson (1988) 79.

[17] D. H. Johnson (1988) 86.

[18] Ayalon (1979) 10.207. I cite Ayalon by essay and page number.

[19] Ayalon (1977) 7.313; (1979) 8. The system of slave soldiers seems to have replaced the use of mercenaries. Just as in classical Greece, both are alternatives to the use of citizens or tribesmen as soldiers (Pipes [1981] 87).

citizens could not own Mamluks.[20] This use of slaves as soldiers bypasses some of the problems with the use of privately owned slaves. There are no slave owners with interests in the slaves different from those of the state; the state is the slave owner.

Several views of the Mamluks attempt to resolve the seeming paradox of slave soldiers. Lapidus doubts that the Mamluks were actually slaves.[21] Pipes does not go this far but argues that slaves in Islam had a relatively high status.[22] The place of war in Islam has also been advanced as an explanation of the Mamluks. War against fellow Muslims was the subject of religious prohibition; yet after the initial conquests, most wars were of this type.[23] In Islamic countries there was little reason to keep warfare, already of dubious value or even blasphemous, pure of slave participation. By way of contrast, in classical Greece, prowess in war was esteemed especially when displayed against worthy opponents. Thus for slaves to take part was anathema.

This line of thought attempts to soften the contrast between the status of slave and of soldier. Three problems keep this explanation for Islamic slave soldiers from being fully convincing.

First, war against fellow Muslims may have originally been against Islamic law, but *ahkam al-bughat*, "judgments pertaining to rebels," were developed which could be used to sanction internecine, Islamic conflicts.[24]

Second, war may be esteemed ever so little, but possession of arms and horses is still a source of power seemingly incompatible with the status of a slave.

Third, the Mamluks were quite definitely slaves.[25] They were often conquered people whose life-long subjection originated in force. The slave recruits were cut off from their families and did not pass their status to their children – in theory and law the children of Mamluks could not become Mamluks; new outsiders had to be brought in.[26] All the respect that the slave soldiers received was due to their status as appendages of their master, the sultan. As individuals they could be and were subject to any number of disgraces. Accordingly the Mamluks were subject to slavery as

---

[20] Ayalon (1977) 10.310.   [21] Lapidus (1981/82 b.) 716.   [22] Pipes (1981) 93.

[23] Keegan (1993) 33–34: Pipes (1981) 75.   [24] El Fadl (1990) 151–152.

[25] Patterson (1982) 309–314.   [26] Ayalon (1977) 7.313.

Patterson defines it: they suffered the "permanent, violent domination of natally alienated and generally dishonored persons."[27]

Some theories for the prevalence of the Mamluks grant that they were slaves and soldiers. The Mamluk institution may be due to factors that made the use of Muslim subjects as soldiers impossible. Both Crone and Pipes view military slavery as the result of a failure in Islamic politics.[28] Crone writes that the Abbasid use of slaves as soldiers took place against the background of failure and grew because of the lack of "legitimating resources" in places where "culturally destructive" conquests had taken place.[29] Pipes explains the coincidence of military slavery and Islam by reference to the nature of this religion. The Islamic creed contained specific political and military prescriptions. When governments ignored these rules, the consequent disillusion made it impossible for them to recruit Muslims.[30]

Turner, however, objects that pious disillusion with politics is universal and lacks explanatory power.[31] Dissatisfaction with Islamic politics could just as easily be a result as a cause of the use of slave soldiers which resulted in a politics consisting of "violent rule by barely civilized warriors."[32]

This impasse leads us to the second type of explanation which looks for the positive factors that led to the choice of military slavery in society after society for a thousand years. Rather than consider the use of citizen soldiers as the norm whose absence must be explained, several scholars have explored why slaves make such good soldiers. For the Mamluk system was a great success militarily. Ayalon argues that the Mamluk army was the "strongest in Islam and one of the most powerful in the world."[33] The Mamluks played a key role in the fight against the Crusaders and the Mongols.[34] In the decisive battle of Ain Jalut in 1260, the Mamluks defeated the Mongols, whom no other Christian or Islamic force had been able to withstand.[35] The intensive professional training that the Mamluks

---

[27] Patterson (1982) 13.   [28] Pipes (1986) 166.
[29] Crone (1980) 80, 83.   [30] Pipes (1981) 75.   [31] Turner (1985) 306.
[32] Turner (1985) 306; Hess (1985) 29. Irwin (1986) 8 objects that Islamic slave soldier systems differed greatly and cannot all be explained by a single factor. But, since Irwin seems to accept that military slavery existed all over the Islamic world and nowhere else, an argument connected with Islam seems to be required. The British use of newly bought and specially trained slaves may be the counterexample Irwin's argument requires.
[33] Ayalon (1977) 6.6.   [34] Ayalon (1977) 10.149.   [35] Keegan (1993) 35.

underwent contributed to their efficiency. The superior military qualities of the people from whom they were recruited – one thinks especially of their familiarity with horses – were another of the reasons for the success of the Mamluks.[36] The lack of Muslim subjects as soldiers was irrelevant; the spread of military slavery was guaranteed by its superiority as a system for winning wars.[37]

The Mamluk system could also work for the political benefit of the ruler. The argument from citizen disillusion seeks to explain the Mamluks by the unwillingness of the Muslim subjects to fight in the army or take part in politics; the argument from the ruler's needs suggests why he might not want his subjects to take part in governing or fighting but rather preferred slave soldiers. For the use of slaves presented internal as well as external advantages: the Mamluks' complete dependence on the sultan made them both safe and useful tools.

Pipes lists four sources of the outstanding loyalty of military slaves: their low status as slaves; their isolation both from their old country and their new home; their position of insecure privilege; and their close identification with their patron.[38] All of these factors kept military slaves from alternative allegiances. The very dishonor in which they were held as slaves made the Mamluks more useful to a ruler than his proud Arab followers.[39] Caliph al-Mahdi defended Mamluk privileges with the following argument:

The mawali deserve such a treatment, for only they combine in themselves the following qualities. When I sit in public audience, I may call a mawla and raise him and seat him by my side, so that his knee will rub my knee. As soon, however, as the audience is over, I may order him to groom my riding animal and he will be content with this and will not take offense. But if I demand the same thing from somebody else he will say: "I am the son of your supporter and intimate associate" or "I am a veteran in your cause" or "I am a son of those who were the first to join your cause."[40]

Absolute rulers often prefer to delegate the power of ruling their realm and impose the necessity of obeying their commands on groups other than their potential rivals in the aristocracy. The

---

[36] Ayalon (1979) 9.55.   [37] Ayalon (1979) 9.56.

[38] Pipes (1981) 89, 184–185. Crone (1980) 74, Patterson (1982) 313, and Hess (1985) 35 make similar arguments. Irwin (1986) 6–7 basically agrees with this list but argues that in practice the Mamluks were no more politically reliable than free soldiers.

[39] Patterson (1982) 311.

[40] In Ayalon (1979) 9.49 and Patterson (1982) 311.

emperor's use of freedmen and *equites* during the principate will come to the mind of classicists. The problem of creating new aristocracies can be avoided if the new administrators can be kept from having families: the use of eunuchs in the Byzantine empire may have resulted from just such a motivation.[41] The natal alienation of Mamluks and exclusive use of first generation Mamluks served just such a purpose. The Mamluks made ideal tools either as administrators or in a strictly military role.

So far the use of slave soldiers seems most similar to the portrayal of Greek tyrants as using slaves and mercenaries because they could not trust their fellow citizens. The function of slave soldiers may be justified both on military and political grounds, but only in a tyrannical and unpopular system of rule.

Hess argues that a political order as violent and illegitimate as such a picture of the Mamluks implies could not have lasted so long. The Mamluks were part of a "underlying structure of great strength" in Islamic politics.[42] The "legend of political failure" is the result of scholars' biases: the agendas of Islamic, Western, and Middle-Eastern scholars have created "a legend of political failure which obscures an appreciation of the stability of Islamic civilization."[43] The withdrawal of Muslims from politics is exaggerated since our evidence primarily reflects the views of religious scholars who refused official positions rather than of the population as a whole.[44]

Although this argument is beyond the competence of this author to judge, the example of the British West Indies regiments (1795–1815) shows that a system of military slavery need not be linked with unstable despotism. After various experiments with the use of slaves acquired from local planters, the British adopted the policy of purchasing newly captured slaves to fight the French. Like the Mamluks the slaves were acquired by the government for specific military purposes. The needs of an insecure or illegitimate ruler played no part in the British decision, which was largely motivated by the belief that Africans fought much better in the tropics – or at least died less often: blacks were thought to be worth three times their number of white troops.[45]

---

[41] Hopkins (1978) 178–197; cf. Patterson (1982) 315–333. Ayalon (1979) 9.50 notes that the eunuchs that occasionally competed with the Mamluks for influence had the same qualities of childless isolation which contributed to their loyalty to their patron.

[42] Hess (1985) 35.   [43] Hess (1985) 39.   [44] Lapidus (1981/82b) 717.

[45] John Vaughan in Buckley (1979) 12.

The "slaves in red-coats" turned out to be extremely successful. Mutinies were no more common among the West Indies regiments than in the British army as a whole – a boisterous organization at this time.[46] Buckley has even argued that a desire to continue recruiting slaves led to a delay in the British abolition of the slave trade.[47]

The systematic use of slave soldiers could be successful both militarily and as a buttress of central power. Some reasons for the success and duration of the system were extrinsic to the notion of slave soldiers. The martial qualities of the peoples from whom the slaves were recruited was a factor in the success of the Mamluks and the West Indies regiments. On the other hand, insofar as the army is a tool of the state, slaves – human tools without outside loyalties – can be considered ideal soldiers.

SLAVES FOR THE CONFEDERACY?

The Confederate debate about arming their slaves to help fight the North is fascinating largely because of the relative abundance of our sources. The concerns of these heated debates evoke many of the issues we have seen in Greek thought about slavery and warfare. Similar arguments may have been used in Athens when the emergency use and emancipation of slaves – such as took place before Arginusae and after Chaeronea – were being discussed. These similarities derive from two sources.

First, the South and Athens share membership in the small circle of true slave societies. They were also similar in the way that a free population with diverse economic interests maintained its tenuous unity by the dichotomy between free and slave. The Confederacy was no Greek city state, but the views expressed about the use of slaves in warfare were solidly in the Athenian tradition.

Second, the South self-consciously patterned itself after classical Greece and Rome. The heyday of neo-Hellenic architecture was the thirty years before the civil war. During this period, apologists for slavery pointed to the example of Athens to show that slavery promoted liberty and equality among the citizens as well as cultural advance.[48] The South's invocation of classical Greece is obvious even in the debates about arming slaves. For example, Major

---

[46] Buckley (1979) 141.   [47] Buckley (1979) 59.   [48] Roberts (1994) 263–264, 273.

General Patrick Cleburne, an early proponent of the policy, headed a host of historical examples with a classical example: "Will the slaves fight? The helots of Sparta stood their masters good stead in battle."[49] Nevertheless, this section will not present a systematic comparison. Similarities will be noted, but the main goal of this section is to provoke the imagination about the debates and arguments we do not have in the Greek historical record, but which are likely to have taken place.

The Confederacy had been using impressed slaves for all sorts of labor necessary for their war effort. This had not occasioned much controversy. By 1864 the South was suffering from inferior manpower, widespread desertion, and increasing Northern incursions. After some individual proposals early in the year, open debate about the use of slaves broke out in the early fall of 1864.

Many felt that, if slaves were actually used to fight, they would need to be promised their freedom. Lee noted that slaves could be given an interest in the issue of the war by "giving immediate freedom to all who enlist, and freedom at the end of the war to the families of those who discharge their duties faithfully (whether they survive or not)."[50]

The outcry against the proposal to arm the slaves came from the racist, ideological concerns which I detail below. In addition, slave owners did not want to give up their valuable property.[51] This concern was unmentionable when hundreds of thousands of non-slave owners were dying for the South and the vastly unpopular "twenty-nigger law" enabled planters to stay home to supervise their slaves.[52] This crude, economic motive may have enabled opposition to arming slaves to prevail until less than one month before the end of the war when the policy was instituted in Virginia – most other states did not cooperate – and a few companies were trained.[53]

The use of slaves was generally admitted, even by advocates of the

[49] Pamphlet of January 2, 1864 signed by General Cleburne and 13 other officers in Durden (1972) 61. The insistence in the final decree of the Confederate Congress that the slaves must volunteer may even derive from Livy, although this stipulation makes practical sense in any case.

[50] Lee to Andrew Hunter in Durden (1972) 209. A factor enabling Sparta's widespread use of Helots appears here too: Lee thought a slave soldier's family would ensure his compliant behavior.

[51] The issue of compensation for slave-owners does not seem to have been stressed, perhaps since the Confederate Government was in no position to offer any.

[52] A. L. Robinson (1980) 291ff.   [53] Durden (1972) 249, 274–275.

measure, to be a last resort whose only advantage was expedience: "a thousand good reasons will be against it; but one imperious consideration will weigh down them all – we shall need men . . . "[54] In the fourth century, Hyperides had claimed that "it was not I who wrote the decree, the battle of Chaeronea did."[55] Southern advocates of state confiscation and emancipation of large numbers of slaves also tread carefully. Even in a society in which three-fourths of the free males owned no slaves, nobody cared to make a positive case for arming and eventually letting slaves go free.

A crucial step in the argument from necessity was implied in the question, "Is it better for the negro to fight for us or against us?"[56] Rather than provoking distrust of slave loyalty, the Northern use of blacks in their army – over 200,000 – was considered a step that needed to be paid back in kind. Lee wrote "I think that the measure is not only expedient but necessary. The enemy will no doubt use them against us if he can get possession of them; and, as his present numerical superiority will enable him to penetrate many parts of the country, I cannot see the wisdom of the policy of holding them to await his arrival."[57] The participation of the slaves was seen as the object of a competition between the North and the South. Just as in the case of the Spartan Helots, the Arginusae slaves, and the Chians freed for the military, an enemy's incitement of slave desertion could prompt rather than discourage the recruitment of slaves.

Despite its advantages, the proposal to arm and free slaves provoked violent outrage. The rabid *Charleston Mercury* went so far as to describe Lee as "an hereditary Federalist, and a disbeliever in the institution of slavery."[58] William W. Holden wrote in his *North Carolina Standard* that to arm slaves would be a "great sin against our slaves, against ourselves, against humanity and against God."[59] One common argument of opponents of arming slaves was that being a soldier was incompatible with being a slave: "You cannot make soldiers of slaves, nor slaves of soldiers."[60] The "negro" was "of all

---

[54] *Charlottesville Chronicle* (reprinted in the *Richmond Sentinel*, December 21, 1864) in Durden (1972) 147.

[55] Hyperides fr. 28 Jensen.

[56] Judah P. Benjamin to Frederick A. Porcher, 21 December 1864 in Durden (1972) 183.

[57] Robert E. Lee to Ethelbert Barksdale, 18 February 1865 in Durden (1972) 206. Similar sentiments were repeated in numerous editorials and letters.

[58] *Charleston Mercury,* 3 February 1865 in Durden (1972) 235–236.

[59] *North Carolina Standard,* 18 October 1864 in Durden (1972) 95.

[60] Howell Cobb to James A. Seddon, 8 January 1865 in Durden (1972) 184.

others the best adapted to slavery, he is therefore of all others the
least adapted for military service."[61] The governor of Georgia
argued that "whenever we establish the fact that they are a military
race, we destroy our whole theory that they are unfit to be free."[62]

These sentiments come out of the view of war as a noble and
liberal profession which could not possibly be practiced by somebody
who deserved to be a slave. This is similar to the contrast in Athens
between the citizen who fights and the cowardly slave. Since the
arming of slaves in the South was usually thought to require their
emancipation, the abhorrence of being "leveled to the equality of
our negroes" was probably exacerbated by racism.[63]

Just as in Thucydides' Athens, the subject of arming slaves was
one to be avoided in the South. Until the final period of the Civil
War it was considered too controversial to discuss. Several papers
found it necessary to apologize for even mentioning the subject: "It
has not hitherto been mentioned . . . because it was a matter to
provoke violent discord of feeling and speech at a period when such
discussion was most undesirable."[64]

The division of the South into slave and free, black and white,
served to unite poor and rich whites whose economic interests were
different and whose doubtful harmony was further threatened by the
conflict, "the rich man's war but the poor man's fight."[65] The
proposal to arm slaves was divisive at a time when unity was
essential. If slaves were armed and freed, planters would be deprived
of their property and the source of their wealth; if they were
reinforced by slaves, non-slave holders would bear less of the burden
of war. On the ideological level, the arming of slaves would have
struck a severe blow to racism in the South, given its emphasis on
military virtues. Racism's unifying force was threatened even by the
suggestion that slaves could be armed.

Even in the South, other views of slavery and the army did not
require the exclusion of slaves from the military or – what good
luck ! – their emancipation. General Francis A. Shoup emphasized

[61] Pamphlet based on speech of Henry C. Chambers, 10 November 1864 in Durden (1972) 142.
[62] Governor Joseph E. Brown of Georgia in Durden (1972) 251.
[63] *Lynchburg Republican*, 2 November 1864 in Durden (1972) 95.
[64] *Richmond Examiner*, 8 November 1864 in Durden (1972) 106. See also *Richmond Dispatch*,
    9 November 1864 (Durden [1972] 111), *Galveston Tri-Weekly News*, 12 December 1864
    (Durden [1972] 119), *Richmond Sentinel*, 2 and 8 November 1864 (Durden [1972] 120).
[65] A. L. Robinson (1980) 282–283; Durden (1972) 23.

that courage was needed only by officers whereas "real soldiers come to have no will of their own, but obey simply because they are ordered by proper authority." Accordingly, he concludes that "the negro is excellently adapted for a soldier."[66] The coincidence of slaves and soldiers in terms of being tools, either of masters or of their officers, is opposite to the usual view of their supposed opposition with respect to courage. Shoup's views are reminiscent of Xenophon's analogy between the command of slaves and command in an army. Both views are decidedly undemocratic in likening common soldiers to slaves.

This discussion has been able to select only a few issues out of many in the debate over the use of slaves by the Confederacy.[67] In many ways, the Southern reaction to the use of slaves in war was similar to that of the Athenians. This was not because of something universal about warfare and slavery, but because both societies, in general, professed an insecure ideal of egalitarianism among free men. This ideal needed to be maintained during the strain of war by adherence in word, if not always in deed, to a rigid distinction between citizen-soldiers and slaves.

CONCLUSION

Conventional wisdom holds that slaves played a very small part in classical Greek warfare. Common sense seems to tells us that chattel slaves, usually non-Greeks held in unwilling bondage, would not fight hard for their city. This seems to find support in a strong link in Greek thought between military service for one's city and rights within it. Elementary logic would seem to forbid the use of slaves, who had almost no rights, in the esteemed field of war.

We have seen that every one of these apparently natural inferences proves upon close inspection to be flawed. Although slaves never replaced the citizen soldier, they played a much more important part than has been generally accepted. In the Persian Wars, in the Peloponnesian Wars, and in various campaigns of the first half of the fourth century slaves and Helots took significant and occasionally decisive parts, either as soldiers, rowers, rebels or deserters. Slaves

---

[66] *Richmond Whig*, 20 February 1865 in Durden (1972) 212–214.

[67] Most conspicuously, I have not dealt at all with the effect that fear of slave revolt had upon the Confederacy (A. L. Robinson [1980]) and with whether the South would have been able to command the loyalty of many slaves with the promise of freedom (Mohr [1974]).

were freed to fight at Marathon. Slaves helped man the Salamis navy. Helots fought and died at Thermopylae and Plataea. In the Peloponnesian War, the campaigns of Brasidas and Pylos turned on the role of Helots. The war was decided by the clash of huge navies, manned in a large part by slaves. Near the beginning of his career Xenophon suggested arming the slaves of the Ten Thousand; at the end of his life he recommended recruiting Athenian mines slaves in case of invasion. Xenophon fought in a Spartan-led army including 3,000 freed Helots and then saw Sparta fade after the liberation of Messenia. The Greeks were much more willing to recruit or incite slaves than they were to talk about the practice.

The vague notion that slaves could not fight for masters whose domination they often hated turns out to be a pious hope.[68] It was no more impossible for slaves to fight for their masters than for resentful slaves to produce profits for their masters in the antebellum South.[69] The modern ideal of fighting for a country or set of beliefs has blinded many scholars to the legion of other motives that have produced effective armies throughout history. Escape from poverty, pride in prowess, hope for advancement or constraint have made as many armies as nationalism or the proverbial stake-in-society.

The ideological link between citizenship and military service is well attested and a large proportion of this work is devoted to detailing its basis and ramifications. The imperative to exclude non-citizens and especially slaves from the military derives from a certain view of the army, of the city, and of the relation between the two. In this ideology the army is conceived of as consisting of equal and interchangeable hoplite-farmers and the citizen body is seen as essentially a unity set in contrast to slaves. Thus an egalitarian army mirrors a citizen body in which every male citizen has equal rights before the law.

But these images of the army and citizen body as homogenous entities were idealizations that aimed at producing unity rather than reflected social reality. For equality before the law at Athens coexisted uneasily with economic differences. Nor was the military

---

[68] Pipes (1981) 27 makes a cursory survey of slave soldiers throughout history and concludes that if slaves were going to turn against their master, they usually did so either before or after a battle. Despite their master's lack of confidence, slaves often fought with vigor and rarely mutinied or deserted.

[69] Stampp (1956); Fogel and Engerman (1974); Fogel (1989).

only a hoplite phalanx. From archaic times, the Athenian army had included the high status cavalry and, from before the Persian Wars, the low status navy. An army which was stratified rather than homogenous could have a place in it for slaves. In fact chattel slaves served in the Athenian navy and Helots in the subordinate rear ranks of the Spartan phalanx.

The military need not even be conceived of as reflecting the citizens. The mercenaries who came into prominence during the period of Xenophon and Thucydides were the tools of the state rather than any reflection of it. What better place for slaves, living tools, than in an army that served exactly this function? So not even in Greek ideology – much less in practice – is the exclusion of slaves from war as simple and obvious as it seems at first.

The subject of slaves in war is a profoundly horrifying one. It combines one of history's worst systems of oppression with the organized mass-murder of war. In practice, the increasing vicious-ness of Greek warfare may have benefited those slaves who were able to run away, revolt, or gain their freedom through military service. Through Theban intervention, Messenia finally gained its freedom from Sparta after ten generations of struggle. The Argi-nusae slaves won a brief Athenian citizenship and the Neodamodeis escaped from Helotage. Nevertheless, the big picture is a grim one. It is hard to rejoice whole-heartedly even with the Chian slaves helping the Athenians ravage their masters' – and their own – plantations.[70] Slaves fighting and dying for the cities of their captivity provide even more bitter contemplation: Helots eager to fight for the Spartans from Sicily to Asia Minor; mine slaves suddenly freed to save Athens at Arginusae.

On the level of ideology, Xenophon's unflinching militarism curbed his elitist tendencies: he condemns the worthless, flabby rich and praises the hardy Persian commons of the *Cyropaedia*. Conversely, Plato and Aristotle make plain elitist dissatisfaction with a society based upon the changeable and difficult ground of military prowess. In the main the ideological legacy of Greece remains pernicious both in its elitist and in its militarist aspects. Plato's philosophers can think pure thoughts, since others, fitted for it, do the work. The superficial pieties of Pericles' appalling funeral oration purify and

---

[70] Compare Southern slaves' anger at Union devastation of their plantations (Genovese [1972] 154).

sanctify death in war. Herodotus, Thucydides, and Xenophon's historical narratives leave much the same taste in the mouth. They systematically play down or omit entirely the role of slaves and Helots in the wars they relate. The baseness of the despised slave and the nobility – however tragic – of patriotic struggle are kept pure.

Bibliography

Abercrombie, N., Hill, S., and Turner, B. S. (1980) *The Dominant Ideology Thesis*. Boston.

Adcock, F. E. (1947) "Epiteichismos in the Archidamian War," *CR* 61: 2–7.

Althusser, L. (1971) *Lenin and Philosophy, and other Essays*, trans. B. Brewster. London.

Amit, M. (1965) *Athens and the Sea: A Study in Athenian Sea Power* (Collection Latomus). Brussels.

Anderson, J. K. (1961) *Ancient Greek Horsemanship*. Berkeley.

(1970) *Military Practice and Theory in the Age of Xenophon*. Berkley.

(1974) *Xenophon*. New York.

(1984) "Hoplites and Heresies: a note," *JHS* 104: 152.

Andreski, S. (1968) *Military Organization and Society*. Berkeley.

Arnim, H. von (1913) ed., *Supplementum Euripideum*. Bonn.

Arnott, G. (1991) "A Lesson from the *Frogs*," *G&R* 38: 18–23.

Ayalon, D. (1977) *Studies on the Mamluks of Egypt*. London.

(1979) *The Mamluk Military Society*. London.

Badian, E. (1993) *From Plataea to Potidaea*. Baltimore.

Barker, E. (1959) *The Political Thought of Plato and Aristotle*. New York.

Barron, J. P. (1986) "Chios in the Athenian Empire," in Boardman and Vaphopoulou-Richardson, edd., *Chios*, 89–103. Oxford.

(1988) "The Liberation of Greece," in J. Boardman, N. Hammond, D. Lewis, M. Ostwald, edd., *Cambridge Ancient History* vol. IV², 592–622. Cambridge.

Beloch, K. J. (1916) *Griechische Geschichte* vol. II.2. Strassburg.

Bernal, M. (1987) *Black Athena* I. New Brunswick, New Jersey.

Best, J. P. (1969) *Thracian Peltasts and their Influence on Greek Warfare*. Groningen.

Betant, E. A. (1961) *Lexicon Thucydideum*, 2 vols. Hildesheim.

Blassingame, J. W. (1979) *The Slave Community*, rev. edn. Oxford.

Boardman, J. (1956) "Delphinion in Chios," *ABSA* 51: 41–54.

Böckh, B. (1886) *Die Staatshaushaltung der Athener* vol. I³. Berlin.

Bosworth, C. E. (1982) Review of *Slave Soldiers and Islam*, by Daniel Pipes, *AHR* 87: 508–509.

Bourdieu, P. (1977) *Outline of a Theory of Practice*, trans. R. Nice. Cambridge.

Bowden, H. (1993) "Hoplites and Homer: Warfare, Hero Cult and the Ideology of the Polis," in J. Rich and G. Shipley, edd., *War and Society in the Greek World*, 45–63. London.

Bradeen, D. W. (1967) "The Athenian Casualty List of 464 BC," *Hesperia* 36: 321–328.

Bradley, K. R. (1987) *Slaves and Masters in the Roman Empire*. Oxford.

(1989) *Slavery and Rebellion in the Roman World 140–70 BC*. Bloomington, Indiana.

(1990) "Servus Onerosus: Roman Law and the Troublesome Slave," *Slavery and Abolition* 11: 135–157.

Breebaart, A. B. (1983) "From Victory to Peace: Some Aspects of Cyrus' State in Xenophon's Cyropaedia," *Mnemosyne* 36: 117–134.

Breitenbach, H. R. (1950) *Historiographische Anschauungsformen Xenophons*. Freiburg.

Bruce, I. A. F. (1967) *An Historical Commentary on the "Hellenica Oxyrhynchia."* London.

Brunt, P. A. (1965) "Spartan Policy and Strategy in the Archidamian War," *Phoenix* 19: 255–280.

(1993) "Aristotle and Slavery," in *Studies in Greek History and Thought*, 343–388. Oxford.

Buckler, J. (1982) "Xenophon's Speeches and the Theban Hegemony," *Athenaeum* n. s. 40: 180–204.

Buckley, R. N. (1979) *Slaves in Red Coats: The British West India Regiments, 1795–1815*. New Haven.

Bugh, R. (1988) *The Horsemen of Athens*. Princeton.

Burn, A. R. (1984) *Persia and the Greeks: the Defense of the West c. 546–478 BC*. Stanford.

Cambiano, G. (1987) "Aristotle and the Anonymous Opponents of Slavery," in M.I. Finley, ed., *Classical Slavery*, 22–39. London.

Cartledge, P. A. (1977) "Hoplites and Heroes: Sparta's Contribution to the Techniques of Ancient Warfare," *JHS* 97: 11–27.

(1979) *Sparta and Lakonia*. London.

(1980) "Euphron and the δοῦλοι again," *LCM* 5.8: 209–211.

(1985) "Rebels and Sambos in Classical Greece: A Comparative View," in P. Cartledge and F. D. Harvey, edd., *Crux: Essays in Greek History Presented to G. E. M. de Ste. Croix*, 16–46. Exeter.

(1987) *Agesilaos and the Crisis of Sparta*. London.

(1988) "Serfdom in Classical Greece," in L. J. Archer, ed., *Slavery and Other Forms of Unfree Labor*, 33–41. London.

(1991) "Richard Talbert's Revision of the Spartan-Helot Struggle: A Reply," *Historia* 40: 379–381.

(1992) Review of *Les Hilotes*, by Jean Ducat., *CPh* 87: 260–263.

(1993a) *The Greeks: A Portrait of Self and Other*. Oxford.

(1993b) "The Silent Women of Thucydides: 2.45.2 Re-Viewed," in R. M.

Rosen and J. Farrell, edd., *Nomodeiktes, Fest. M. Ostwald*, 125–132. Ann Arbor, Michigan.

(1993c) "Like a Worm i' the Bud? A Heterology of Greek Slavery," *G&R* 40: 163–180.

Casson, L. (1966) "Galley Slaves," *TAPhA* 97: 35–44.

(1994) *Ships and Seafaring in Ancient Times*. Austin.

Cawkwell, G. (1963) "Eubulus," *JHS* 83: 47–67.

(1966) "Introduction," in *Xenophon: A History of My Times*, trans. R. Warner, 7–48. Harmondsworth.

(1970) "The Fall of Themistocles," in B. F. Harris, ed., *Auckland Classical Essays presented to E. M. Blaiklock*, 39–58. Oxford.

(1975) "Thucydides' Judgment of Periclean Strategy," *YClS* 24: 53–70.

(1983) "The Decline of Sparta," *CQ* 33: 385–400.

Chambers, J. (1977/78) "On Messenian and Lakonian Helots in the Fifth Century," *The Historian* 40: 271–285.

Chambers, M. (1957) "Thucydides and Pericles," *HSPh*, 79–92.

Chroust, A-H. (1957) *Socrates: Man and Myth: the two Socratic Apologies of Xenophon*. Notre Dame, Indiana.

Cizek, A. (1975) "From the Historical Truth to the Literary Convention: the Life of Cyrus the Great viewed by Herodotus, Ctesias and Xenophon," *AC* 44: 531–552.

Clausewitz, C. von (1968) *On War*, trans. J. Graham. Harmondsworth.

Cogan, M. (1981) *The Human Thing*. Chicago.

Cohen, D. (1989) "Seclusion, Separation, and the Status of Women in Classical Athens," *G&R* 36: 3–15.

Cohen, E. E. (1973) *Ancient Athenian Maritime Courts*. Princeton.

Connor, W. R. (1984) *Thucydides*. Princeton.

(1988) "Early Greek Land Warfare as Symbolic Expression," *P&P* 119: 3–27.

(1994) "The Problem of Athenian Civic Identity," in A. Boegehold and A. Scafuro, edd., *Athenian Identity and Civic Ideology*, 34–44. Baltimore.

Cook, J. M. (1983) *The Persian Empire*. London.

Cornelius, F. (1973) "Pausanias," *Historia* 22: 502–504.

Cornford, F. M. (1907) *Thucydides Mythistoricus*. London.

Crane, G. (1996) *The Blinded Eye: Thucydides and the New Written Word*. London.

Crone, P. (1980) *Slaves on Horses*. Cambridge.

Culler, J. (1982) *On Deconstruction: Theory and Criticism after Structuralism*. Ithaca.

David, E. (1989) "Laughter in Spartan Society," in A. Powell, ed., *Classical Sparta: Techniques behind her Success*, 1–25. London.

Davies, J. K. (1971) *Athenian Propertied Families: 600–300 BC*. Oxford.

Davis, D. B. (1966) *The Problem of Slavery in Western Culture*. Ithaca.

Degler, C. (1959) "Starr on Slavery," *JEH* 19: 271–277.

Delbruck, H. (1975) *History of the Art of War*, trans. W. J. Renfroe. Westport, Connecticut.

Delebecque, E. (1957) *Essai sur la Vie de Xénophon*. Paris.

Delorme, J. (1960) *Gymnasion*. Paris.

Den Boer, W. (1956) "Political Propaganda in Greek Chronology," *Historia* 5: 162–177.

Detienne, M. and Vernant, J. P. (1974) *Cunning Intelligence in Greek Culture and Society*, trans. J. Lloyd. Chicago.

DeVoto, J. G. (1992) "The Theban Sacred Band," *AncW* 23.2: 3–19.

Diels, H. (1903) *Die Fragmente der Vorsokratiker*. Berlin.

Dillery, J. (1995) *Xenophon and the History of His Times*. London.

Dindorf, L. (1857) *Xenophontis Institutio Cyri*. Oxford.

Dobbs, D. (1994) "Natural Right and the Problem of Aristotle's Defense of Slavery," *Journal of Politics* 56: 69–94.

Douglas, M. (1966) *Purity and Danger: An Analysis of the Concepts of Pollution and Taboo*. New York.

Dover, K. J. (1965) *Thucydides' Book VI*. Oxford.

(1972) *Aristophanic Comedy*. Berkeley.

(1973) *Thucydides (Greece and Rome: New Surveys in the Classics* 7). Oxford.

(1974) *Popular Morality in the Time of Plato and Aristotle*. Berkeley.

(1993) *Aristophanes: Frogs*. Oxford.

Dubois, P. (1991) *Torture and Truth*. London.

Ducat, J. (1974) "Le Mépris des Hilotes," *Annales (ESC)* 29:2: 1451–1464.

(1990) *Les Hilotes (BCH* sup. vol. 20). Paris.

Ducrey, P. (1968) *Le Traitement des Prisonniers de Guerre dans la Grèce Antique*. Paris.

Due, B. (1989) *The Cyropaedia: Xenophon's Aims and Methods*. Copenhagen.

Durden, R. F. (1972) *The Gray and the Black*. Baton Rouge.

Dyer, G. (1985) *War*. New York.

Eagleton, T. (1991) *Ideology. An Introduction*. London.

Edmunds, L. (1975) *Chance and Intelligence in Thucydides*. Cambridge, Mass.

(1993) "Thucydides in the Act of Writing," in R. Pretagostini, ed., *Tradizione e innovazione nella cultura greca da Omero all'età ellenistica: Scritti in onore di Bruno Gentili* vol. II. Rome.

Edmunds, L. and Martin, R. (1977) "Thucydides 2.65.8: ἐλευθέρως," *HSPh* 81: 187–193.

Ehrenburg, V. (1951) *The People of Aristophanes*. Oxford.

Ehrhardt, C. (1970) "Xenophon and Diodorus on Aegospotami," *Phoenix* 24: 225–228.

El Fadl, K. A. (1990) "Ahkam Al Bughat: Irregular Warfare and the Law of Rebellion in Islam," in J. T. Turner and J. Kelsay, edd., *Cross, Crescent and Sword: The Justification and Limitation of War in Western and Islamic Tradition*, 149–176. New York.

Evans, J. A. S. (1982) *Herodotus*. Boston.

(1991) *Herodotus: Explorer of the Past*. Princeton.

Ewbank, L. (1982) *Plutarch's Use of non-literary Sources in the "Lives" of Sixth- and Fifth-Century Greeks*. Ph.D. diss., University of North Carolina at Chapel Hill.

Farber, J. J. (1979) "The Cyropaedia and Hellenistic Kingship," *AJPh* 100: 497–514.

Farrar, C. (1988) *The Origins of Democratic Thinking*. Cambridge.

Fehling, D. (1989) *Herodotus and His "Sources,"* trans. by J. G. Howie. Liverpool.

Ferrill, A. (1985) *The Origins of War: From the Stone Age to Alexander the Great*. London.

Figueira, T. J. (1984) "Mess Contributions and Subsistence at Sparta," *TAPhA* 114: 87–109.

   (1986) "Population patterns in Late Archaic and Classical Sparta," *TAPhA* 116: 165–213.

Finley, J. H. (1963) *Thucydides*. Ann Arbor.

Finley, M. I. (1980) *Ancient Slavery and Modern Ideology*. New York.

   (1982a) "Was Greek Civilization based on Slave Labor?" in B. Shaw and R. Saller, edd., *Economy and Society in Ancient Greece*, 97–115. New York.

   (1982b) "Sparta and Spartan Society," in B. Shaw and R. Saller, edd., *Economy and Society in Ancient Greece*, 24–40. New York.

   (1982c) "The Freedom of the Citizen in the Greek World," in B. Shaw and R. Saller, edd., *Economy and Society in Ancient Greece*, 77–94. New York.

   (1982d) "The Slave Trade in Antiquity: The Black Sea and Danubian Regions," in B. Shaw and R. Saller, edd., *Economy and Society in Ancient Greece*, 167–175. New York.

   (1982e) "Debt-Bondage and the Problem of Slavery," in B. Shaw and R. Saller, edd., *Economy and Society in Ancient Greece*, 150–166. New York.

   (1982f) "Between Slavery and Freedom," in B. Shaw and R. Saller, edd., *Economy and Society in Ancient Greece*, 116–132. New York.

   (1982g) "Land Debt and the Man of Property in Classical Athens," in B. Shaw and R. Saller, edd., *Economy and Society in Ancient Greece*, 62–76. New York.

   (1985) *The Ancient Economy*. Berkeley.

Fisher, N. R. E. (1989) "Drink, Hybris and the Promotion of Harmony in Sparta," in A. Powell, ed., *Classical Sparta: Techniques behind her Success*, 26–50. London.

Flory, S. (1987) *The Archaic Smile of Herodotus*. Detroit.

Fogel, R. W. (1989) *Without Consent or Contract: the Rise and Fall of American Slavery*. New York.

Fogel, R. W. and S. Engerman (1974) *Time on the Cross*. Boston.

Fornara, C. W. (1971) *Herodotus: An Interpretive Essay*. Oxford.

Forrest, W. G. (1960) "Themistokles and Argos," *CQ* n. s. 10: 221–241.

   (1968) *A History of Sparta: 950–192 BC* London.

Foucault, M. (1980) *Knowledge/Power*, trans. C. Gordon. Brighton.

   (1990) *The History of Sexuality* vol. II: *The Use of Pleasure*, trans. R. Hurley. New York.

Foxhall, L. (1993) "Farming and Fighting in ancient Greece," in J. Rich and G. Shipley, edd., *War and Society in the Greek World*, 134–145. London.

Frazer, J. G. (1965) *Pausanias's Description of Greece*, 6 vols. New York.

Fredrickson, G. M. and Lasch, C. (1971) "Resistance to Slavery," in A. J. Lane, ed., *The Debate over Slavery: Stanley Elkins and his Critics*, 223–244. Chicago.

Freeman, E. A. (1892) *The History of Sicily from the Earliest Times*. Oxford.

Fuks, M. (1984) "Slave War and Slave Troubles in Chios," in *Social Conflict in Ancient Greece*, 260–269. Leiden.

Funke, P. (1980) *Homónoia und Arché*. Wiesbaden.

Gabriel, R. A. and Metz, K. S. (1991) *From Sumer to Rome: the Military Capabilities of Ancient Armies*. New York.

Gabrielsen, V. (1994) *Financing the Athenian Fleet: Public Taxation and Social Relations*. Baltimore.

Gallant, T. W. (1991) *Risk and Survival in Ancient Greece: Reconstructing the Rural Domestic Economy*. Cambridge.

Gagarin, M. (1996) "The Torture of Slaves in Athenian Law," *CPh* 91: 1–18.

Garlan, Y. (1972) "Les Esclaves Grecs en Temps de Guerre," in *Actes de Colloque d'Histoire Sociale 1970 (Besançon)*, 29–62. Paris.

(1974a) "Quelques Travaux Récents sur les Esclaves Grecs en Temps de Guerre," in *Actes de Colloque d'Histoire Sociale 1972 (Besançon)*, 15–28. Paris.

(1974b) *Recherches de Poliorcétique Grecque*. Paris.

(1975) *War in the Ancient World*, trans. J. Lloyd. London.

(1987) "War, Piracy and Slavery in the Greek World," in M. I. Finley, ed., *Classical Slavery*, 7–21. London.

(1988) *Slavery in Ancient Greece*, trans. J. Lloyd. Ithaca.

(1989) *Guerre et économie en grèce ancienne*. Paris.

(1995) "War and Peace," in J.-P. Vernant, ed., *The Greeks*, trans. C. Lambert and T. Fagan, 53–85. Chicago.

Garnsey, P. (1996) *Ideas of Slavery from Aristotle to Augustine*. Cambridge.

Garver, E. (1994) "Aristotle's Natural Slaves: Incomplete Praxeis and Incomplete Human Beings," *JHPh* 32: 173–195.

Gauthier, P. (1976) *Un Commentaire Historique des Poroi de Xenophon*. Paris.

Gay, P. (1974) *Style in History*. New York.

Geertz, C. (1973a) "Ethos, World View and the Interpretation of Sacred Symbols," in Geertz, ed., *The Interpretation of Cultures*, 126–141. New York.

(1973b) "Ideology as a Cultural System," in Geertz, ed., *The Interpretation of Cultures*, 193–233. New York.

(1973c) "After the Revolution: the Fate of Nationalism in the New States," in Geertz, ed., *The Interpretation of Cultures*, 235–254. New York.

Genovese, E. D. (1971) "Rebelliousness and Docility in the Negro Slave: a Critique of the Elkins Thesis," in A. J. Lane, ed., *The Debate over Slavery: Stanley Elkins and his Critics*, 43–74. Chicago.

(1972) *Roll Jordan Roll.* New York.

(1979) *From Rebellion to Revolution.* Baton Rouge.

Georges, P. (1994) *Barbarian Asia and the Greek Experience: From the Archaic Period to the Age of Xenophon.* Baltimore.

Gera, D. L. (1993) *Xenophon's Cyropaedia: Style, Genre and Literary Technique.* Oxford.

Gill, C. (1995) *Greek thought.* Oxford.

Golden, M. (1984) "Slavery and Homosexuality at Athens," *Phoenix* 38: 308–324.

(1985) "Pais, 'Child' and 'Slave'," *AC* 54: 91–104.

Goldhill, S. (1990) "The Great Dionysia and Civic Ideology," in J. Winkler and F. Zeitlin, edd., *Nothing to Do with Dionysus*, 97–129. Princeton.

Gomme, A. W. (1933) *The Population of Athens in the Fifth and Fourth Centuries* BC. Oxford.

Gomme, A. W., Andrewes, A., Dover, K. J. (1956–1981) *Historical Commentary on Thucydides*, 5 vols. Oxford.

Goodman, M. D. and Holladay, A. J. (1986) "Religious Scruples in Ancient Warfare," *CQ* 36: 151–171.

Gould, J. (1989) *Herodotus.* New York.

Graham, A. J. (1992) "Thucydides 7.13.2 and the Crews of Athenian Triremes," *TAPhA* 122: 257–270.

Gray, V. J. (1985) "Xenophon's Cynegeticus," *Hermes* 113: 156–172.

(1989) *The Character of Xenophon's "Hellenica."* London.

Green, P. (1970) *Armada from Athens.* Garden City, New Jersey.

(1970) *Xerxes at Salamis.* New York.

Greenhalgh, P. A. L. (1973) *Early Greek Warfare: Horsemen and Chariots in the Homeric and Archaic Ages.* Cambridge.

Griffin, J. (1987) *Homer. The Odyssey.* Cambridge.

Grote, G. (1848) *History of Greece* vol. V. New York.

Grundy, G. B. (1901) *The Great Persian War.* London.

(1908) "The Population and Policy of Sparta in the Fifth Century," *JHS* 28: 77–96.

(1911) *Thucydides and the History of his Age.* London.

Guthrie, W. K. C. (1969) *A History of Greek Philosophy*, vol. III. Cambridge.

Gutman, H. (1976) *The Black Family in Slavery and Freedom: 1750–1925.* New York.

Haarmann, U. (1982) Review of *Slave Soldiers and Islam*, by Daniel Pipes, *Religious Studies Review* 8: 392.

Habicht, C. (1985) *Pausanias' Guide to Ancient Greece.* Berkeley.

Hall, E. (1993) "Asia Unmanned: Images of Victory in Classical Athens," in J. Rich and G. Shipley, edd., *War and Society in the Greek World*, 108–133. London.

Halperin, D. M. (1990) "The Democratic Body: Prostitution and Citizenship in Classical Athens," in David Halperin, ed., *One Hundred Years of Homosexuality*, 88–112. London.

Hamilton, C. D. (1991) *Agesilaus and the Failure of Spartan Hegemony*. Ithaca.

Hammond, N. G. L. (1988) "The Expedition of Xerxes," in J. Boardman, N. Hammond, D. Lewis, M. Ostwald, edd., *Cambridge Ancient History* vol. IV², 518–591. Cambridge.

(1992) "Plataea's relations with Thebes, Sparta and Athens," *JHS* 112: 143–150.

Hansen, M. H. (1985) *Demography and Democracy*. Denmark.

(1991) *The Athenian Democracy in the Age of Demosthenes*. Oxford.

(1993) "The Battle Exhortation in Ancient Historiography," *Historia* 42: 161–180.

(1994) "The Number of Athenian Citizens secundum Sekunda," *EMC* n. s. 13: 299–310.

Hanson, V. D. (1983) *Warfare and Agriculture in Classical Greece*. Pisa.

(1989) *The Western Way of War*. New York.

(1991a) "The Ideology of Hoplite Battle Ancient and Modern," in V. Hanson, ed., *Hoplites: The Classical Greek Battle Experience*, 3–11. London.

(1991b) "Hoplite Technology in Phalanx Battle," in V. Hanson, ed., *Hoplites: The Classical Greek Battle Experience*, 63–84. London.

(1992) "Thucydides and the Desertion of Attic Slaves during the Decelean War," *ClAnt* 11: 209–228.

(1995) *The Other Greeks: The Family Farm and the Agrarian Roots of Western Civilization*. New York.

Harder, M. A. (1985) *Euripides' Kresphontes and Archelaos*. Leiden.

Hardy, W. G. (1926) "The Hellenica Oxyrhynchia and the Devastation of Attica," *CPh 21*: 346–355.

Harris, M. (1971) "The Myth of the Friendly Master," in A. J. Lane, ed., *The Debate over Slavery: Stanley Elkins and his Critics*, 191–209. Chicago.

(1977) *Cannibals and Kings*. New York.

(1979) *Cultural Materialism: The Struggle for a Science of Culture*. New York.

Hartog, F. (1988) *The Mirror of Herodotus*, trans. J. Lloyd. Berkeley.

Harvey, F. D. (1981) Review of *The Athenian Navy*, by B. Jordan, *CR* n. s. 31: 83–87.

(1988) "Herodotus and the Man-Footed Creature," in L. J. Archer, ed., *Slavery and Other Forms of Unfree Labor*, 42–52. London.

Havelock, E. A. (1957) *The Liberal Temper in Greek Politics*. New Haven.

(1972) "Heroism and History," in E. Gareau, ed., *Valeurs Antiques et Temps Modernes*, 19–52. Ottawa.

Heath, M. (1990) "Thucydides' Political Judgement," *LCM* 15.10: 158–160.

Henderson, B. W. (1927) *The Great War between Athens and Sparta*. London.

Henderson, J. (1987) *Aristophanes, Lysistrata*. Oxford.

Henry, W. P. (1967) *Greek Historical Writing: A Historiographical Essay Based on Xenophon's Hellenica*. Chicago.

Herington, J. (1991) 'The Closure of Herodotus' Histories', *ICS* 16: 149–160.

230   *Bibliography*

Hess, A. C. (1985) "Islamic Civilization and the Legend of Political Failure," *JNES* 44: 27–39.

Higgins, W. E. (1977) *Xenophon the Athenian*. Albany.

Hignett, C. (1963) *Xerxes' Invasion of Greece*. Oxford.

Himmelmann, N. (1971) *Archäologisches zum Problem der griechischen Sklaverei*. Mainz.

Hirsch, S. W. (1985) *The Friendship of the Barbarians: Xenophon and the Persian Empire*. Hanover.

Hodkinson, S. (1983) "Social Order and the Conflict of Values in Classical Sparta," *Chiron* 13: 239–281.

(1986) "Land Tenure and Inheritance in Classical Sparta," *CQ* 36: 378–406.

(1989) "Inheritance, Marriage and Demography: Perspectives upon the Success and Decline of Classical Sparta," in A. Powell, ed., *Classical Sparta: Techniques behind her Success*, 79–121. London.

Holden, H. A. (1887–1890) *The Cyropaedia of Xenophon with Introduction and Notes*, 4 vols. Cambridge.

Holladay, A. J. (1978) "Athenian Strategy in the Archidamian War," *Historia* 27: 400–427.

(1982) "Hoplites and Heresies," *JHS* 102: 94–103.

Holwerda, D. (1977) *Prolegomena de Comoedia; Scholia in Acharnenses, Equites, Nubes* vol. III.1. Groningen.

Hooker, J. T. (1980) *The Ancient Spartans*. London.

(1989) "Spartan Propaganda," in A. Powell, ed., *Classical Sparta: Techniques behind her Success*, 122–141. London.

Hopkins, K. (1967) "Slavery in Classical Antiquity," in A. de Rueck and J. Knight, edd., *Caste and Race*, 166–177. London.

(1978) *Conquerors and Slaves*. Cambridge.

(1989) *Death and Renewal*. Cambridge.

Hornblower, S. (1983) *The Greek World, 479–323*. London.

(1987) *Thucydides*. London.

(1991) *A Commentary on Thucydides* vol. I. Oxford.

(1994) "Narratology and Narrative Technique in Thucydides," in S. Hornblower, ed., *Greek Historiography*, 131–166. Oxford.

How, W. W. and Wells, J. (1912) *A Commentary on Herodotus* vol. II. Oxford.

Howard, M. (1991) *The Lessons of History*. New Haven.

Hude, K. (1927) ed., *Scholia in Thucydidem ad optimos codices collata*. Leipzig.

Hunt, P. (1994) Slaves and Soldiers in Classical Ideologies. Ph.D. diss., Stanford University.

(1997) "Helots at the Battle of Plataea," *Historia* 46.2: 129–144.

Hunter, V. J. (1973) *Thucydides, the Artful Reporter*. Toronto.

(1994) *Policing Athens: Social Control in the Attic Lawsuits, 420–320 BC*. Princeton.

Imber, M. (1995) Cops, Robbers and Democratic Ideology. Paper presented at 127th Annual Meeting of the American Philological Association. San Diego.

Immerwahr, H. R. (1966) *Form and Thought in Herodotus*. Cleveland.

Irwin, R. (1986) *The Middle East in the Middle Ages: The Early Mamluk Sultanate 1250–1382*. Carbondale, Illinois.

Jackson, A. H. (1970) "Some Recent Work on the Treatment of Prisoners of War in Ancient Greece," *Talanta* 2: 37–53.

— (1991) "Hoplites and the Gods: The Dedication of Captured Arms and Armour," in V. Hanson, ed., *Hoplites: The Classical Greek Battle Experience*, 228–249. London.

Jacob, O. (1928) *Les Esclaves Publiques à Athènes*. Liège.

Jaeger, W. (1944) *Paideia: The Ideals of Greek Culture vol. III*. New York.

Jameson, F. (1981) *The Political Unconscious: Narrative as a Socially Symbolic Act*. Ithaca.

Jameson, M. H. (1963) "The Provisions for Mobilization in the Decree of Themistocles," *Historia* 12: 385–404.

— (1977) "Agriculture and Slavery in Classical Athens," *CJ* 73: 122–141.

— (1980) "Apollo Lukeios in Athens," *Archaiognosia* 1: 213–136.

— (1990) "Space in the Greek City State," in S. Kent, ed., *Domestic Architecture and the Use of Space: An interdisciplinary cross-cultural study*, 92–113. Cambridge.

— (1991) "Sacrifice before Battle," in V. Hanson, ed., *Hoplites: The Classical Greek Battle Experience*, 197–227. London.

— (1992) "Agricultural Labor in Ancient Greece," in B. Wells ed., *Proceedings of the Seventh International Symposium at the Swedish Institute at Athens*, 135–146. Stockholm.

— (forthcoming) *Halieis I.*

Jeffery, L. H. (1949) "Comments on Some Archaic Greek Inscriptions," *JHS* 69: 25–38.

Jensen, C. (1917) ed., *Hyperidis orationes sex*. Leipzig.

Johnson, D. H. (1988) "Sudanese Military Slavery from the Eighteenth to the Twentieth Century," in L. J. Archer, ed., *Slavery and Other Forms of Unfree Labor*, 142–156. London.

Johnson, M. (1989) "Runaway Slaves and the Slave Communities in South Carolina," in P. Finckelman, ed., *Rebellions, Resistance and Runaways within the Slave South*, 230–253. New York.

Johnston, S. (1994) "Virtuous toil, Vicious Work: Xenophon on Aristocratic Style," *CPh* 89: 219–240.

Jones, A. H. M. (1957) *Athenian Democracy*. Oxford.

— (1956) "Slavery in the Ancient World," *Economic History Review*, 2nd ser. 9: 185–199.

Jordan, B. (1975) *The Athenian Navy in the Classical Period*. Berkeley.

— (1990) "The Ceremony of the Helots in Thucydides IV, 80," *AC* 59: 37–69.

Just, R. (1989) *Women in Athenian Law and Life*. London.

232   *Bibliography*

Kagan, D. (1969) *The Outbreak of the Peloponnesian War.* Ithaca.
  (1974) *The Archidamian War.* Ithaca.
  (1987) *The Fall of the Athenian Empire.* Ithaca.
Kahrstedt, U. (1922) *Griechische Staatsrecht* vol. I. Göttingen.
Kallet-Marx, L. (1993) *Money Expense and Naval Power in Thucydides' History 1–5.24.* Berkeley.
Keegan, J. (1993) *A History of Warfare.* New York.
Kelly, T. (1976) *A History of Argos to 500 BC.* Minneapolis.
  (1979) "Peloponnesian Naval Strength and Sparta's Plans for Waging War against Athens in 431 BC," *Alter Orient und Altes Testament* 203: 245–255.
Kelsey, F. and A. Zenos. (1956) *Xenophon, Anabasis I–IV.* Boston.
Konstan, D. (1987) "Persians, Greeks, and Empire," *Arethusa* 20: 59–73.
Knight, D. W. (1970) "Thucydides and the War Strategy of Perikles," *Mnemosyne* n. s. 4.23: 150–161.
Krentz, P. (1980) "Foreigners against the Thirty: *IG* II²10 Again," *Phoenix* 34: 298–306.
  (1982) *The Thirty at Athens.* Ithaca.
  (1989) *Xenophon, Hellenica I–II.3.10.* Warminster.
  (1995) *Xenophon, Hellenica II.3.11–IV.2.8.* Warminster.
Krentz, P. and Wheeler, E. L. (1994) edd. and trans. *Polyaenus: Stratagems of War,* 2 vols. Chicago.
Kromayer, J. and G. Veith (1928) edd. *Heerwesen und Kriegführung.* Munich.
Kurke, L. (1992) "The Politics of ἀβροσύνη in Archaic Greece," *Classical Antiquity* 11.1: 91–120.
Laing, D. R. (1966) *A New Interpretation of the Athenian Naval Catalogue IG II² 1951.* Ann Arbor.
Lamb, W. R. M. (1914) *Clio Enthroned: A Study of Prose-Form in Thucydides.* Cambridge.
Lane, A. (1971) ed., *The Debate over Slavery: Stanley Elkins and His Critics.* Chicago.
Lapidus, I. M. (1981/82a) Review of *Slaves on Horses,* by Patricia Crone. *Journal of Interdisciplinary History* 12: 560–563.
  (1981/82b) Review of *Slave Soldiers and Islam,* by Daniel Pipes. *Journal of Interdisciplinary History* 12: 716–718.
Lateiner, D. (1989) *The Historical Method of Herodotus.* Toronto.
Lauffer, S. (1979) *Die Bergwerksklaven von Laurion.* Wiesbaden.
Lawton, C. (1995) *Attic Document Reliefs: Art and Politics in Ancient Athens.* Oxford.
Lazenby, J. F. (1978) *Hannibal's War.* Warminster.
  (1985) *The Spartan Army.* Warminster.
  (1991) "The Killing Zone," in V. Hanson, ed., *Hoplites: The Classical Greek Battle Experience ,* 87–109. London.
  (1993) *The Defense of Greece: 490–479 BC.* Warminster.
Lengauer, W. (1979) *Greek Commanders in the 5th and 4th Centuries BC: A Study of Militarism.* Warsaw.

Levy, E. (1974) "Les Esclaves Chez Aristophanes," in *Actes de Colloque d'Histoire Sociale 1972 (Besançon)*, 29–46. Paris.

Lévi-Strauss, C. (1963) *Structural Anthropology*, trans. C. Jacobson and B. G. Schoepf. New York.

Levy, R. (1997) "Purity/Pollution," in Barfield, T. J. ed., *Blackwell Dictionary of Anthropology*. Oxford.

Lewis, D. M. (1977) *Sparta and Persia*. Leiden.

(1992a) "The Archidamian War," in D. Lewis, J. Boardman, J. Davies, and M. Ostwald, edd., *The Cambridge Ancient History* vol. V², 370–432. Cambridge.

(1992b) "Mainland Greece 479–451 BC," in D. Lewis, J. Boardman, J. Davies, and M. Ostwald, edd., *The Cambridge Ancient History* vol. V², 96–120. Cambridge.

(1992c) "The Thirty Years' Peace," in D. Lewis, J. Boardman, J. Davies, and M. Ostwald, edd., *The Cambridge Ancient History* vol. V², 121–146. Cambridge.

Lichtenstein, A. (1989) " 'That Disposition to Theft, with which They have been branded': Moral Economy, Slave Management, and the Law," in P. Finckelman, ed., *Rebellions, Resistance and Runaways within the Slave South*, 255–282. New York.

Lintott, A. W. (1981) *Violence, Civil Strife and Revolution in the Classical City, 750–330 BC*. Baltimore.

Little, D. P. (1982) Review of *Slaves on Horses*, by Patricia Crone. *Religious Studies Review* 8.3: 299.

Littman, R. J. (1968) "The Strategy of the Battle of Cyzicus," *TAPhA* 99: 265–272.

Lloyd, G. E. R. (1966) *Polarity and Analogy*. Cambridge.

(1990) *Demystifying Mentalities*. Cambridge.

Loraux, N. (1986) *The Invention of Athens: The Funeral Oration in the Classical City*, trans. A. Sheridan. Cambridge, Mass.

Losada, L. A. (1972) *The Fifth Column in the Peloponnesian War*. Leiden, Netherlands.

Lotze, D. (1959) *Metaxy eleutheron kai doulon*. Berlin.

(1970) "Selbstwusstsein und Machtpolitik," *Klio* 52: 255–275.

Luccioni, J. (1948) *Les Idées politiques et sociales de Xénophon*. Orphys.

Macan, R. W. (1895) *Herodotus 4–6*. 2 vols. London.

(1908) *Herodotus 7–9*. 2 vols. London.

MacDowell, D. M. (1978) *The Law in Classical Athens*. Ithaca.

Mactoux, M.-M. (1980) *Douleia: Esclavage et Pratique Discursive dans L'Athènes Classique* (Annales Littéraires de L'Université de Besançon 250). Paris.

Malkin, I. (1994) *Myth and Territory in the Spartan Mediterranean*. Cambridge.

Manville, P. B. (1990) *The Origins of Citizenship in Ancient Athens*. Princeton.

Marchant, E. C. (1900–1920) *Xenophontis Opera Omnia*. 5 vols. Oxford.

McKechnie, P. (1988) *Hellenica Oxyrhynchia*. Warminster.

(1989) *Outsiders in the Greek Cities of the 4th Century*. London.

McNeill, W. H. (1995) *Keeping Together in Time: Dance and Drill in Human History*. Cambridge, Mass.

Meier, C. (1990a) "Die Rolle des Krieges im Klassischen Athen," *HZ* 251: 555–605.

(1990b) *The Greek Discovery of Politics*, trans. D. McLintock. Cambridge, Mass.

Meiggs, R. and Lewis, D. (1988) *Selection of Greek Historical Inscriptions to the end of the Fifth Century* BC, rev. edn. Oxford.

(1972) *The Athenian Empire*. Oxford.

Meyer, E. (1892) *Forschungen zur Alten Geschichte*. Halle.

Miller, M. (1970) *The Sicilian Colony Dates*. Albany.

Millett, P. (1993) "Warfare, Economy, and Democracy in classical Athens," in J. Rich and G. Shipley, edd., *War and Society in the Greek World*, 177–196. London.

Mohr, C. L. (1974) "Southern Blacks in the Civil War: A Century of Historiography," *Journal of Negro History* 59: 177–195.

Moles, J. (1992) Review of *The Character of Xenophon's Hellenica*, by Vivienne Gray. *CR* 42: 281–284.

Momigliano. (1944) "Sea-Power in Greek Thought," *CR* 58: 1–7.

(1990) *The Classical Foundations of Modern Historiography*. Berkeley.

Moore, J. M. (1975) ed., *Aristotle and Xenophon on Democracy and Oligarchy*. Berkeley.

Morris, I. (1987) *Burial and Ancient Society: the Rise of the Greek City*. Cambridge.

(1994) "Everyman's Grave," in A. Boegehold and A. Scafuro, edd., *Athenian Identity and Civic Ideology*, 67–101. Baltimore.

Morrison, J. S. (1984) "Hyperesia in Naval Contexts in the Fifth and Fourth Centuries BC," *JHS* 104: 48–59.

Morrison, J. S. and Coats, J. F. (1986) *The Athenian Trireme*. Cambridge.

Morrow, G. R. (1939) "Plato and Greek Slavery," *Mind* 47:186–201.

(1960) *Plato's Cretan City: A Historical Interpretation of the Laws*. Princeton.

Mossé, C. (1985) "La Role Politique des Armées dans le monde Grec à l'époque classique," in P. Vernant, ed., *Problèmes de la Guerre en Grèce ancienne*, 221–229. Paris.

Munn, M. (1993) *The Defense of Attica*. Berkeley.

Munro, J. A. R. (1904) "Some Observations on the Persian Wars 3: The Campaign of Plataea," *JHS* 24: 144–165.

Murray, O. (1980) *Early Greece*. Glasgow.

Nichols, M. P. (1983) "The Good Life, Slavery, and Acquisition: Aristotle's Introduction to Politics," *Interpretation* 11: 171–183.

Nickel, R. (1979) *Xenophon*. Darmstadt.

Nightingale, A. (1995) *Genres in Dialogue: Plato and the Construct of Philosophy*. Cambridge.

Notopoulos, J. A. (1941) "The Slaves at the Battle of Marathon," *AJPh* 62: 352–354.

Nussbaum, G. (1959) "The Captains of the Ten Thousand." *C&M* 20: 16–29.

(1967) *The Ten Thousand: A Study in Social Organization and Action in Xenophon's Anabasis.* Leiden.

Ober, J. (1985a) *Fortress Attica.* Leiden.

(1985b) "Thucydides, Pericles and the Strategy of Defense," in J. W. Eadie and J. Ober, edd., *The Craft of the Ancient Historian,* 171–188. Lanham, Maryland.

(1989) *Mass and Elite in Democratic Athens: Rhetoric, Ideology and the Power of the People.* Princeton.

(1991) "Hoplites and Obstacles," in V. Hanson, ed., *Hoplites: The Classical Greek Battle Experience,* 173–196. London.

(1994) "The Rules of War in Classical Greece (ca. 600–300 BC)," in G. Andreopoulos, M. Howard, and M. Shulman, edd., *The Laws of War: Constraints on Warfare in the Western World,* 12–26. New Haven.

Ochberg, F. (1978) "The Victim of Terrorism: Psychiatric Considerations," *Terrorism* 1: 147–168.

Oliva, P. (1971) *Sparta and her Social Problems.* Amsterdam.

Ollier, F. (1934) *Xénophon: La République des Lacédémoniens.* Lyon.

Orwin, C. (1994) *The Humanity of Thucydides.* Princeton.

Osborne, M. J. (1981) *Naturalization at Athens.* Brussels.

Osborne, R. (1995) "The Economics and Politics of Slavery at Athens," in A. Powell, ed., *The Greek World,* 27–43. London.

Ostwald, M. (1986) *From Popular Sovereignty to the Sovereignty of Law.* Berkeley.

(1991) "Herodotus and Athens," *ICS* 16:137–148.

Parke, H. W. (1930) "The Development of the Second Spartan Empire (405–371 BC)," *JHS* 50: 37–79.

(1933) *Greek Mercenary Soldiers.* Oxford.

Parker, R. (1989) "Spartan Religion," in A. Powell, ed., *Classical Sparta: Techniques behind her Success,* 142–172. London.

Parker, V. (1993) "Some Dates in Early Spartan History," *Klio* 75: 45–60.

Patterson, O. (1971) "Quashee," in A. J. Lane, ed., *The Debate over Slavery: Stanley Elkins and his Critics,* 210–219. Chicago.

(1982) *Slavery and Social Death.* Cambridge, Mass.

(1991) *Freedom in the Making of Western Culture.* New York.

Pearson, L. (1962) "The Pseudo-History of Messenia and its Authors," *Historia* 11: 397–426.

Pease, S. J. (1933–4) "Xenophon's Cyropaedia: the Compleat General," *CJ*: 436–440.

Pipes, D. (1981) *Slave Soldiers and Islam: The Genesis of a Military System.* New Haven.

(1986) Review of *Slaves on Horses: The Evolution of the Islamic Polity,* by Patricia Crone. *JNES* 45.2: 165–167.

Pohlenz, M. (1966) *Freedom in Greek Life and Thought: The History of an Ideal.* Dordrecht, Holland.

Pomeroy, S. B. (1975) *Goddesses, Whores, Wives, and Slaves.* New York.

(1994) *Xenophon, Oeconomicus: A Social and Historical Commentary.* Oxford.

Poole, W. (1994) "Euripides and Sparta," in A. Powell and S. Hodkinson, edd., *The Shadow of Sparta,* 127–181. London.

Pope, M. (1988) "Thucydides and Democracy," *Historia* 37: 276–296.

Popper, K. R. (1966) *The Open Society and Its Enemies* vol. I, 5th rev. edn. Princeton.

Porzio, G. (1898) "Gli Schiavi nelle Milizie dal principio della guerra Peloponnesiaca sino alla battaglia di Mantinea (432–362 a. C.)," *RFIC* 26: 564–585.

Powell, A. (1989) "Mendacity and Sparta's Use of the Visual," in A. Powell, ed., *Classical Sparta: Techniques behind her Success,* 173–192. London.

(1994) "Plato and Sparta: modes of rule and of non-rational persuasion in the *Laws,*" in A. Powell and S. Hodkinson edd., *The Shadow of Sparta,* 273–321. London.

Powell, J. E. (1966) *A Lexicon to Herodotus.* 2nd edn. Hildesheim.

Pritchett, W. K. (1956) "The Attic Stelai, Part II," *Hesperia* 25: 178–317.

(1957) "New Light on Plataea," *AJA* 61: 9–28.

(1965) "Plataea Revisited," in *Studies in Ancient Greek Topography 1,* 103–121. Berkeley.

(1971–1991) *The Greek State at War,* 5 vols. Berkeley.

(1985) "The Topography of Tyrtaios and the Messenian Wars," in *Studies in Ancient Greek Topography 5,* 1–68. Berkeley.

(1993) *The Liar School of Herodotus.* Amsterdam.

Proietti, G. (1987) *Xenophon's Sparta.* Leiden.

Quinn, T. J. (1981) *Athens and Samos, Lesbos and Chios: 478–404 BC.* Manchester.

Raaflaub, K. A. (1983) "Democracy, Oligarchy and the Concept of the 'Free Citizen' in Late Fifth-Century Athens," *Political Theory* 11.4: 517–544.

(1985) *Die Entdeckung der Freiheit.* Munich.

(1987) "Herodotus, Political Thought and the Meaning of History," *Arethusa* 20: 221–248.

Randall, R. H. (1953) "The Erechtheum Workmen," *AJA* 57: 199–210.

Raubitschek, A. E. (1941) "The Heroes of Phyle," *Hesperia* 10: 284–295.

Rawlings, H. (1981) *The Structure of Thucydides' History.* Princeton.

Rawlinson, G. (1880) *The History of Herodotus.* 6 vols. London.

Redfield, J. (1985) "Herodotus the Tourist," *CPh* 80: 97–118.

Rhodes, P. J. (1987) "Thucydides on the Causes of the Peloponnesian War," *Hermes* 115: 154–165.

(1994) "In Defence of the Greek Historians," *G&R* 41: 156–171.

(1995) "The Acephalous Polis," *Historia* 44: 153–167.

Ridley, R. (1979) "The Hoplite as Citizen: Athenian Military Institutions in their Social Context," *AC*: 508–548.

Rihll, T. (1993) "War, Slavery and Settlement in Early Greece," in J. Rich and G. Shipley, edd., *War and Society in the Greek World*, 77–107. London.

Robert, L. (1935) "Sur des Inscriptions de Chios," *BCH* 59 (1935): 453–470.

Roberts, J. T. (1994) *Athens on Trial: The Antidemocratic Tradition in Western Thought*. Princeton.

Robinson, A. L. (1980) "In the Shadow of Old John Brown: Insurrection Anxiety and Confederate Mobilization, 1861–1863," *Journal of Negro History* 65: 279–297.

Robinson, E. W. (1992) "Oracles and Spartan Religious Scruples," *LCM* 17: 132.

Roebuck, C. (1941) *A History of Messenia from 369 to 146 BC*. Ph.D. diss., University of Chicago.

(1986) "Chios in the Sixth Century BC," in Boardman and Vaphopoulou-Richardson, edd., *Chios*, 81–88. Oxford.

Roisman, J. (1993) *The General Demosthenes and his Use of Military Surprise* (Historia Einzelschriften 78). Stuttgart.

Romilly, J. de (1956) *Histoire et Raison chez Thucydide*. Paris.

(1963) *Thucydides and Athenian Imperialism*, trans. P. Thody. Oxford.

Rose, P. W. (1992) *Sons of Gods, Children of Earth*. Ithaca.

Rosivach, V. J. (1985) "Manning the Athenian Fleet, 433–426," *AJAH* 10.1: 41–66.

(1993) "Agricultural Slavery in the Northern Colonies and in Classical Athens: Some Comparisons," *CSSH* 35.3: 551–567.

(forthcoming) "The Athenian Ideology of Slavery," *Historia*.

Rouland, N. (1977) *Les Esclaves Romains en Temps de Guerre*. Bruxelles.

Roy, J. (1967) "The Mercenaries of Cyrus," *Historia* 16: 287–323.

Ruschenbusch, E. (1979) "Zur Besatzung Athenischen Trieren," *Historia* 28: 106–110.

Rusten, J. S. (1989) ed., Thucydides, The Peloponnesian War: Book 2. Cambridge.

Rüstow, W. and Köchly, H. (1852) *Geschichte des griechischen Kriegswesens*. Aarau.

Sainte Croix, G. E. M. de (1957) Review of *The Slave Systems of Greek and Roman Antiquity*, by William L. Westermann. *CR* 7: 54–59.

(1972) *Origins of the Peloponnesian War*. Ithaca.

(1981) *Class Struggle in the Ancient Greek World*. Ithaca.

(1988) "Slavery and Other Forms of Unfree Labor," in L. J. Archer, ed., *Slavery and Other Forms of Unfree Labor*, 19–32. London.

Sallares, R. (1991) *The Ecology of the Ancient Greek World*. Ithaca.

Salmon, J. B. (1977) "Political Hoplites?" *JHS* 97: 84–101.

(1984) *Wealthy Corinth*. Oxford.

Sargent, R. L. (1924) *The Size of the Slave Population at Athens*. Urbana, Ill.

(1927) "The Use of Slaves by the Athenians in Warfare," *CPh* 22: 201–212, 264–279.

Schaps, D. (1982) "The Women of Greece in Wartime," *CPh* 77: 193–213.
Schlaifer, R. (1936) "Greek Theories of Slavery from Homer to Aristotle," *CPh* 47: 165–204.
Schwartz, E. (1899) "Tyrtaeos," *Hermes* 34: 428–468.
(1937) "Die Messenische Geschichte bei Pausanias," *Philologus* 92: 19–46.
Scott, J. C. (1985) *Weapons of the Weak: Everyday Forms of Peasant Resistance.* New Haven.
Seymour, P. A. (1922) "The 'Servile Interregnum' at Argos," *JHS* 42: 24–30.
Shero, L. R. (1938) "Aristomenes the Messenian," *TAPhA* 69: 500–531.
Shipley, G. (1993) "Introduction: The Limits of War," in J. Rich and G. Shipley, edd., *War and Society in the Greek World*, 1–24. London.
Shrimpton, G. S. (1971) "The Theban Supremacy in Fourth Century Literature," *Phoenix* 25: 310–318.
Silverthorne, M. (1973) "Militarism in the Laws?" *SO* 49: 29–38.
Snodgrass, A. M. (1965) "The Hoplite Reform and History," *JHS* 85: 110–122.
Sommerstein, A. H. (1978) "Notes on Aristophanes' *Acharnians*." *CQ* n. s. 28: 383–395.
(1987) *Birds*. Warminster.
Spence, I. G. (1990) "Pericles and the Defense of Attica," *JHS* 110: 91–109.
Stadter, P. A. (1973) ed., *The Speeches in Thucydides*. Chapel Hill.
Stalley, R. F. (1983) *An Introduction to Plato's Laws*. Oxford.
Stampp, K. (1956) *The Peculiar Institution: Slavery in the Ante-Bellum South*. New York.
Stanford, W. B. (1958) *Aristophanes: Frogs*. London.
Starr, C. (1958) "An Overdose of Slavery," *JEH* 18: 17–32.
(1965) "The Credibility of Early Spartan History," *Historia* 14: 257–272.
(1977) *The Economic and Social Growth of Early Greece, 800–500 BC*. Oxford.
(1978) "Thucydides on Sea Power," *Mnemosyne* 31: 343–350.
Stein, Heinrich (1889) ed., *Herodotos*. Berlin.
Stephenson, N. W. (1912/13) "The Question of Arming the Slaves," *AHR* 18: 295–308.
Strassler, R. B. (1990) "The Opening of the Pylos Campaign," *JHS* 110: 110–125.
Strauss, B. S. (1986) *Athens after the Peloponnesian War*. Ithaca.
Strauss, L. (1963) *On Tyranny*. New York.
(1970) *Xenophon's Socratic Discourse*. Ithaca.
Synodinou, K. (1977) *On the Concept of Slavery in Euripides*. Joannina.
Talbert, R. J. A. (1989) "The Role of the Helots in the Class Struggle at Sparta," *Historia* 38: 22–40.
Tannenbaum, F. (1946) *Slave and Citizen: The Negro in the Americas*. New York.
Tatum, J. (1989) *Xenophon's Imperial Fiction*. Princeton.
Tigerstedt, E. N. (1965) *The Legend of Sparta in Classical Antiquity*. Stockholm.
Todd, J. M. (1968) *Persian Paedia and Greek Historia: An Interpretation of the Cyropaedia of Xenophon, Book One*. Ph.D. diss., University of Pittsburgh.

Todd, S. C. (1990) "Lady Chatterley's Lover and the Attic Orators: The Social Composition of the Athenian Jury," *JHS*: 146–173.

Tomlinson, R. A. (1972) *Argos and the Argolid: From the End of the Bronze Age to the Roman Occupation*. Ithaca.

Toynbee, A. (1969) *Some Problems of Greek History*. London.

Treggiari, S. (1969) *Roman Freedmen during the Late Republic*. Oxford.

(1991) *Roman Marriage*. Oxford.

Treves, P. (1944) "The Problem of a History of Messenia," *JHS* 64: 102–106.

Tucker, T. G. (1906) *The Frogs of Aristophanes*. London.

Tuplin, C. (1979) "Thucydides 1.42.2 and the Megarian Decree," *CQ* 29: 301–307.

(1994) "Xenophon, Sparta and the *Cyropaedia*," in A. Powell and S. Hodkinson, edd., *The Shadow of Sparta*, 127–182. London.

Turner, B. S. (1985) "State, Religion, and Minority Status. A Review Article," *CSSH* 27.2: 304–311.

Turney-High, H. H. (1971) *Primitive War: Its Practice and Concepts*. 2nd edn. Columbia, SC.

Underhill, G. E. (1900) *Commentary on the Hellenica of Xenophon*. Oxford.

Usher, S. (1968) "Xenophon's Critias and Theramenes." *JHS* 88: 128–135.

Vagts, A. (1959) *A History of Militarism*. Rev. edn. London.

Van der Veer, J. A. G. (1982) "The Battle of Marathon: A Topographical Survey," *Mnemosyne* 35: 290–321.

Van de Maele, S. (1980) "Démosthène et Cleon à Pylos (425 av.J.-C.)," in J. B. Caron and M. Fortin, edd., *Mélanges d'Etudes Anciennes offerts à Maurice Lebel*, 119–124. Quebec, Canada.

Van Wees, H. (1994) "The Homeric Way of War: The Iliad and the Hoplite Phalanx (II)," *G&R* 41: 131–155.

Vidal-Naquet, P. (1986a) "Reflections on Greek Historical Writing about Slavery," in *The Black Hunter*, trans. A. Szegedy-Maszak, 168–18. Baltimore.

(1986b) "Slavery and the Rule of Women in Tradition, Myth and Utopia," in *The Black Hunter*, trans. A. Szegedy-Maszak, 205–223. Baltimore.

(1986c) "The Black Hunter and the Origin of the Athenian Ephebia," in *The Black Hunter*, trans. A. Szegedy-Maszak, 106–128. Baltimore.

(1986d) "The Tradition of the Athenian Hoplite," in *The Black Hunter*, trans. A. Szegedy-Maszak, 85–105. Baltimore.

(1986e) "Were Greek Slaves a Class?" in *The Black Hunter*, trans. A. Szegedy-Maszak, 159–167. Baltimore.

Vlastos, G. (1941) "Slavery in Plato's Republic," *PhR* 50: 289–304.

Vogt, J. (1975) *Ancient Slavery and the Ideal of Man*, trans. T. Wiedemann. Cambridge, Mass.

Wade-Gery, H. T. (1967) "The Rhianos-Hypothesis," in *Ancient Society and Institutions: Studies presented to Victor Ehrenberg on his 75th birthday*, 289–302. New York.

Wallace, W. P. (1954) "Kleomenes, Marathon, the Helots and Arkadia," *JHS* 74: 32–35.

Walzer, M. (1992) *Just and Unjust Wars*. 2nd edn. New York.

Wardman, A. E. (1959) "Tactics and the Tradition of the Persian Wars," *Historia* 8: 49–60.

Waters, K. H. (1985) *Herodotus the Historian*. London.

Watson, A. (1987) *Roman Slave Law*. Baltimore.

Weiler, I. (1968) "The Greek and Non-Greek World in the Archaic Period," *GRBS* 9: 21–29.

Welskopf, E. C. (1973) "Loisir et Esclavage dans la Grèce Antique," *Annales Littéraires de l'Université de Besançon* 182: 161–168.

Welwei, K. W. (1974–1988) *Unfreie im Antiken Kriegsdienst*, 3 vols. Wiesbaden.

(1979) "Das Sogenannte Grab der Plataier," *Historia* 28: 101–106.

Westermann, W. L. (1955) *Slave Systems of Greek and Roman Antiquity.* Philadelphia.

Westlake, H. D. (1945) "Seaborne Raids in Pericles' Strategy," *CQ* 39: 75–84.

(1968) *Individuals in Thucydides*. Cambridge.

(1969a) "Hermocrates the Syracusan," in *Studies in Greek Historians and Greek History*, 174–202. New York.

(1969b) *Thessaly in the Fourth Century* BC. Groningen.

(1989) "Ionians in the Ionian War," in *Studies in Thucydides and Greek History*, 113–153. Bristol.

Wet, B. X. de. (1969) "The So-Called Defensive Policy of Pericles," *AClass* 12: 103–119.

Wheeler, E. L. (1988) *Stratagem and the Vocabulary of Military Trickery*. Leiden.

(1991) "The General as Hoplite," in V. Hanson, ed., *Hoplites: The Classical Greek Battle Experience*, 121–170. London.

Whitby, M. (1994) "Images of Spartans and Helots," in A. Powell and S. Hodkinson, edd., *The Shadow of Sparta*, 87–126. London.

White, J. W. (1914) *The Scholia on the Aves of Aristophanes*. Boston.

Whitehead, D. (1977) *The Ideology of the Athenian Metic*. Cambridge.

(1980) "Euphron, Tyrant of Sikyon: an unnoticed problem in Xenophon, Hell. 7.3.8," *LCM* 5.8: 175–178.

Wiedemann, T. E. J. (1987) *Slavery* (Greece and Rome: New Surveys in the Classics 19). Oxford.

Wiles, D. (1991) *The Masks of Menander: Sign and Meaning in Greek and Roman Performance*. Cambridge.

Wiley, B. I. (1938) *Southern Negroes 1861–1865*. New Haven.

Willetts, R. F. (1954) "The Neodamodeis," *CPh* 49: 27–32.

Williams, B. (1993) *Shame and Necessity*. Berkeley.

Wilson, J. B. (1979) *Pylos 425 BC*. Guildford, Surrey.

(1987) *Athens and Corcyra: Strategy and Tactics in the Peloponnesian War*. Bristol.

Winkler, J. J. (1990a) "The Ephebes' Song," in J. J. Winkler and F. I. Zeitlin, edd., *Nothing to Do with Dionysus*, 20–62. Princeton.

(1990b) "Laying Down the Law: The Oversight of Men's Sexual Behavior in Classical Athens", in J. Winkler, ed., *The Constraints of Desire*, 45–70. London.

Wood, E. M. (1983) "Agricultural Slavery in Classical Athens," *AJAH* 8.1: 1–47.

(1988) *Peasant-Citizen and Slave*. New York.

Wood, N. (1964) "Xenophon's Theory of Leadership," *C&M* 25: 33–66.

Woodcock, E. C. (1928) "Demosthenes, Son of Alcisthenes," *HSPh* 39: 93–108.

Woodhouse, W. J. (1898) "The Greeks at Plataiai," *JHS* 18: 33–59.

Index

Abercrombie, Hill, and Turner, 23
Abydos, 90
Acanthus, 73
Aegina, 39, 66, 114, 123
Aegospotami, battle of, 93, 94, 114
Aeneas Tacticus, 6, 177
Aeschylus, 132
Aetolia, 67, 79
Africa, sub-Saharan, 209
Ageladas, 30
Agesilaus, 149, 154, 163, 169–175 *passim*, 204
agon, hoplite: 11, 195–196; *see also* warfare,
   Archaic limitations on
ahkam al-bughat, 210
Alcibiades, 112, 114–115, 135, 140
Alcidamas, 182
Amphipolis, 59, 198
Amphitryon, 9
Anabasis: see Ten Thousand
Anaxilas, 30
Anderson, J., 156
Apollonides, 158, 169
Arcadians, 30, 65, 78, 79, 156, 196
"Archaeology," the: *see under* Thucydides
archers, 9, 187, 190
Archidamian War, 58, 71, 72, 75, 107–108
Arginusae, battle of, 83, 89–95, 111, 116, 134,
   138, 207, 216
Argos, 26 n. 1, 30, 72, 118
Arimnestus, 29
Aristagoras, 30
Aristides, 76
Aristomenes, Messenian folk hero, 78
Aristophanes, 48, 73–74, 83, 92–93, 99, 102,
   108, 110, 124–125, 128, 161
Aristotle: 6 n. 12, 27, 64, 65, 83–84, 119, 132,
   137, 138, 156, 177 n. 57; on natural slavery,
   200–202
Athens: 40–41, 50; citizenship at, 133–134;
   gives citizenship to Arginusae slaves,
   92–93; ideology and social structure,
   121–138 *passim*; oligarchic coup of 411 at,

   123, 133, 134, 135, 140, 141; pro-Spartan
   sentiments, 76–77, 134, 150; second naval
   alliance of, 179; the Thirty at, 95,134, 136,
   138; *see also* slaves and thetes; *see under* naval
   warfare and hoplite
atimia, 122

Badian, E., 66
baggage carriers: 166–169; *see also* hoplite,
   attendants
bandaka, 49
barbarians: *see* non-Greeks
Beloch, K. J., 35
binaries: *see* dichotomies and slavery,
   metaphor of
Blassingame, J., 162–163
body, control of,151–153
Bradley, K., 161
Brasidas: 73, 128; helot soldiers with, 57,
   58–60, 61, 116–117, 174
Breitenbach, H., 149
Britain, 213–214
Buckley, 214
Byzantine empire, 213

Caliph al-Mahdi, 212
Cannae, battle of, 207, 208
Carthage, 207, 208
Cartledge, P., 63, 65, 67, 173
cavalry, 8, 123, 125,126, 151, 165, 169–170,
   186, 189, 190
Cawkwell, G., 37, 58, 120
Cephisodotus, 190
Chaeronia, 216
Chambers, J., 119
Charleston Mercury, 216
Chios, 40, 45–46, 85–86, 95, 103–105, 110,
   116, 134, 216
Cimon, 76, 138, 180
Cinadon, 65, 119, 120, 172
Civil War, U.S., 214–218
Clearidas, 59

Cleisthenes, 137
Cleomenes, 26 n. 1, 65
Cleon, 75, 79, 81, 135, 138
Cnidus, battle of, 172
Cobb, H., 206
cock-fighting, 155
comedy: *see* Aristophanes *and under* slaves
Confederacy, 214–218
Connor, W., 10, 73, 93, 141
Conon, 67, 89, 90, 91, 94
Corcyra, 84, 85, 96, 110, 135, 138, 140, 141–142
Corinth, 84, 85
Cornelius, F., 35
Cornford, F., 74–75, 140
Coronea, battle of, 172, 174
Cranii, 67
Cresphontes, mythical king of Messene, 78–79
Crete, 65
Critias, 137
Crone, P., 211
Crusades, 211
Cynossema, battle of, 90
Cyropaedia, of Xenophon: 147–158, 203–205; Spartan parallels, 204
Cyrus the Great, 50, 106, 107, 147–158, 187, 189, 195–196, 203–204
Cyrus the Younger, 94, 108, 114, 154–155, 158
Cythera, 80, 119

dangers of recruiting slaves: *see* motivation of slave soldiers
Darius, king of Persia, 47
Decelea, desertion to, 12, 95, 111–115, 116, 175
Delium, battle of, 74
Demaratus, 49
Demosthenes, the general, 67, 73, 75, 79 , 81, 108, 138, 186
Demosthenes, the orator, 92, 113, 127, 133, 197–198
desposionautai, 85
dichotomies: 129–130, 158–160, 181; *see also under* slavery, metaphor of
Dinarchus, 182
Diodorus Siculus, 32, 69, 87, 91, 96, 178
Dionysius I, tyrant of Syracuse, 87
Dipaea, battle of, 37
Douglas, M., 21, 129, 153
Dover, K., 202–203
Ducat, J., 15, 17, 29–30, 61, 79–81
Ducrey, P., 104, 109

Eagleton, T., 23

Egypt, 130
elite troops, 38, 156, 106, 188–189
Ellis, 174, 196
Epaminondas, 68, 70, 171, 178, 179, 182–183
epilektoi, 196
equites, 209
Erechtheum, slave workmen at, 94, 99
Eretria, 47
Eubulus, 197–198
eunuchs, 213
Euphron, 91
Euripides, 78–79, 121, 122

Finley, J., 72
Finley, M., 50, 131
fortifications, 10, 64
Foucault, M., 24 n. 103, 152 n. 32
Four Hundred: *see* Athens, oligarchic coup of 411 at
front-rank man: 33, 35, 37, 188
funeral orations, 138–139
Funke, P., 133

Garlan, Yvon, x, 7, 118, 175–177
Geertz, C., 20–22, 24–25, 131
Genovese, E., 63
Gitiadas, 30
Gomme, A., 59, 60, 69, 102, 140
Gorgopas, 171
Gorgos, 182
Graham, A., 88
Gylippus, 57, 128–129
gymnastics, 151

Hannibal, 208
Hanson, V., 8, 9
Hartog, F., 51 n. 35, 130
Havelock, E., 201
Hellanicus, 92
Helots: precedent for Confederate slave soldiers, 215; and the *Cyropaedia*, 203; freed to defend Sparta, 171; equated with slaves, 16, 17; families and homes of, 14, 18, 38–39; as hoplites, 61; Laconian, distinguished from Messenians, 119–120; motivation of, 38–39, 118, 119–120; numbers, 18–19; in Peloponnesian War, 53, 56–62; at Plataea, 32–39, 45; problems with military use of, 16–18; rebelliousness, *see* Messenians; status and treatment, 13–19; at Thermopylae, 31–32; *see also* Neodamodeis
Henderson, B., 85–86
Heracles, 9
Hermocrates, 105–106

Herodotus, Chapters 2–3, 70, 80, 130, 132, 141
Hess, A., 213
hierarchy, within military forces, 185–189, 205, 217–218
Hiero, 154
historiography, modern: intellectual and political background of, 5–7; underestimates slave participation, 44–46
Holden, W., 216
Homer, 122, 191, 198
hoplite: attendants, 27, 32, 34, 36, 41, 55, 57, 166–169; class at Athens, 124–126, 132, 144, 159, 175–176; egalitarian ideology, 8, 185–186, 190–194; hierarchies within phalanx, 188; warfare of, 8–11, 153–155, 185–205; *see also* warfare
Hunter, V., 74, 141
hunting, 151, 157, 193, 195–196

ideology: of Herodotus, 46–52; limits of, 22–23, 80; theory of, 19–25; of Thucydides, 121–143; of Xenophon, 144–164, 181–184, 185–196, 203–205
India, 209
Ionians, 48
Iphicrates, 103–104, 155, 167, 186, 196
Islamic slave soldiers, 209–214
Isocrates, 32, 37, 79, 183–184, 197
Ithome, revolt: *see under* Messenians

Jason of Therae, 172
Jewish dietary prohibitions, 21, 129
Jordan, B., 118

Kallet-Marx, L., 100–101
Kallias, Peace of, 143
Kerameikos, 139
Krentz, P., 90, 178

Lacedaemonian: meaning of term, 34 n. 39, 37; *see also* Helots and Sparta
Lade, battle of, 48
Lamachus, 108
Laurium: *see* slaves, in mines
Lechaeum, battle of, 167
Lee, Robert E., 215, 216
Lenaea, 125
Leotychidas, 28
Lepreum, 174
Leuctra, battle of, 68, 179, 180, 188, 200
light-armed soldiers: 34, 35, 176, 186; *see also* archers, peltasts, and slingers
Livy, 44, 206–208
Loraux, N., 6 n. 11, 138–139

Lycurgus, 154, 156, 160
Lycus, 9
Lysander, 114
Lysias, 191

Macedonia, 198
Macronia, 169
Malea, 178–179
Mamluks, 209–214
Mannheim's Paradox, 24
Mantiklos, 182
Mantinea: 34, 36; battle of, 60–62
Mantitheus, 191
Manville, P., 131
Marathon, battle of, 26–28, 42–43, 124, 207
Marines, on ships, 83–84
Marxism, 22, 23
McNeill, W., 117 n. 68
Megalopolis, 179
Megara and the Megarian Decree, 102–103, 107, 109, 110, 112
Megillus, 199
Meier, C., 8
Melos, 128, 139
mentalities, emphasis on, 5–6
mercenaries, 13, 126, 146, 165, 169, 174, 190, 196–197, 199
Messene: foundation of, 177–184; Thebes and, 179–183; various judgments of, 181–184, 200; walls of, 64, n. 50; Xenophon on, 181, 183–184; *see also* Messenians.
Messenians: and Athens, 66–68, 76–79,136, 138; mythology of, 62, 77–79, 182; name of, 68–69; in Peloponnesian War, 62–82; rebelliousness of, 12, 63–65, 116, 118, 119–120; revolt in 490 BC, 28–31, 65, 76; revolt at Ithome in 464 BC 29, 29 n. 16, 64, 65, 66, 69–70, 76, 81, 106, 119, 180; Second Messenian War, 76, 77; Thucydides on, 68–82, 130; *see also* Messene and Naupactus
methodology, 19–25, 42–46, 53–56, 179
metics, 97, 98,113, 126, 138, 159, 191
military forces, hierarchy within, 185–189, 205, 217–218
military service and political rights: in many societies, 2–3; in Herodotus, 46–52; in Thucydides, 122–126; in Xenophon, 146–158
military training, 196
Miltiades, 27
Mnasippus, 110
Momigliano, A., 141
Mongols, 211

motivation of slave soldiers, 38–39, 83–84, 86, 92–93, 115–120, 202
Mycale, battle of, 41
Mytilene, 79, 89, 98

Naupactus, 64–65, 66, 67, 68, 70, 72–73, 77
naval warfare: Decelean slaves in Peloponnesian navy, 111, 114; escalation of warfare, 11–12; slaves and Helots in non-Athenian navies, 83–87, 171; slaves in Athenian navy, 40–41, 83, 87–101, 175–176; status of navy at Athens, 123–126, 175–176, 188, 191
Neodamodeis: 2, 13, 117, 120, 146, 164, 172; in Peloponnesian War, 57, 59, 60; after Peloponnesian War, 179–175; Xenophon and, 174–175
Nepos, C., 96
Nestor, 194
Nicias: 96, 99, 108, 135; Peace of, 67, 72, 82
non-Greeks: 108, 130, 131–132, 158, 159, 191; *see also under* slavery
Notium, battle of, 90

Ober, J., 133
officers, 189
oligarchic coup of 411: *see under* Athens
omission and suppression: *see* methodology
Osborne, M., 93

Paralus, 97, 100, 125
Patterson, O., 14, 17, 50, 161, 208, 211
Pausanias, geographer, 26–27, 30, 182
Pausanias, Spartan regent, 29, 35, 65
Pearson, L., 77
Peisander, 157
Pelopidas, 179, 182
Peloponnesian League, 71, 76
Peloponnesian War, 53–143 *passim*
peltasts, 169, 187, 190
penestai, 194
Pentecontaetia, 139
Pericles, 6, 56, 71, 75, 84, 92, 103, 111, 114, 123, 126, 134, 135, 200, 220–221
perioeci, 32, 37, 172–173
Persia: 94–95, 131–132, 163–164, 167, 181, 182; Thucydides' treatment of, 142–143; *see also Cyropaedia* and non-Greeks; *see under* slavery, connected with non-Greeks
Persian Wars, 26–41, 47
Pheraulas, 203–204, 205
Philon of Byzantium, 177
Phormio, 85, 123
Phrygia 131–132
Pipes, D., 210, 211, 212

Plataea: 66, 73, 74, 92–93, 114, 134, 141–142; battle of, 32–39, 42, 45, 50, 61, 188
Plato: 28, 64, 79, 91, 128, 130, 136, 137, 155, 182, 202; criticizes militarism, 198–200, 220
Plutarch, 42
Pohlenz, M., 50
Polyaenus, 103, 105–106, 110
Polydamas, 172
ponos, 150, 152
Poroi: see *Ways and Means*
Poseidon, 74, 125
Pritchett, W. K., 9, 113
Punic War, Second, 44, 206–208
Pylos, 57, 67, 71–75, 76, 77, 140, 177–179, 180

Raaflaub, K., 50, 136
racism: 217; *see also* non-Greeks
Rawlings, H., 140
Redfield, J., 130
rewards for slave soldiers: *see* motivation
Roebuck, C., 45
Rome, 206–209
Romilly, J. de, 140

Salaminia, 97, 125
Salamis, battle of, 40–41
Sambo: *see* slaves, stereotype of personality
Samos, 93, 123, 134
Sargent, R., 88 n. 32, 96, 99
Sarpedon, 122
Scillus, 174
Scione, 93, 128
Scott, J., 23
Scythians: 48, 51–52, 131–132: archers, 122 n. 6
Sepeia, battle of, 26 n. 1
Seuthes, 149
sexuality: *see* body *and* women
Shoup, General Francis, 217–218
Sicilian Expedition, 57, 74, 75, 87, 89, 98, 99, 105–106, 116, 123, 124, 128–129, 133, 167
silver mines: *see under* slaves
slavery: and certain jobs, 151, 168; and cowardice, 47–48, 51, 129, 162; and loss in war, 47–48, 128–129; and non-Greeks, 46, 48–50, 158–159, 191; and softness, 48, 150, 152–153; metaphor of, 46–51, 128–129; *see also* slaves *and* women
slaves: childishness of, 160–163: in comedy, 127, 161; desertion and flight of, 102–120; enslavement, 47–48,155, 201; feelings not shown by military service, 115–120; in mines, 40, 94, 111–112, 121; numbers at Athens, 11; punishment of, 127–128; revolts

slaves (*cont.*)
(*see also* Messenians), 103–106; status
changes due to military service, 202–203;
stereotype of slave personality, 121, 145,
160–163; and tyrants, 90, 91, 212–213; in
vase paintings 127; *see also* slavery, naval
warfare; *see also under* the names of
individual campaigns, battles, and
authors.
slingers, 165, 187, 190
Socrates, 148
Solon, 133
Sophocles, 132
Soteridas, 149
South, the U.S., 109, 137, 162, 214–218
Spain, 209
Sparta: 15, 18, 41, 64, 65, 72, 128, 150, 199;
army of, 36–38, 58, 60, 159, 189; failure to
arrive at Marathon, 28–31; fears of Helot
revolt, 79–8, 116, 119–120; after Leuctra,
180–184, 200; strengths and weaknesses,
57, 172–174; at Thermopylae, 31–32; *see also*
Helots *and* Messenians
speeches, 42 n. 2, 54, 59, 81
Sphacteria, 57–58, 71–75
spies, 107, 110,112
Stenyclerus, battle of, 29
Stockholm Syndrome, 117
Strabo, 30
Strauss, B., 133
structuralism, 5–6
Sybota, battle of, 84, 85
symbolic systems: *see* ideology
Syracuse, 44, 57, 75, 86–87, 99, 105–106, 110 ,
116, 128–129, 167

Taenarus, temple at, 74
Talbert, R., 119
Tegea, 33
Ten Thousand, the, 149, 155, 157, 158–159,
165–169, 186, 189
Thebes: 31, 49, 71, 107, 112, 113, 141, 173;
founds Messene, 179–183; the Sacred
Band, 38, 196
Themistocles: 40, 96; Decree of, 40
Theramenes, 137
Thermopylae, battle of, 31–32
Thespians, 31

Thessaly, 194
thetes: 97, 99, 132, 137, 144–145; not at
Marathon, 27; role in navy, 8, 124–126
Thirty, the: *see under* Athens
thranatai, 124
Thucydides: 30, 35, 36, 44, 46; chapters 4–7,
144, 217; "Archaeology," 55, 111, 126
Thurii, 86
Tisamenus, 29
Toynbee, A., 60
training, military, 196
Treves, P., 77
trierarchs, 94, 97, 98,124
Turner, B., 211
"twenty-nigger law," 215
tyrants: *see under* slaves
Tyrtaeus, 198–199

Van de Maele, S., 72
vase painting: *see under* slaves
Vidal-Naquet, P., 8, 128
Volones, 44, 206–209

Wallace, W. 65
walls: *see* fortifications
warfare: Archaic limitations on, 8–11;
escalation in the 5th century, 11–13;
escalation in the 4th century, 195–197;
Homeric, 9, 10; in Islamic societies, 210;
prestige of, declines, 194–202; primitive, 9,
10 n. 35; trickery in, 9–11, 195–196; *see also*
naval warfare
Ways and Means of Xenophon, 175–177
Wellington, Duke of, 185
Welwei, K., x, 60–61, 88, 93, 118
West Indies, British, 213–214
whips, 49, 51
Williams, B., 160 n. 85
Winkler, J., 8, 152 n. 32
women: rule of, 128, 148; and slaves, 26 n. 1,
51, 127, 142, 158; unwarlike,159, 164

Xenophon, 60, 70, 89–95, 106–107, 110, 123,
125, 131, 136, 137; chapters 8–10, 218
Xenophon, pseudo-, 124, 136, 137, 186
Xerxes, 31, 49

Zankle, 30, 77, 182

Printed in the United Kingdom
by Lightning Source UK Ltd.
2854